RESTLESS SPIRIT

RESTLESS SPIRIT

The Story of Rose Quinn

MARGARET HAWKINS

ⴍERCIER PRESS

MERCIER PRESS
Douglas Village, Cork
www.mercierpress.ie

Trade enquiries to Columba Mercier Distribution,
55a Spruce Avenue, Stillorgan Industrial Park, Blackrock, Dublin

1 85635 496 2

10 9 8 7 6 5 4 3 2

Mercier Press receives financial assistance from
the Arts Council/An Chomhairle Ealaíon

Printed and Bound by J. H. Haynes & Co. Ltd, Sparkford

CONTENTS

For John Quinn

PROLOGUE

Blue flowers in the graveyard. Patricia Quinn Murphy gripped the handle of the rusty entrance gate as a tiny shiver ran down her spine. So another detail of what her daughter, Catherine, had seen was correct.

Catherine had a gift – a psychic one. Patricia had no doubt about that now.

When Catherine had connected with Rose for the first time, ten months earlier, in September 1999, Catherine, then twenty-eight, had seen her long-dead relative standing in this graveyard. Blue flowers lay on the ground then beside the emaciated figure of Rose, marking the spot where the Clongeen woman had been buried, without coffin, without priest, in May 1907. It had been the proof Patricia needed that there was a burial plot at St Senan's psychiatric hospital in County Wexford, formerly known as the Enniscorthy District Lunatic Asylum for the Insane Poor. It was also proof that her great-aunt Rose was buried there.

Patricia couldn't wait to tell Catherine about the blue flowers – it would be another unusual phone call from this quiet place.

Patricia was glad to have been invited to attend the July 2000 pattern that day. 'At least they have some kind of service here once a year,' she said to herself. She doubted, though, if many came near the place in the intervening months. This was a big day for her – and for Rose. Today Rose Quinn would be prayed for here for the first time. Patricia had even been invited to read a prayer herself during the service – she hoped now that emotion wouldn't overcome her as she spoke.

She looked again at the flowers. The blue hydrangeas sat at

the base of the framed poem that she had placed in the cemetery six months before:

Discarded,
Disowned ...
Suffering
Untold

She'd written the poem in memory of her great-aunt who had been committed to the asylum, sent there having refused to live with the man she was forced to marry. A woman who, for most of her life, Patricia hadn't known existed.

*

Who could have put the blue flowers there? Someone from the hospital? A kind-hearted local resident? Any other colour and Patricia wouldn't have batted an eyelid but these were different.

Were the blue flowers a sign from Rose that her goal was on the way to finally being achieved? Were they a 'thank you' from the next life and encouragement to complete the task? Patricia decided they were.

Patricia's first real visit to the graveyard in Enniscorthy was still heavily imprinted on her memory. She had visited it less than twenty-four hours after she and Catherine had returned from Spain. At the time she had wondered why they had had to go to Spain for such a thing to happen, for Catherine to connect with her dead great-aunt. It was probably that they were so relaxed in one another's company, they had decided, enjoying a post-illness break, mother and daughter free to think and talk about family roots and mysteries.

'Anyway, spirits don't need airline tickets,' Catherine said at the time.

Patricia couldn't argue with her on that one.

Catherine's 'connection' meant they had known for the first time that there *was* a graveyard attached to the hospital. Up to that, Patricia's queries had fallen on deaf ears. There had been no communication, no admission that there was such a graveyard, never mind that Rose Quinn was interred there.

On Patricia's first visit the graveyard had been as Catherine had described it – neglected, the burial ground raised on one side, no headstones but instead 'little white monuments' or crosses strewn in the thick grass. It had been the strangest of nights, strange but yet not frightening, an experience that few knew about as yet.

'Still, without it I might never have found this place,' Patricia said to herself before joining the priest, staff and elderly patients who had now arrived by mini-bus.

'Rose is no longer a skeleton in the Quinn family cupboard,' she thought. 'Thank God for that.'

At first the story had only been an amazing string of coincidences. Patricia had discovered that she and Rose shared the same birthday – 11 July. They had married men with the same surname too, from the same parish, in the same church. They had both lived and worked on the Rosegarland estate owned by the Leigh family near Wellingtonbridge, County Wexford – an estate that had employed generations of Quinns.

Catherine's experience in Spain had confirmed that Rose was trying to 'connect' with Patricia. To get a score settled, two generations on.

'She will be remembered,' said Patricia to herself, 'in an even bigger way than at this pattern today.'

Plans were already in motion to erect a headstone in this graveyard before the end of the millennium year as a memorial to Rose and all the forgotten people buried there.

'Then Rose need be a restless spirit no longer,' Patricia thought as the priest began the prayers.

1

'AND THEN THERE WAS ROSE ...'

John Quinn, now almost ninety-four, paused to tap his pipe on the palm of his hand in the cottage at Ballylannon, Wellingtonbridge, County Wexford.

It was New Year's Eve 1993 and he stood, back to the fire, not making eye contact with his fifty-year-old daughter, Patricia.

She sat alongside in an armchair, notebook in hand and pen poised. 'That's all your dad's side of the family then. Have I got them all – Jack, Mary, Elizabeth, Johanna and your dad, Patrick?'

John Quinn shifted his weight from one foot to the other as Patricia waited for an answer, the clock ticking loudly in the silence.

'And then there was Rose ...' he said.

'Rose? Where does she fit in? I never heard of an aunt Rose.'

John Quinn cleared his throat, shifting uneasily again. 'She was a year younger than my father.'

'But if she was in the family why haven't we heard of her before?'

John Quinn cleared his throat again.

'She was made to marry a man,' he said eventually. 'When she wouldn't go live with him she was put in the asylum.'

Patricia sat up straight.

'The asylum? In Enniscorthy – St Senan's?'

'Yes.'

'Good God! She was put in there just because she wouldn't go live with her husband?'

'Yes.'

'It doesn't bear thinking about,' Patricia said, mental pictures of her great-aunt's suffering forming in her mind.

'Goddamn it, it should never have happened,' her father said quietly, turning to place his unused pipe on the mantelpiece.

'What happened to her? Did she get out?' Patricia asked.

'No. She died within a year.'

'Dear God! What did she die of – do you know?'

'Disease, probably. You didn't live long in them places them times. If disease didn't get you, starvation did.'

'Do you remember anything about her – about what happened?'

'I was at the wedding. We all were.'

'What age were you then?'

'About six, so it must have been 1906. Winter time, I remember; there was frost on the ground.'

'What happened?'

'I was standing outside with my mother,' he said quietly. 'Aunt Rose was crying and my mother was trying to persuade her to go in.'

Tears stung Patricia's own eyes as she imagined the scene. She had stood outside the church in Clongeen herself on her own wedding day in 1964. She had gone there of her own free will. To go there against it would have been unthinkable.

'Who did she marry?' she asked.

Her father paused again.

'A Murphy from Carrig-on-Bannow.'

Patricia felt a shiver run down her spine. She had married a

Murphy from Carrig-on-Bannow herself!

'Is he related to Michael?' she asked, almost in shock.

'Well, Michael's family moved to the village years after, so I don't think so.'

'Gracious! Do you know his first name – the husband's?

'Patrick. Pat the Pumper he was called,' said her father. 'He pumped the water for the engines when they were building the railway in Wellington Bridge – that's probably how he got the nickname. He worked on building the track same as your grandfather did. That's probably how the match was made, with the two of them knowing one another from the job.'

Patricia had heard talk many times of the railway being built between Waterford and Rosslare Harbour. Why wouldn't she when it ran through the Rosegarland estate where she'd been reared, when the building of it had been a monumental time in the lives of the people of her area? Hadn't she crossed it too most days of her life?

Now she didn't know what to say. As well as the shock of this new information, the injustice of what had happened to her great-aunt struck her deeply. Put in a mental institution just because she wouldn't live with someone she was forced to marry – Patricia felt both sad and angry at the thought of it.

'But surely the family tried to get her out? Surely Granny and Granddad tried?'

Her father looked straight ahead.

'I don't know that they did – or could. Times were different then,' he said. 'The husband put her in – that's the way we were told it. Maybe they could do nothing after that.'

'No matter, her family shouldn't have turned their backs on her,' said Patricia to herself, her mind now preoccupied with the story of a relative she had never known.

*

As her father's health declined in the days and weeks that followed, Patricia wondered many times why he had told her the story of Rose. Was it to free himself, before death, of the burden of a secret that he had carried too long? She felt sad at the thought of a grown man carrying such a load with him throughout his lifetime. The shame of having a family member in the asylum had obviously struck deep. Stigma – there was still too much of it.

Rose's story was seldom far from Patricia's mind from that day on, even though family concerns prevented her from immediately doing the research she swore that night in 1993 that she would do.

Thoughts of Rose stayed with her through her father's final months and the grieving that followed, through the years of caring for her mother who had developed Alzheimer's, through subsequent days when she was ill herself. Fibromyalgia had set in during her days of caring for her mother, making her physically unable to cope. The fatigue was chronic, muscles pained and joints stiffened, making daily life difficult.

'You pushed your body too far for too long,' Catherine said. 'In the end it forced you to slow down.'

For two years life wasn't easy but as she came to terms with coping with the condition thoughts of Rose increased.

Every time she drove past St Senan's hospital on the way to Enniscorthy, for instance, she would wonder about Rose's life and death in the place. Had anyone visited her? Had she been brought home for burial?

The day she eventually rang the priest in Clongeen to check if he had found Rose's baptismal and marriage records still stood out in her mind.

Yes, he had found a record of the marriage between Rose Quinn, spinster, of Rosegarland and Patrick Murphy, bachelor, of Ballyfrory, Carrig-on-Bannow. He had found her baptismal records too.

'That's wonderful,' said Patricia, feeling that Rose was now becoming more and more a real person. She wasn't prepared for what he would say next, however.

'She was born in 1870,' he said. 'The eleventh of July.'

The eleventh of July? That was her birthday!

Patricia marvelled at the coincidences – the same birthday, marrying a man with the same name from the same parish in the same church.

'What was her address on the marriage certificate, please? Did it say what her occupation was?' she asked.

'Yes. Her address is Rosegarland. She's listed as "house servant".'

So, Rose had worked in Rosegarland just like she had. Another coincidence. Patricia had worked there as cook for four years before she got married. All that matching detail and she had never heard of Rose.

In other circumstances she probably would have been named after her because of their coinciding birthdays. Hadn't all the other names in the family – John, Patrick, Elizabeth, Catherine – come down through the generations? Rose's incarceration had wiped her out of the family history books, making her a namesake of none.

Patricia now felt a great sense of connection with the grandaunt she had never known. She felt a huge curiosity also. What sort of person was she? What did she look like? What had her life been like? How had she felt having a marriage arranged for her? What had happened to her in the asylum? Where had she been buried? There was a lot to find out.

*

Patricia was glad to get back to the hotel bedroom in the south-eastern Spanish resort of Roquets De Mar. It had been a long but enjoyable day.

Catherine followed behind, holding their wine glasses as her mother unlocked the door. Patricia was glad to see Catherine so happy. This September 1999 holiday was a good idea.

'You know, I've never felt so relaxed in my life,' Patricia said, throwing her bag on the bed.

'Me neither,' said Catherine. 'I bags the shower first.'

'OK, as long as you don't take too long – my feet are covered in sand.'

It was a holiday they had both looked forward to – the holiday abroad promised to themselves when they had both recovered from illness.

'A celebration of life, that's what it is,' said Patricia. 'It was a good job nobody saw us when we got off the plane, though, or they'd have said we were a right pair of mad eejits.'

Catherine laughed, grabbing her wash-bag. 'They'd have been right too.'

When the plane had touched down and the warm Mediterranean wind hit them, they had run, arms outstretched, to the arrivals building, revelling in the heat and their delight that they had arrived. Why shouldn't they enjoy a hard-saved-for holiday now that they had both recovered – Patricia from her initial illness, Catherine after surgery.

'You can't keep good things down,' said Patricia, looking out the window at the picturesque scene below.

The bus tour of Almira had gone well. She and Catherine had been talking all day about family, close in a way that only mother and daughter can be. They had visited castle ruins and ancient buildings and talk had turned to places of importance in their own lives.

The Rosegarland estate, the place that Patricia knew so

well from being reared there and the place that Catherine knew so well from visiting her grandparents there so often, featured strongly as usual. They talked of all the Quinns that had worked there, of who had married whom, of the aunts and uncle of her father's who had lived there too.

Rose was mentioned, seldom far from Patricia's mind, especially as in the preceding months she had tried to get information from St Senan's hospital by telephone and letter. Was there a graveyard attached to the former asylum, she had asked? Were there records of Rose Quinn or Rose Murphy as a patient or of her being buried in the hospital grounds?

A trawl through Clongeen parish records and those of Kilcavan, the graveyard where Rose's husband was buried, had yielded nothing, leading Patricia to conclude that Rose was more than likely buried in Enniscorthy.

There had been no reply from the hospital.

'They probably threw the letter in the bin hoping you'd go away,' Catherine said.

'You can't blame them really. They probably think they have enough to do looking after the present patients without worrying about someone who died almost a hundred years ago.'

'Probably,' said Catherine.

As she waited for her daughter to wash, Patricia sat on the bed, unable to stop thinking about Catherine's gift. Today they had spoken of it again as Catherine walked among the historic buildings of Almira, picking up 'feelings' about the place.

Patricia had been aware of Catherine's being different long before now. One day when she was five they had picnicked at St Mullins in Carlow. Catherine had insisted that she had been there before. Patricia knew she hadn't.

As a child, Catherine also had an awareness of people that no one else could see. In Rosegarland, when visiting, she never played in front of her grandparents' cottage because of the 'people there', she said. Patricia had looked and saw no one.

Catherine had often told her mother of feelings she got when she visited other people's houses – happy feelings, sad feelings, depending on what had happened there. She liked to play a game too, even still, of describing a house that she had never visited – *before* she got there. She would exchange a secret smile with her mother, then, when the details of her description proved correct.

She hadn't told many people about what she could do, though, fearing what they'd say. Seeing things as she did wasn't normal, she felt, and for many years she tried to shut it out.

Patricia wasn't unsettled by what her daughter could do, however. Hadn't she 'seen' her own grandfather, Patrick Quinn, one day in the cottage in Rosegarland herself? He had died years before she was born. Her father told her years later that she had described 'the old man' down to a tee but that he had been afraid to tell her so at the time in case she was frightened and wouldn't sleep in the house any more.

Did she have a gift too, one that was simply more finely tuned, one generation down, in Catherine?

Patricia herself always had strong feelings about places and objects. Walls attracted her – stones too. She found herself drawn to them. Her kitchen window at home was full of them, brought back from places she'd visited, better souvenirs for her than anything you could buy in a shop, she always said. She only brought back the ones that felt good, though. Occasionally when she picked one up from some ancient site it seemed to spit at her and she immediately replaced it.

She had never witnessed anyone connecting properly with a spirit, though.

*

Both now washed and ready for bed, Patricia and Catherine sat up talking in the bedroom of the Hotel Playa Capricho.

As the minutes passed and the conversation deepened to talk of Rose, Catherine lay back against the headboard, her eyes taking on a look that Patricia wasn't familiar with.

'Do you know where I am now?' Catherine said, looking to one side.

'Where?' Patricia asked, watching her closely.

'In Rosegarland, looking up the lane at Uncle Willie's cottage.' Willie Quinn was the youngest of Patricia's uncles.

'That's near where Rose lived after the family was evicted from Newcastle. What else do you see?' asked Patricia, unsure now of what was happening but feeling the urge to ask questions.

Rose had been on her mind a lot in the last few weeks. What was on her mind was often on Catherine's too – she had learned that much over the years. Was it empathy, telepathy? Whatever it was, it was real.

Rose's family had been evicted from the house and farm in Newcastle in 1881. Rose was eleven years old when her father had been reduced from tenant farmer to estate labourer.

'Who do you see now?'

'I see the names – the shapes of the names – all the family ones – Patrick, Kate, Johanna, Elizabeth. I see riding boots – a man wearing them.'

'Is he small? Is it Jack?' Patricia asked, having heard that her grand-uncle Jack had been small in stature and that as coachman at Rosegarland he had seldom been seen in anything but riding boots.

She saw Catherine look up and down the length of herself. 'Not that small, he says!'

Patricia laughed. It was the first time she had insulted a spirit!

'Ask him about Rose – does he know where she is?'

The next few moments were very strange – Catherine speaking all the time, listing the places that Jack was taking her, as if he was showing her the Rosegarland estate and all the Quinns who lived there.

'There's a woman beside him now. He says it's Rose. He says he knows you have been thinking about her.'

'What's she like? Tell me!'

Catherine stared to one side of her mother, as if checking for more detail, then looked back and grinned. 'She's not good-looking. She's handsome, she says – a Quinn, just like you.'

'Ouch!' Patricia didn't know whether to laugh or cry. At least Rose had a sense of humour.

Catherine was looking away again.

'She's got a child beside her. A boy with fair hair, maybe five or six years old.'

A child!

'She had a child? Was that why they were trying to marry her off?'

'She won't say. She says it's not about the child.'

'Oh.'

Patricia was now keeping eye contact with her daughter. 'Ask her where she is – where she's buried.'

'She says you've been told where she is,' said Catherine.

'Is she at St Senan's?'

Catherine was concentrating hard, her eyes wide open. It was an odd sensation. Later she would describe it as feeling as if she was a few feet to the right of herself – of her own reality.

'She's buried in the graveyard behind the hospital. I can see her there now.'

'There *is* a graveyard! I knew it!' said Patricia.

She listened now as Catherine continued to talk.

'She's about your height but thin, very thin – her cheek-bones are almost sticking out. She's got dark clothes on – long and rough looking. And boots. Her hair is tied up but there are wisps of it straggling round her face.'

'The graveyard – what's it like?'

'Not like a normal one,' said Catherine. 'It looks like part of a field. There are walls on three sides and a ditch on the lower side. There's a bank of ground on the upper side, covered in grass that's falling over.'

'There are no individual graves?' Patricia asked, trying to create her own mental picture of the place.

'There's a stone wall behind where Rose is standing. I can see one of the hospital's towers over it.'

Patricia hardly dared to breathe in case she disturbed her daughter.

'Yew trees too – four of them and a big cross on the upper side with steps going up to it.'

'Where is Rose?'

Catherine looked straight ahead of her, but into some unknown distance. 'She's on the high side, near the path. Past the cross with the steps up to it.'

So – Catherine knew exactly where she was buried!

'What else can you see?'

Catherine concentrated again. 'There are little white monuments – odd things – lying in the grass and flowers. And there are blue flowers on the ground beside Rose.'

Patricia was amazed. 'What's Rose doing? Is she saying anything?'

'She's got her fists clenched, like she's frustrated about something. Ha! She says she's been trying to connect with you for years but you wouldn't listen. She says she realised I could hear her so she's making contact through me instead.'

21

So, the coincidences had a purpose – if only she'd been able to go beyond them – but, never mind, Rose was doing so now through Catherine.

'Ask her what it is she wants of us – why she feels the need to contact us.'

Catherine waited for the feelings and words of her great-great-aunt to come through. 'She wants two things, she says.'

'Tell me!'

'Recognition by family. And her story told.'

So, Rose did feel let down by her family. She wasn't at peace because no one had tried to help her. The injustice of what had been done to her had driven her to seek acknowledgement now, two generations down.

'Ask her was it her husband that committed her?' said Patricia.

Catherine concentrated again. 'She says the man is not important. It's family she wants recognition from.'

Did that mean that her family had been involved in her committal? Or that they hadn't supported her when she needed it? There were still so many questions.

Catherine moved in the bed. 'She's gone,' she said, the unfamiliar look now leaving her face.

Looking at her watch, Patricia saw that it was five o'clock in the morning. The drinks they had brought with them to the room at 11 p.m. sat there untouched.

The next morning at breakfast they were both subdued, shocked almost.

'Did that really happen?' they asked one another.

'The only way to find out is to go to the hospital as soon as we get home and see if there is a graveyard,' said Patricia, butterflies in her stomach at the thought of it. 'I bet there will be – just like you said.'

'It'll be something if there is,' said Catherine, not sure how she would feel if there was – or how devastated she would be if there wasn't. 'Pity I have to go to Galway for the diving course – I'd go with you if I didn't have to go straight there from the airport.'

'Don't worry,' said her mother. 'I'll ring you as soon as I find it so keep your phone switched on all Monday afternoon.'

Would Catherine be right? Had she a powerful gift? They would have to wait three days to find out. The flight home seemed an eternity long.

*

The following Monday at half past two Patricia put her apron away, then locked the storeroom door at the Franciscan friary in Wexford town where she was employed, part-time, as cook. Seven friars to feed, five days a week – that was her work. Lunch was over now for another day. Now it was time to walk the few hundreds yards to her home in John Street.

After she had given her husband, Michael, some lunch, they drove to Enniscorthy to St Senan's hospital.

Michael knew about her obsession with finding out more about Rose. He would go too. Nothing had been said about Spain, however. For now, what had happened was a secret between herself and Catherine. She knew Michael felt a bit uneasy about such things – there was no point annoying him until they knew if Catherine really was right.

The hospital was an imposing building; there was no doubt about it. Standing high in a field overlooking the Slaney river on the Wexford side of Enniscorthy town, its red-brick exterior dominated the landscape. Two huge towers marked its perimeter at each end and three smaller ones rose from the rear.

It was built in 1868 – Patricia knew that. Most people dreaded it – she knew that too – looking away as they passed, trying not to think of its significance. The red brick ... The madhouse.

Some said the building was too grand looking for an asylum – that plans had got mixed up and a building meant for India had been built here by mistake. Maybe the story was right. Patricia couldn't help wondering what India had got instead – a big grey barracks like St Otteran's hospital in Waterford or St Loman's in Mullingar, maybe?

Patricia couldn't help wondering too what Rose's feelings had been the day she was first brought here. Fear? Terror? Shame? Torment? Despair? How could she have felt anything else knowing she was going to be locked up, perhaps forever? 'I'm glad she lived only a year here. Death would have been an escape for her,' Patricia said to herself as Michael parked the car.

She told the male nurse in the outpatients' ward that she wanted to know where the hospital's graveyard was. She explained that she had been in touch with hospital management about a relative of hers, Rose Quinn, who had been a patient there many years before. Asking her to wait the nurse departed to speak with someone in authority.

Eventually he returned.

'I'll send one of the patients to show you where it is,' he said. 'It's at the back of the hospital. He'll give you directions.'

Patricia's stomach did a somersault as she heard the words 'it's at the back of the hospital'.

Michael drove slowly up the lane towards the rear entrance to the hospital, the patient sent to give them directions sitting in the back. So, there was a graveyard!

'Turn right here,' said the man when they reached the top of the lane.

Michael did so, knowing that he must now be on the road that ran between the Roadstone quarry and Templeshannon.

24

The high wall that once edged the walled gardens of the hospital ended at the field gateway where the patient now told them to stop. 'That's it,' the man said, pointing into the field.

Patricia got out of the car and stood there in shock. The graveyard, its entrance about ten feet in from the main field gate, was as Catherine had described it.

There was a ditch on the lower side and a raised area on the right. A cement cross stood on the right, with steps going up to it. The place looked overgrown, with grass tumbling over.

Saying nothing, Patricia followed the patient and Michael over the stile beside the main field gate and across the few feet of ground to the graveyard entrance. The small entrance gate creaked as she opened it. Scanning the place, she saw there were no headstones, no marked graves, as Catherine had said. Walking along the pathway Patricia noticed small, rusty white crosses strewn in the grass – the 'little white monuments'? She bent down to examine one. There were no names on any of them, not even numbers.

The elderly patient now waved his hand and smiled. 'Them's the graves,' he said, pointing at the raised area on the right. 'Them's the graves.'

'Thank you,' said Patricia. 'Thank you very much for showing them to us.'

'It's in a bit of a state all right,' Michael said, echoing what Patricia was thinking. 'I wouldn't say too many people come here.'

Patricia felt desolate, tuned into the sadness of the place. How many people had been buried here, she wondered? What terrible things had they suffered before they died? The asylum had opened in 1868 – were there hundreds buried here, thousands maybe, unclaimed by family after death? It struck her now that Rose was only one of the forgotten people.

Blue flowers – Patricia found herself somehow expecting them, given that so many other details were correct, but there was no sign of any flowers.

Catherine had said there were blue flowers on the spot where Rose had been buried. Today there were none.

'How could there be?' Patricia asked herself. She wondered how long it had been since anyone had been there with any kind of decoration.

Patricia now looked across at the far wall. She couldn't see a tower of the hospital over it. So Catherine got that bit wrong too. Still, she had been spot on with so much. No one could be 100 per cent correct.

She dialled Catherine's number on her mobile phone. 'Guess what? It's like you said in so many ways!'

The next few minutes were full of excited talk, going over and over the description of the place, comparing the expectation with the reality. It was a day they would both remember forever.

'There are no blue flowers, though,' she said when Catherine asked.

'They'll turn up yet – don't worry,' said her daughter.

*

Patricia was scarcely aware of the road as Michael drove home.

'Something will have to be done,' Patricia said eventually.

'How do you mean?'

'All those people deserve to be remembered – not just Rose. Something should be done to atone for what they suffered.'

'True,' said Michael. 'The hospital mightn't want to do anything, though.'

'We'll see,' said Patricia, now lost in thought.

How could she get the graveyard cleaned up, maybe get a headstone erected in memory of those who are buried there? It was only right, she felt. She thought of Rose, buried there with no family near her, dying with no one she loved to comfort her.

Once again, Patricia longed to know everything about her great-aunt's life. What kind of existence had she had before she went into the asylum? How could she have been committed so easily? Surely no doctor would have certified her as a lunatic just because she refused to go live with her husband? Had she become hysterical when they tried to force her? Patricia knew things were different then but surely such injustices didn't happen?

'There's probably a graveyard like that beside every psychiatric hospital in the country,' said Michael as they neared Ferrycarrig.

'Probably,' said Patricia, saddened even more at that thought.

Taking out a notebook, she began to jot down a list of what she would need to do.

*

As soon as Catherine returned from Galway, she, Patricia and Patricia's older sister, Maura, went to visit the graveyard again.

They chatted happily in the car on the way up, Catherine looking forward to her first physical sight of the graveyard.

Going in through the gate, however, Catherine felt as if she had hit a wall of emotion. As the weight of the sadness overwhelmed her she began to cry. Feeling then as if she was being pulled in a particular direction, she walked along the pathway past the cross and up to a particular spot on the sloping ground beyond it.

Reaching the place where she felt Rose was buried, she went down on her knees and sobbed inconsolably.

*

Rose was seldom far from Patricia's thoughts as she went about her daily routine in the weeks that followed.

Up at eight, prepare the vegetables for their own dinner, get to the friary for work at ten. Do the shopping for the friars' meals, prepare and cook the lunch, ready to serve it at one o'clock, get home by half past two to prepare Michael's lunch before he returned from Pettitt's supermarket where he worked as a bacon butcher.

Patricia's workload wasn't as great as it used to be, however. There was a time when her three children filled the house, keeping her busy. But as soon as they had grown and moved out to make lives for themselves, and she had recovered from her care tasks and illness, she had updated her culinary skills and taken the part-time job at the friary.

At the age of twenty-one, marriage had meant leaving her job as cook in Rosegarland, the estate owned by the Leigh family where she had been reared. She still missed the place – the trees, the fields, the woods and the beauty of the estate.

It had been such a change to move into the bustle of Wexford town when she married, where one house looked across upon another and traffic passed a few feet from the door.

'How are you going to get the graveyard cleaned up?' Michael asked as she sat scribbling in the sitting-room.

'Contact politicians. See if they can help.'

'Might work,' he said, turning a page of the newspaper.

Patricia wrote down another name. Writing to these people would mean Rose's story going public. Was she ready for that? Part of her didn't want to make Rose's story known. It was a private story after all. A story about family. She wasn't immune from the stigma herself. Would other members of the Quinn family resent her making it public?

She thought again of Rose. Rose wanted recognition from

family, even this far down the line. A wrong had to be righted. The Quinns hadn't taken Rose in when she refused to live with her husband. No one supported her when she needed it.

The next time Patricia went to visit her parents' grave she stopped outside Clongeen church on the way home.

Rose's marriage had been an arranged one. Was the deal done in the snug of the pub across the road, she wondered. More than likely – it would have been there in 1906. Patricia found it hard to imagine what it would have been like being told to marry someone – your life planned out for you by someone else and having no power to do anything about it.

'Rose's parents would have been dead at this stage so she would have had no help from them,' Patricia thought. They were buried in the old graveyard that overlooked the church car park.

Patricia's grandfather, Patrick, Rose's elder brother, as head of the family, would have been the organiser of the wedding – she was sure of that. The fact that he had worked on the railway with Patrick Murphy made it likely, as her father had said.

Patricia wondered what Patrick Murphy, the husband, was like. Was he a good man? Was he offensive in character or looks? Was Rose in love with someone else? Had she had an illegitimate child by him or by someone else years before? Who was the child that Catherine had seen with her on that night of connection? If that child had been taken from her, the family would probably have wanted to marry her off before she'd get into trouble again.

Was that what was in their minds when they were making the match?

She hoped Patrick Murphy was a kind man. Surely Rose's brother would not have picked someone unacceptable for his sister?

She wished she knew more about her grandfather, Patrick, too. He was a small man, fond of a drop by all accounts. Could he not have done anything to stop Rose's husband committing her to the asylum? Surely no one would stand by and let that happen easily?

'People probably thought differently then,' said Michael when she voiced her opinions.

Anger tinged her reply. 'They were still human beings. Her family should have stood by her.'

'Maybe they hadn't got the money to. How many children did they have – six? They would have been hard set to rear them without taking in anyone else to look after – especially if she was depressed and couldn't work. There was no dole in them days.'

Maybe Michael was right. Maybe they had more than enough to be looking after. The Quinns had never been rich. What land they had, they had been evicted from in 1881.

In 1909, she knew, her grandfather, Patrick, had finally received a few acres and a house from the Land Commission after legislation had forced landlords to sell land cheaply to the families of those who had been evicted.

It was strange. Her father had told the story of the eviction to her many times down through the years. She had been to the field in the townland of Newcastle where the house stood too. Resentment of English and landlord rule had gone deep with him as a result, she felt, culminating in his involvement in the Rising in 1916 when he was only sixteen years old. He fought the Black and Tans too, then was active on the side of De Valera in the civil war that followed.

So deeply had he been involved that he had had to emigrate to Wales for ten years until the dust settled, as he put it. He only returned in the 1930s when his mother was ill, later getting married and finding work as a stockman in Rosegarland.

The eviction had definitely sown the seed of resentment against a foreign ruler. Rose surely must have felt that too. She would have been eleven at the time of the eviction – a traumatic day for the Quinn family if the newspaper reports of the time were to be believed. Patricia had read them and been upset by them.

Twelve evictions had taken place on the Rosegarland estate that wet and bitterly cold day. One hundred and fifty armed police escorted the five bailiffs from one tenant farm to the next, reaching Patrick Quinn's homestead at ten o'clock in the morning.

'This was an extremely hard case,' the newspaper report said, 'Quinn owed two-and-a-half years rent: £20 8s 8d. His land was poor and marshy and out of this Quinn endeavoured to support a household of ten. The roof of the house was thatch and the interior comprised a kitchen and one room.'

Guns, neighbours shouting and heaping curses on the heads of the police and the landlord, raw fear – Patricia could only imagine the desperation as the family's belongings were left on the side of the road and they were helped to an old barn down the road by the representatives of the Ladies' League, the Misses Keating and the Misses Murphy – women subjected to 'disrespectful sneers from the bailiffs and policemen' for their trouble.

Patricia didn't know how long it was before her great-grand-father got a job and a labourer's cottage on the Leigh estate but that was what had happened. The gate lodge the Quinns had lived in was still there.

All that was left now to show the Quinns had lived in the townland of Newcastle was the field named after them.

Funny how the eviction could be talked about in the family but not what happened to Rose:

Abandoned in life
And then in death.

Patricia went back to compiling the list of all the people she would contact: TDs, county councillors, the South Eastern Health Board, priests, the bishop of Ferns, Brendan Comiskey – surely he'd be concerned about the state of the graveyard? There were seventeen names in all. All she needed to do now was to write the letter.

She would send a copy of the letter to the local papers too. A wave of nervousness swept over her at the thought of it being published. Rose's story would be in the public domain. There would be no turning back.

*

'You starting a campaign?' the girl in the card shop said as she photocopied the letter Catherine had typed.

'Something like that,' said Patricia.

But now would she have the courage to pop the letters in the post when she had stuck them in envelopes?

Back at home she painstakingly addressed them all.

'The Editor, the *Echo* newspaper ...' she wrote.

The gum stuck to her lips as she dampened the flaps of the envelopes. Carefully she put a stamp on each one and, before she could talk herself out of it, she grabbed her bag and headed for the post office in Anne Street.

She stood there for a few minutes before letting the envelopes go. 'This is for you, Rose!' she said as the letters clunked on the bottom of the box.

They were gone. There was no going back now. Rose's story

was public. Feeling a mixture of excitement and apprehension she left the post office and headed home.

She woke early the following Wednesday morning. Today was paper day. Would her letter be in the *Echo* or *The People*? She hurried to Morris' shop to look. Had her letter been included? No luck with the first paper but a quick turn of the pages of the *Echo* brought her to the letters page. The heading jumped out at her – 'Sadness at Cemetery'. Her letter was there, word for word. All she had to do now was wait and see if it brought any reaction.

She had several phone calls within days from family, from neighbours, from independent county councillor Padge Reck and local historian Nicky Furlong, who promised to help. Long conversations centred on what had happened to people years ago. Yes, something should be done to remember them, they all agreed.

Acknowledgement letters from TDs came next – Fianna Fáil TDs John Browne and Hugh Byrne, Ivan Yates of Fine Gael and Labour TD Brendan Howlin. They would pass her letter on to the manager of the hospital, they said, and to the South Eastern Health Board and get back to her as soon as they received a reply.

'God help the manager of the hospital,' Patricia thought. She had visions of him or her being swamped with copies of the same letter but how was she to know that the politicians would each have sent a copy on? Maybe Michael was right. Maybe she should just have picked a party and contacted one politician.

There was more chance of getting help, she had thought, though, by contacting everybody. Maybe that way something would be done.

*

Several weeks passed and there was still no reply from St Senan's hospital. How long more would it take? Patricia felt frustrated by the wait. She needed information about Rose – every scrap that could be found. What was her exact condition when she went into the asylum? What did the doctor's records say?

It was just before Christmas that the letter with the Enniscorthy postmark arrived.

'From the hospital?' said Catherine who had called in.

Patricia scanned the lines rapidly. 'It says there are no records, that the county council might have records and that no one has been buried there since the 1940s.'

'Does it say how many were buried there before that?' asked Catherine.

'No.'

'Why doesn't that surprise me?' said Catherine. 'Give us a look.'

Patricia felt as if she had hit a brick wall. Catherine read the short letter quickly.

'There must be records somewhere,' Patricia said.

'See what the county council says. We won't give up yet,' her daughter said.

'I bet they're there somewhere – propping up tables or stuck in some dusty old storeroom.'

Unspoken between them was the hope that the records hadn't been burned.

'Don't worry, they haven't – they're in the hospital,' said Catherine.

The letter said that the staff and patients of the hospital didn't forget the patients buried in the hospital graveyard. The hospital chaplain held a pattern there every summer, weather permitting, it added. Patricia was welcome to go to the next one if she wanted.

'Yes, I want to,' Patricia said. 'Definitely.'

The fact that they held a pattern was something. At least a few prayers were said there once a year.

'The management probably think I'm making a fuss about nothing,' she said. 'That I'm an over-sentimental busybody.'

'You're not. They don't know what we know.'

Of course they couldn't. All the coincidences, what Catherine had seen, no one else knew about it.

At mass in the friary later Patricia prayed that Rose would find peace.

Where was God when Rose was being committed, she wondered? Why did He forsake her and so many others? Sometimes it was hard to figure it all out, to excuse all the bad things in the world, hard not to blame a God who is supposed to be compassionate, but then the God that Rose would have known would have been one of fear, of retribution. How much of the blame for what happened had she taken on herself?

'It wasn't God who put her in the asylum,' said Patricia as she walked home. 'His will didn't come into it.'

*

The next few weeks went by quickly – and disappointingly. Most of the politicians hadn't actually done anything. They had just passed her letter on to the hospital. Their letters didn't mention the cemetery being tidied up.

'They aren't even listening,' said Patricia to herself. Right now she felt like going up there with a slash hook and cutting back the weeds and ivy herself but that might cause a stir. Would she be trespassing? She could see the headlines now – 'Wexford Woman Fined for Graveyard Trespass'.

It was almost Christmas now and the days were full of the routine of work, of preparations for the festive season, of present buying and meal planning.

After Christmas she would try to find out more about Rose. Right now the streets of Wexford were full of shoppers rushing to get their last minute bits and pieces. All the family would be calling at some stage on Christmas Day – John, her eldest, with his wife and daughters, David and his family and Catherine, her daughter, with her fiancé.

'I love Christmas,' she thought as she put the last pudding on to steam. 'This year will be like two Christmases together with the millennium celebrations as well. The end of another century!'

Patricia couldn't help wondering how Rose had celebrated the end of the century she had seen out. She would have been thirty years of age then. She could not have had any idea then that she would live only seven years into the new one.

What was going on in her life as the bells rang in the first few minutes of the twentieth century? Was she pregnant around that time? Catherine said the child who was with Rose was five or six …

Patricia set the timer to remember to check the saucepan for water in half an hour's time.

'What are you doing for the millennium?' That's what everyone was asking. It was almost a cant at this stage. Everywhere was the feeling that you had to do something significant to mark the end of the old century and the beginning of the new one. For most people it would be a good night out but Patricia had her own plans for the coming year.

If she did nothing else she would have the graveyard improved and a monument erected – even if she had to pay for it herself.

*

She visited the graveyard again on Christmas Eve. The wreath of flowers that she had placed there a few weeks before was still in the same place – no one had touched it. There were no other wreaths.

The winter wind blew through the graveyard making Patricia wrap her coat tighter around her. It was still a desolate place – the grass had lodged even further, the ivy and briars covering even more of the walls. She thought of all the graveyards where wreaths would be laid especially for Christmas, a family time.

In talking to people about Rose since – friends and neighbours who had seen the letter in the paper – story after story had come out about people being put in the asylum. Whispered rememberings of a pregnant woman put in to get rid of her, of illegitimate children who spent their lives there, of brothers put in after rows over land.

'So many stories. Rose's is only one of them.'

Patricia took one last look back at the graveyard. She would say a special prayer at midnight mass. Leaving, she was frustrated by the big holes in her knowledge about Rose. No records, no records. Surely there must be.

She stood there for a few minutes wondering again what Rose's life had been like as a young woman. She could imagine her going about her work in Rosegarland – making butter, feeding pigs, picking fruit in the gardens day after day, letting cows out into Byron's field.

She imagined Rose as a woman of thirty-six, taking shortcuts to the village on her evening off, just as Patricia herself had, walking through Hinks' field, crossing the ditch into Curry's Hill and the railway line down to Wellingtonbridge.

Somehow, imagining Rose's life brought her closer.

2

SUMMER 1906

R ose! Over here!' shouted one of the men cocking hay in Hinks' field as she crossed the ditch into Curry's Hill – a shortcut to the village from the Rosegarland estate where they all worked.

Rose Quinn did not look back.

This time the man whistled.

'Getting stuck up now, are we? Miss High and Mighty Quinn, is it? Thinks she's a cut above buttermilk.'

She could hear the guffaws of the other men but still she didn't turn.

'If it was Ted Jameson who was calling she wouldn't be ignoring him, lads, would she?'

A burst of laughter rose from the men as she hurried on, scratching herself on briars as she did so. She could see them in her mind's eye – sweat making damp patches under their arms as they pitched the hay in the hot July sun, big leery grins on their faces. God only knows what else they were saying about her. Their eyes burnt holes in her back as she continued down the field towards the railway line. 'That's what I get for taking a shortcut.'

If she'd remembered that they were working there she would have gone to Wellingtonbridge the long way round. She wished they hadn't mentioned Ted, though. That meant the staff were talking about her. Watching her. 'If Jack hears of it, he'll not be pleased,' she thought.

Her coachman brother, Jack, worked with Ted, a groom on the estate, every day. Nice and all as Ted was, Jack wouldn't want her having anything to do with someone who dug with the other foot.

Rose automatically blessed herself as she heard the early bell ring in Ballymitty church. She hurried down toward the new railway station, shading her eyes from the sun as she tried to spot her sister-in-law, Mary, but no, there was no sign yet. It would be the first time the children had seen the train close up, even though they had lived on stories of it for years.

Her brother Patrick had held their attention many's the night with stories of his job working for the Great Southern and Western Railway-people who'd built the line through Rosegarland land. Tales of horses being killed when they were building the viaduct at Taylorstown. Rocks disappearing in Leighs' marsh until they never thought they'd find the bottom of it. Half the parish had been employed as well as some outsiders. Now at last the huge task was finished.

'No sign of Jack yet,' she said to herself, looking round, but she didn't worry – she'd have a few more minutes with the children.

Jack had promised to meet her at the station and give her a lift to the New Ross agricultural show. As long as she wasn't spotted getting into the pony and trap in the village no one would be any the wiser. Mary's husband, Rose's eldest brother, Patrick, would already be at the show.

'Quenching his thirst, no doubt,' she said to herself. Patrick was short of work but had a few days now and again helping with the stock at Rosegarland.

'Aunt Rose!' Six-year-old John was running towards her.

She caught him, lifting him up high in the air, and swung him round.

'And how's my little chap?' she said, giving him a hug.

'I'm well, thank you,' he said as his mother and brothers and sisters joined them. Mary Quinn looked flushed from her task of keeping an eye on her six offspring but she seemed pleased to see Rose at the same time. Too pleased, almost.

'Is it coming yet?' The children were anxiously waiting, watching the turn of the track. The stationmaster was checking his pocket watch, rising up and down on the balls of his feet as he did so. No one in the village was used to the sound of the locomotive yet. They could hear the whistle of it now in the distance.

'It's coming! It's coming!'

'Come on!'

Mary and Rose took the younger children's hands. Cattle and sheep in Rosegarland fields scurried away from the big black monster that was now smoking across their territory.

'The world will be a smaller place, they say,' said Mary.

'Not for the likes of us, though,' said Rose.

Lately, she wondered what it would be like to travel beyond Wellingtonbridge, beyond Campile, beyond Waterford even. Across the sea to places she'd only seen on a map.

Boston, New York, London, Fishguard. Fish-guard. New-York. She even liked the sound of the words. Was she only fooling herself thinking that she'd ever get to places like that, even with a train now running from Waterford to Rosslare and linking up with the world? She had lived here all her life – was she too rooted in this place?

In a few weeks' time the official opening of the Rosslare to Fishguard steamboat route would take place. The master, Mr Leigh, was invited, so Cook said.

'Wake in London and sleep in Killarney the same day – that's what they say.'

Rose couldn't even imagine it. It would take her long enough to get by horse and trap to New Ross.

'I'm going to drive a train when I grow up,' young John said as she handed the children some sweets. When the others weren't looking Rose slipped him the string ball she had made.

'You shouldn't spoil him,' said Mary, seeing what she had done. 'It's not right making fish of one and flesh of the other.'

Rose felt the blood rise to her cheeks. 'I'm not …'

Mary put a protective arm around her son's shoulders. Rose looked away. Was Mary laying claim to what was hers?

Rose tried to quell the thoughts of her own child. What was he doing now – eating dry bread and sour milk in the workhouse along with all the other scantily dressed children who bore the name 'bastard'?

'You'll come over to the house tonight for a bite to eat, Rose?'

The invitation surprised her. She'd never had a formal one before.

'What's the big occasion?'

'Well, it's your birthday, isn't it?'

'Yes.' Rose was thirty-six. She hadn't remembered it until now.

'It'd be nice to mark the day, even in a small way.'

Odd. They had never fussed before.

'You will come over?'

'Please, Aunt Rose,' said John, hearing what his mother had said.

'If you want.'

'Good,' Mary said, visibly relieved. 'You'll walk up straight after you get back from the show?'

'If you like.'

'Good.'

'It's coming!'

All along the station people stretched their necks to see the train arrive. Neighbours most of them, people who had worked on the railway, still eager to see what their work had culminated in. Although few had the money to travel on it, it was still drawing a crowd of onlookers every day. Those who could afford it would have to wait to travel on it, though. It would only carry goods until August – so said the paper.

'Stand clear.' The stationmaster's voice rang out as the train chuffed to a halt. The children were speechless at the sight and the sound of it.

'Where's the coal kept, Aunt Rose?'

'At the back, I think. In the tender.'

'The ten-der,' young John said, as if the word had some magic in it.

A few minutes later the goods that were sitting ready on the platform were loaded into the carriages, the whistle was blown and the new train chuffed out of the station.

Rose's brother Jack arrived in the pony and trap, staying at the station entrance and whoa-ing the horse into steadiness as the train departed.

*

The journey to New Ross was all uphill. Ross, the town she shared a name with. It was called after Strongbow's sister, Rose, or so they said. Maybe that's why her mother had chosen the name for her. She was glad of it if it was the case. It made her feel special. There were plenty of Marys and Lizzies and Pegs around.

Maybe her mother had given her a more unusual name because she thought she wasn't going to live. She had been baptised *subconditionae* – in danger of death. Her mother's naming fancy had not pleased her father, though. Rose had the ring of an Englishwoman's name, he said, and no daughter of his would ever be that.

Rose … Rose …

Her fingers suddenly curled around her rosary beads as she tried to repress the thought of someone saying her name very, very softly one cold winter's night several years before. Persuading her. Insisting.

She blessed herself. 'Hail Mary, full of grace, the –'

'How's work?'

Jack's words interrupted her prayer. She would burn in hell for stopping.

'Same as usual. Hard.'

'At the blackcurrants, are you?'

'Aye,' she said, showing him her stained hands.

For several days herself and Bridget Rowe had been picking fruit after they'd finished their regular jobs of feeding the hens and pigs, making butter and helping in the fields. The long days of hard work seemed to roll into one another but at least she had a job. There were those who hadn't.

Some said they were lucky to work on the Leigh estate. Others muttered 'Leigh the Leveller' as they passed the gate and told tales of yards being paved with the stones of evicted tenants' houses.

She was glad to have the day off. It was only by catching the steward when he was in a good humour that she'd managed to get it on the day of the show. That and the fact that her chances of winning a prize in the milking competition that all the estate girls entered were high. It would mean an extra shilling in her wages if she won.

'I suppose you've no choice but to put up with it for the moment,' Jack said, flicking the reins to make the mare go faster.

'What?' she asked.

'Being in service.'

'How do you mean?'

'Your not being wed. You've no choice but go on working.'

'I don't need a husband. I'm all right as I am.'

Jack shifted himself in his seat and corrected the horse that needed no correction. 'There's women your age'd like to settle. Have a family.'

'I'm a bit long in the tooth for that. Is it because you're not long married yourself that you want the rest of us following suit?' she asked, laughing at his seriousness.

'No. I was only thinking of your future.'

Rose brushed away a horsefly that was determined to bite her. 'Everyone seems very concerned about me today for some reason. First an invitation to supper at Patrick and Mary's and now you talking all serious – is it that my brothers are all going cracked? It'll be the red brick for the lot of you if you're not careful!'

Jack laughed. 'Divil the fear of that!'

'Good.'

The road to Ross was busy – ponies and traps, donkeys and carts, people on foot. The closer they got to the town the busier it was. Barefoot children ran after Leigh's trap for a while after they passed, laughing as the mare broke wind as she walked uphill.

'Looks like there's a delay of some sort,' said Jack. Ahead of them everyone had come to a full stop. The people on foot were craning their necks to see what the delay was.

Jack checked his pocket watch. Five minutes to ten. He was supposed to meet the master soon. 'See what the problem is, Rose. There'll be trouble if I'm late for the judging.'

Rose jumped down from the trap and onto the dusty street.

Other pedestrians turned to watch as she strode purposefully to the front of the crowd to speak to the RIC officer. 'What's the hold up? We have to get to the show,' she said to the officer.

'Military pipe band coming up from the station, miss. The Cameron Highlanders. No one's moving until they've gone by.' As he spoke she heard the familiar sound of bagpipes. Her head turned instantly, her foot already stirring to a tap at the sound of the drum major marking time. Piping had always excited her. The estate had a piper and she loved waking to the sound of the reveille being played each morning. The Highlanders were playing a march, a tune she had never heard before. What a sound! She pushed nearer the front of the crowd to get a glimpse of them.

'Bagpipes, you can't beat them,' the officer said, seeing her enthusiasm.

'No.'

The music was getting closer now. Rose could feel the excitement building in her chest. She wanted to walk, march, follow them wherever they were going.

Within minutes the soldiers with the green kilts and red jackets appeared. They were led by a drum major, the plume on his busby dancing as he twirled the mace in front of him in time to the music. The brass buttons of the uniforms glinted in the sunlight.

Rose's heart beat faster as they passed within feet of her, her ears filling with the sound, her eyes with the colourful spectacle. She wished the music would go on forever.

'Can't beat a man in a uniform for catching a woman's eye,' said the RIC officer to his colleague as he watched Rose.

The other officer smiled. 'No.'

'I think I'll walk the rest of the way,' Rose said to Jack, after she had run quickly back to him. 'Follow the band up.'

'Don't let Patrick see you or he won't be happy.'

'What's it got to do with him? I'm a grown woman, for God's sake.'

'That won't stop him telling you what to do. He's not too pleased about that shower coming here.'

'He takes everything too seriously. There's no law against listening to music.'

'Still, it'd be better if he didn't see you.'

Parting company with Jack, she caught up quickly with the crowd behind the band. Her spirits felt a bit dampened but her eldest brother had always been able to do that. Jack was right. Patrick wouldn't want her, or any of the family, being part of an audience for any band of English soldiers. He'd drive the invaders out of the country if he could. Every time he got drunk he sang Fenian songs and ranted about the eviction. As if none of the rest of them remembered it. She remembered it. How could she not, seeing her sick grandfather carried out to the side of the road before the bailiffs took possession of the house, listening to her mother and her siblings cry, not knowing what fate would now befall them. Still, the memory hadn't festered in her like it had with Patrick. Now she preferred not to think about what kind of planning and plotting went on among men like her brother in the forge on dark winter's evenings.

He was wrong about this music, though. This music didn't belong to anyone, even the English. It belonged to the world.

As the tune ended the band continued to march along the street, starting another one a few yards further on and drawing shop workers from their labours as they passed. Now they filed down the hill towards the show field.

After she'd joined the crowds waiting to pay their penny admission into the show, she felt her arm being grabbed tightly from behind.

'Have you no shame?' It was Patrick, the rims of his eyes already red. Rose knew better than to argue with him when he was like this.

'I wasn't doing any harm.'

'We'll not march to the beat of their music – we have our own. Now get over to the milking – they'll be looking for you.'

Rose shook with anger as she parted company with him. So he had taken lately to going to céilís organised by the Gaelic League in the village, even speaking a few words of Irish when he got the chance – that didn't mean he had to shut out the music she liked.

Still angry, she made her way over by the hundreds of sheep who were bleating in pens as well-dressed judges marked down their scores on sheets of paper.

Patrick could always do this to her. 'You'd think you'd have more sense than to mind him,' she said to herself. Even though she was thirty-six he could still dominate her. She felt like lashing out at him for giving her orders. Why shouldn't she – weren't women fighting for the vote, weren't women entitled to have minds of their own now? Still, she knew it was a battle she would lose. Jack wouldn't even stand up to him. Since their parents had died Patrick was the head of the family – and he liked everyone to remember it. He didn't care what age the rest of them were.

Reluctantly putting distance between herself and the Cameron Highlanders, she soon reached the ring where she was to meet Bridget Rowe, her friend. Bridget worked with her in Rosegarland and lived in Clongeen but she had stayed overnight with her aunt Maggie in New Ross and so would have a head start on Rose.

'She promised she'd be here.' Rose removed the wrapped piece of bread and cheese she'd brought with her while she waited – it would fill her stomach for a while. She'd have enough to buy a penny bun later on.

From her standpoint she could see down onto the show field. People were milling about like ants, some enjoying the sideshows, the farmers gathering in groups at agricultural-implement stands where salesmen showed off the finer points of Pierce mowers and O'Dwyer Bros Binders. Animals stood tied to posts and in pens waiting their turn in the show rings – cattle, sheep, pigs, purebred bulls that everybody but their handlers was keeping a respectable distance from.

That's where Patrick would be. The Leighs often called him in to help with the bulls because he showed no fear of them. 'Rather him than me,' she thought.

There'd be prizes for the best stock today, much-sought-after prizes that would mean higher prices on fair days. Mrs Kinsella from Ballycullane was there with her best jennet too. Rose smiled at the thought of the fuss last year when the judges announced Mrs Kinsella's jennet was a mule and disqualified it from the competition. Mrs Kinsella could be heard cursing in Newbawn.

Rose tried to stop herself thinking of the workhouse that stood above the town.

'There's no good dwelling on him and where he is,' she thought, yet she fingered the beads in her pocket, praying for the health of her child and for her soul. She had brought great shame upon herself and upon her family but God was a merciful God, wasn't He? Not a vengeful one like the priests at retreats said.

'Boo!'

Rose almost jumped out of her skin as someone shouted loudly in her ear. It was Bridget, laughing at the fun of surprising her.

'Jesus, you'll never grow up!' said Rose, recovering from the fright.

'And your face would stop a clock. What were you thinking about?' Bridget said, linking Rose's arm as they walked in the direction of the milking ring.

'Nothing.'

Bridget looked sideways at her. 'Good. It's not a day for moping. Not when you have important work to do. And when Ted Jameson'll be watching you.'

'He will not!'

'He will so. I heard him asking the steward if he could have a few minutes off when the horse judging is over. I'll bet you anything he'll turn up when you're milking.'

Rose said nothing but secretly she was pleased. Ted made the days bearable at Rosegarland. Smiling at her from a distance, always a kind word. He was a good man.

'See, there he is,' said Bridget pointing.

Bridget was right. Ted was leaning over the fence waiting for the milking competition to start. He saw her and smiled. She looked away. It wouldn't do to be seen making friendly with him by either of her brothers.

Bridget handed her the bucket. Ten cows were lined up in a row at the far side of the ring. Once the judge blew the whistle all the women entering the competition had to pick up their buckets and stools and go to the cows. The first one to empty the cow's udder was the winner.

'I can't wait to see Lizzie Conway's face when you beat her. She can't stand anyone winning except her.'

Lizzie Conway worked on Major Boyce's estate near Carrig-on-Bannow, a few miles from Rosegarland. Rose had never been able to beat her before.

With the blast of the whistle, Rose took her bucket and

stool and hurried towards cow number nine. Placing the stool on the grass, she quickly seated herself and placed the bucket under the cow's udder. The cow was long overdue being milked. Already milk had begun to stream from her teats. Grabbing the two at the far side, Rose squeezed on the soft flesh and pulled down hard as she did so. Now milk squirted out, making noise as it hit the bottom of the wooden bucket.

Rhythmically she continued her work, expertly pulling the white liquid from its store. Froth built up on the top of the milk that was now filling the bucket. The heat from the cow's body became almost unbearable as her hands moved to the second set of teats. She could hear the crowd shouting, women's voices, men's voices, as she neared the end of her task. Was one of the voices Ted's?

'Come on, Rose! Faster, Rose!'

After finally checking that every teat was empty, Rose stood up.

No, she hadn't won – she was a few seconds behind number three, the girl from Horetown House, but at least she'd beaten Lizzie. She might be in her thirties but she wasn't over the hill yet.

One of the judges strode quickly over, stopping his watch and checking that the udder was empty.

'The winner! Mary Dillon, Horetown. Second, Rose Quinn, Rosegarland.'

Bridget was grinning from ear to ear. 'Tough luck but you did well. The competition was stiff.'

Rose could see Ted Jameson smiling at her from the far side of the ring. Even Jack was there.

'A blessing to any man – that's what she'd be, with hands on her like that.' It was her brother Patrick bragging to the man beside him.

'Who's that with your brother?' Bridget asked as she gave Rose a bucket of water to wash her hands.

'I don't know,' said Rose, looking over. 'Someone he worked with on the railway maybe.'

The man continued to stare at her and grinned suddenly as he listened to something else Patrick was saying.

'I wouldn't like waking up to look at his face of a morning,' said Bridget.

'Neither would I.'

'Put me off getting up at all.'

Rose laughed as she glanced back. The man was still watching her.

*

Rose was glad to be back in Wellingtonbridge. She was hungry, tired and thirsty now and glad that the journey on Redmond's donkey and cart was over. It wasn't nearly as comfortable as Leighs' trap but she was grateful for the lift. No one could travel in style all the time.

Right now she would prefer to go back to Rosegarland where Cook would give her something to eat as she threw questions about the show and all that went on at her. Still, she could tell the staff about it later. She had promised she'd go to Patrick's. If she didn't the children would never forgive her.

Rose left the village and turned right for Clongeen opposite the Norman ruins at Clonmines. It was hard to get used to crossing the railway tracks. They were odd steel things, foreign to the ground. She crossed quickly even though she knew that the train probably hadn't yet left Waterford.

As she walked toward the townland of Rochestown, not far from the farmyard entrance to Rosegarland, she hummed the tune she'd heard the pipers play that day. She was glad she had heard the Cameron Highlanders. Good music was good music, no matter what the players' allegiance was. Patrick took all this Fenian stuff too seriously. Still, she stopped humming as she came within sight of the house.

The children were at the end of the lane watching out for her: two, four, six, including young John. Such a big family to feed. Rose felt afraid for them with the winter coming on and their father not in permanent work. Even though there had been talk of the government giving some land back at low rent to people who had been evicted for years now, the landlords weren't eager to hand it over.

How would Patrick and his family survive over the winter with nothing?

Banishing such thoughts, she greeted the children as they ran towards her.

'Aunt Rose, Aunt Rose! Will you teach me to milk cows when we get some?' John asked.

So their father was filling them with tales of becoming farmers. She hoped they wouldn't be disappointed.

'Of course I will,' said Rose, sorry that she hadn't been back to Rosegarland first and got a few turnips or apples or some gooseberries from the garden. If she was careful, no one saw her, and she wasn't the only staff member to take the odd thing or two – didn't she work hard enough to have earned a few benefits?

*

Mary Quinn was putting the kettle on the fire when Rose entered, her face flushed from the heat in the small kitchen. 'Rose – sit down. John, get your aunt a drink of water. She's thirsty after her long day.'

'You shouldn't have gone to so much trouble.'

It was obvious Mary had taken great care with the pre-parations. Several of her highly valued wedding gifts were sitting on the table, replacing the normal tin mugs they drank out of.

'It's no trouble,' Mary said, shooing out the curious hen that had perched on top of the half door.

'Where's Patrick?'

'He'll be along in a minute,' Mary said, cutting up the soda loaf. 'He's out in the yard with someone.'

A few minutes later her brother entered, accompanied by the man who had been with him at the show.

'Rose,' said Patrick, nodding and looking almost embarrassed. 'This is Pat Murphy.'

Mary fussed finding him a stool.

Rose suddenly felt as if a stone had lodged in her chest.

Now she knew what was going on, why they had invited her to supper. They wanted her to meet this man – the man they wanted her to marry.

3

EXTRAORDINARY STORY

Patricia Murphy's letter to the *Echo* newspaper was photo-copied and placed in the 'Possible Topics' folder at South East Radio the day it came out. Local woman trying to right a wrong – it was a good story, worthy of time on the current affairs programme, *Regional Express*, that I researched for.

Still, an old graveyard behind St Senan's psychiatric hospital – did I really want to go rooting around there? I would have to see the place to know what she was talking about. St Senan's – even the name of the place made me uneasy or was I simply tarred with a stigma brush too, one that made me shy away from unsavoury subjects?

Then there was the other complication of the chairman of the board of the radio station being chief nursing officer at St Senan's. How would management feel about me turning a negative focus on his place of work? Maybe it would be better to leave the subject alone.

Yet every time I looked through the folder the title 'Sadness at Cemetery' caught my eye and I re-read the letter.

A woman being forced to marry someone then being locked up in an asylum because she wouldn't go live with him – the feminist in me bristled at the thought of such treatment. She had died so quickly too – what exactly had happened to her in that red-brick fortress?

I read the letter again. It was well written: that was immediately obvious. I could picture the writer taking time over it, wishing to make every word count. There was no doubt about the sincerity behind it. I wondered what she was like – this Patricia Murphy (*née* Quinn).

Over Christmas Rose's story kept coming back to me. If there were hundreds of people like her in that graveyard something should be done about it. To hell with it – I was a journalist, wasn't I? I'd have to get over any personal ghosts and, when it came to highlighting subjects on the programme, we had editorial independence, didn't we?

The thought of it not being known exactly who or how many were buried in that cemetery appalled me. Women, especially, were unjustly treated in the past – an interest and qualification in history had taught me that much. My knowledge of the period of Rose's life centred on men, though, I realised: Parnell and the Land Wars, the elusiveness of Home Rule and the build up to world war and rebellion. Asylums hadn't featured much in my educational landscape except as a by-the-way feature of the Poor Law system under which Britain and Ireland were governed until 1898.

I would call to see Patricia as soon as I returned to work, I decided. With any luck she would have made some progress in having the graveyard done up and would want to talk about it on air.

*

Michael Murphy answered the door. I was taken aback momentarily by seeing a familiar face. Where had I seen him before?

'Pettitt's – the meat counter,' he said smiling.

'Exactly!'

He was on a late lunch break. Yes, Patricia was there, he said. She appeared immediately, still in her chef's uniform having just returned from work at the friary.

She doesn't look mad, I thought, and immediately hated

myself for thinking such a thing. It was the sceptic in me coming out again.

The thought that perhaps Rose really had been mentally ill and rightfully committed had crossed my mind. Perhaps there was a family predisposition towards psychiatric illness and perhaps her great-niece's version of the story was a manicured version of events that simply squared with family dignity.

Our conversation lasted over half an hour. I left the house in John Street knowing that the story of Rose Quinn would dominate my life for a long time to come.

I also left the house knowing that I had just met a remarkable person. There was no doubt about her sincerity and no doubt about the scale of the story. This story was bigger than a ten-minute slot on any daily radio programme. This was documentary material.

The coincidences, unmentioned in the letter to the newspaper, clinched it – Patricia's birthday being the same day as Rose's (11 July), her having married a man with the same surname, from the same parish, in the same church. What was going on here?

'It's as if there is a psychic link between you,' I said. 'Rose is trying to get you to tell her story.'

'Yes, there are a lot of coincidences,' Patricia said smiling. 'I believe she wants her story told.'

Having asked her how much documentation she had found already, my mind raced forward, quantifying what research would be needed. There had been no real progress since the letter was published, she said. Hospital management had written to say there were no records for this period. She had received a few phone calls from politicians and supporters but she was no nearer achieving her goal.

'But there must be records somewhere,' I said. 'We'll have

a go at finding them – between us you'd never know what we could come up with.'

I headed back down Abbey Street, into Cornmarket and back to the station on Custom House Quay. I had to talk to the programme's producer and presenter, Alan McGuire. He was in the downstairs office with *Echo* journalist Conor Breen.

'Well, how did it go?' Alan asked.

'Amazingly,' I said, telling them about the details the letter hadn't mentioned.

'What was Patricia like?'

'Articulate, sincere and sane,' I said.

'Excellent,' Alan said.

The story was worthy of a documentary – they both agreed on that.

'I can see it now,' said Conor. 'Documentary, book, who knows? In years to come we'll remember this day.'

The foundation for the documentary *Forgotten People* was laid.

The next nine months were to be a time of research, of logging the progress of Patricia's campaign to have the graveyard cleaned up.

I would visit places of significance in both her and Rose's lives, follow leads, get lost down research cul-de-sacs, speak to historians to help paint a picture of life at the time and seek the hospital management's opinion.

St Senan's wasn't the baddie – I knew that. If there was a paupers' graveyard behind that former asylum there were certain to be such graveyards all over the country. Those places, I knew, had opened in the mid-1800s, all under the Poor Law system. What was done in one would have been done in them all. Nameless people could have been buried in them for seventy or eighty years. Multiply that and the number could run into hundreds of thousands of people whose deaths, at that time, society didn't care about.

Yes, there was a score to settle – somebody should remember these people. Tell the story of one, as a friend said, and you tell the story of a thousand.

That day was the beginning of a bond between Patricia Murphy and me that, in time, was to sideline journalistic distance. I was helping with the research on Rose to add to her knowledge and deepen the thrust of the documentary. I was also fascinated by what life would have been like for Rose before she was committed. What was the build up to the story? What were the family dynamics? I wanted to know every detail. Could I rebuild Rose's story in an objective way down the line? Such was the hold of the story on me that I wanted to try.

More startling coincidences followed as the research gathered momentum. A meeting with Patricia for coffee one afternoon in April was to fundamentally shock me, while at the same time telling me of the trigger that sent Patricia to the hospital that day the previous September.

Experience told me that there is usually some event, some last straw or first realisation that pushes a person to go forward. This was it and what a trigger it was. For several years this had remained a secret. In 2004 Catherine finally became more open about her gift and took the leap of faith that goes with disclosing such a gift.

The documentary would tell most of Rose's story but not all. It would also bring forth a similarly remarkable story of another Wexford woman, Mary Farndon, and her search for the grave of her grandfather who died in the asylum in 1926.

It is my privilege to include that story and to tell the story of three Quinn women – Rose, Patricia and Catherine.

4

BREAKTHROUGH

Patricia's New Year resolutions were made – visit old friends and neighbours more often, watch the cholesterol, walk in the women's mini-marathon for charity in June, perhaps. It would be such an achievement to do that – even though she'd be more tortoise than hare performance wise, but so what? Slow and steady gets there in the end.

Patricia wished she could simply make a resolution to have good health and, hey presto, she'd have it. Then she could throw medication out the window and inflamed joints and 'sick tiredness' would be no more.

If only life was that simple.

As it was, few people knew she had medical problems and those who did said they wouldn't have thought it to look at her. On a good day they were probably right. On a good day she could 'beat herself into shape', as she called it – do her hair, put on make-up and get ready to face the world. That was one thing being ill had taught her – never judge the book by the cover. Just because a person looks well doesn't necessarily mean that they are.

On bad days, though, she knew they'd hardly recognise her and it was then that she didn't want anyone to see her. She'd rather hole up until the bad time had passed. The important thing to do, though, was to refuse to let it get you down. If there were several bad days they were only that – a few bad days. Tomorrow was a new day. Fresh. She would be better tomorrow.

Right now she was sorry Christmas and the millennium fuss were over. The house looked bare with the clutter of decorations gone. She wasn't looking forward to a cold January. Roll on February and the promise of spring!

*

After the researcher from the radio station had left Patricia felt both apprehensive and excited.

Funny, she hadn't sent the letter directly to the radio station. It was the one place she hadn't sent it. Strange the way things work out sometimes. Although she was a bit anxious about being on radio she felt maybe that was the way it was meant to be.

Rose's story would be told on the airwaves. 'She must be grinning up there – she'll be getting her story told in style.'

Patricia felt that she would win this battle to get at the records about Rose now that she had some help.

She walked over to the stereo and put on a CD of bagpipe music – one of the many that stood in a rack in her kitchen. She was a big fan of piping, an addict almost, though she couldn't explain where that addiction came from. Maybe Rose had been a fan too, for all she knew. The music filled the small room – the Gordon Highlanders playing 'The Battle is O'er'. It was a triumphant tune, one that always lifted her spirits.

'If I get the graveyard cleaned up I'll have a piper play that tune the day the headstone is unveiled,' she said.

Right now, though, that seemed a very long way away. She had a lot of work to do.

There must be things she could find out about the times Rose had lived in, the kind of Ireland she was born into, the kind of society that would treat people like that. She added another resolution to her list. She would spend as much time as she could spare in the library.

The county council was in charge of the asylums until the 1970s, she'd found out, until the responsibility was handed over to the newly formed health boards. Perhaps they did have records stashed somewhere? Perhaps the books had been removed from the hospitals after the change-over. She hoped against hope that there hadn't been a bonfire and they'd all gone up in flames.

But first she would go to the clinic to ask for a copy of Rose's death certificate. The researcher said it should be there. Why hadn't she thought of that before?

*

Patricia watched the girl in Wexford County Clinic copy out the details with ink pen. She got a lump in her throat when she read the certificate. Rose had died of phthisis – what disease was that? She'd had it for 'some months' before death, the certificate said.

And then the part that really upset her. Rose's death was registered by one Patrick Donnelly – an inmate, residence: District Asylum. The words shocked her. Rose didn't even have the dignity of an asylum staff member to register her death.

How many deaths had this inmate registered that day, 24 May 1907, she wondered? The death was registered in the town of Enniscorthy. How would an inmate, who was seriously mentally ill, be allowed out to do that? Surely that proved that many people were wrongly incarcerated? Her mind was full of questions.

Her eyes scanned the certificate for 'occupation'. Rose was listed as servant. That was confirmation that Rose had never gone to live with her husband. If she had she would have been down as housewife, surely?

Patricia clutched the certificate as she left the clinic – now she had birth, marriage and death records. How long, and what, would it take to get the records of Rose's admission to the asylum?

*

The Wexford librarian and historian Celestine Rafferty had no good news for her when she called seeking help.

'Phthisis was TB – tuberculosis of the lungs,' she said. 'It was rife in asylums and workhouses at the time. It would have killed her very quickly.'

'She gave up the will to live when she went there anyway,' Patricia said, as the two people with her wondered at her certainty.

'People died like flies in those places at the turn of the century. The sanitation was dreadful in that era,' said Celestine.

The thoughts of Rose dying in squalor and pain filled Patricia with sadness – that on top of her family turning their backs on her. How could anyone bear such a fate?

'Asylums were packed to bursting point in the early 1900s,' said Celestine. 'Most of them had many more inmates than they were built to take. Irish people were fond of locking family members up given the slightest reason in those times.'

Patricia asked how much information she could find out in the library.

'Well, you're at a disadvantage straight away because it's a woman you're looking for information about.'

'Why is that?'

'Women don't feature much in the records of the time, unless they had property. Property-owning men are the easiest to track. You could try the census of 1901, though. It might tell you where she was living at the time.'

'Thank you. I will.'

Hours in front of the microfiche machine followed, scrolling through records. Patricia found the listing for her grandfather, Patrick, his wife, Mary, and their six children, including her father who was one at the time. The record was there for the townland of Rochestown.

Her grandfather was listed as an engine driver. That was correct enough. The railway was being built at the time and he had driven a steam lorry to draw stones while the land was cleared for the building of the line.

Perhaps Rose was living with her sisters in Rospile? She checked out that townland but no luck – Kate, Lizzie and Johanna were listed but there was no entry for 'Rose'.

She would surely find her in Rosegarland then, living in, she thought. Maybe she was already working there in 1901.

Patricia was disappointed to find no mention of her.

'Perhaps it's tied in with the child that Catherine saw with Rose,' thought Patricia. 'Wasn't he five or six? That meant that he could have been born in 1901.' Rose would most likely have been shut away somewhere until he was born. Was she in the workhouse or in the Good Shepherd convent in New Ross, Patricia wondered, shut away until he was old enough to be weaned and taken from her? Her having had a child would explain why Rose's family were so eager to get her married off – to get a bit of respectability back into the family.

But why bother to get her married off at thirty-six – her childbearing years were nearly over, surely? Why bother to make a match for her? Still, marriage would keep her out of harm's way.

When asked, Catherine couldn't throw any more light on this. Rose had given her no more information since, she said.

'I've probably done my part,' said Catherine. 'It's up to you to do the research, that's the way I feel Rose wants it.'

Patricia searched the records for the asylum. She had to put another theory to rest. What if Rose had really been mentally ill and she had been in the asylum, then let out again? The asylum census records yielded nothing. There were no names for inmates, just initials, and no sign of an R. Q. or R. M., she was relieved to see. She looked at the causes of the inmates' insanity listed in a column to the right – reversal of fortune, affairs of the heart, disease …

She then searched the census records for the convent. Only the nuns were named. The women who would have been there didn't even have the dignity of initials.

There were no names for the workhouse residents either.

It was a sad state of affairs but yet it didn't surprise her. Her own mother, a generation later, had her own fears of such places. 'You two better mind yourselves,' she had said to Patricia's sister, Maura, and herself, 'I don't want either of you ending up in the county home.'

The county homes were the old workhouses, still sheltering those who had 'fallen'.

Patricia watched as a young mother checked out her books in the library while her child watched from his pushchair. There was no ring on the girl's finger. How times had changed. No more secrets like Rose's baby. No more women hiding away. Thank God for a healthier society.

*

It was the end of January. How much longer would it take to find records of Rose's admission to the asylum? Without them she had no written proof that Rose had ever been there. The letter from the county council said they had no records from the former asylum – their guess was that they were still in the hospital somewhere.

Ping-pong, back and forth the buck was passing. How would she ever get her hands on Rose's records if the hospital wouldn't give her access?

The lack of progress was frustrating. All those letters and nothing real to show for it and the graveyard no nearer to being cleaned up. All those empty words: 'Please do not hesitate to contact me if I can be of any further assistance ...' Maybe she would put them under pressure to give her more assistance. She would meet the TDs in person.

By seven o'clock that evening she had travelled to meet the first one.

He was the most obvious choice – hadn't she been reared a Fianna Fáil supporter? Hadn't her dad been a De Valera man to the backbone? Hadn't he done things that were within the call of duty, as he saw it at the time, then paid the price for his participation in the Troubles by having to leave the country after 1922?

The TD wasn't sure that anything could be done, he said. There were problems – obstacles. Who would cover the cost for a garden of remembrance, for instance? What about insurance? The county council had given him the impression, he said, that they didn't want anything done about the graveyard – neither did the hospital. Patricia wondered what they were afraid of. Was it fear of setting a precedent for cleaning up other old graveyards in the county and it all costing too much money?

'I see,' she said as she left the room, 'but thank you for your time. I'm not sure what I can do but luckily the radio station is interested in the story – maybe something will come of that.'

*

Two days later Patricia returned to the cemetery. In her hand she held the small framed plaque she was going to put up somewhere for Rose. It contained a poem she had written herself, scribbled in hurried moments one day while at work in the friary:

Rose Quinn
11/7/1870 – 4/5/1907

Discarded,
Disowned
A desolate feeling
Suffering
Untold
But a special person

A person with dignity
A person with feelings
Dealt with a cruel hand
But loved

Loved and cherished by Someone Greater
Taken from the suffering to love and peace

And now
Years later
Found
Your story unfolding

A special person in my family
My purpose
To say
You were special
You were loved
Your life was of value
An expression of sorrow
For treatment by family
And thanksgiving to the Greater Power
For your life
For a special Rose.

She couldn't believe the sight that met her eyes when she parked in the gateway. The place was being tidied up! All the ivy had been removed from the walls. The ditch had been trimmed. The laurels had been cut back.

A man, a patient of the hospital, she suspected, was in the field below the graveyard burning all the ivy and rubbish from the graveyard. The fire crackled and the smoke hung heavy on the crisp January air. So the clean up had started! She was delighted.

Had it anything to do with it becoming known that the media was interested, she wondered? Had one politician or other put pressure on or had the hospital simply got round to doing something they had intended to do for a while? Patricia didn't care which it was. She was just glad it had happened.

The walls on two sides had been completely stripped. Now she could see the rusty nails and the broken glass clearly sticking up on top of the walls. Was that to keep people in or to keep people out? The former, she decided.

The grass had been cut with a scythe, probably, because it had been so heavy. The plant that she had placed on the spot where Catherine believed Rose was buried was still there.

Her eyes kept going back to the far wall – the wall behind Rose that Catherine had described that hadn't been quite right in reality. Patricia had never noticed the stonework before but then how could she have with all the ivy and briars covering them?

The hairs now stood up on the back of Patricia's neck as she looked at the wall. It was built from two types of stone – the top three feet or so were different, a darker stone than the rest of the wall. So! The wall had been raised.

Catherine had said she could see one of the towers of the hospital over the wall behind Rose. The wall must have been lower in 1907 and the tower could be seen. Until now it was the only detail that hadn't been correct. Now she knew it was right.

Eventually settling to her task she placed the framed poem at the bottom of the cross. Tears came as she thought of the death that Rose must have had. To die so alone – discarded, disowned; at least now her story was unfolding. Patricia blew her nose. 'Better pull myself together.'

The graveyard had been tidied up in the 1960s, she'd been told, but no one had been buried there since the 1940s. The ground rose to a slope against the wall on the right-hand side. Had the ground always been sloped or had the ground been pushed up in the 1960s clean up? The cement cross must have been erected then. The gateway separating the graveyard from the rest of the field looked like its contemporary too.

Patricia left the graveyard feeling excited. She had to ring Catherine. She'd be delighted by the news about the wall. She would also be delighted that the clean up had started. 'I'll get a memorial up here by Christmas, if it kills me,' Patricia said to herself before closing the rusty gate behind her.

*

It was 8 February. Stooping to pick up the envelope in the hall she saw it had an Oireachtas stamp on it. Would it be good news this time?

It was. Ivan Yates TD had decided to table a written question in the dáil asking the minister for health, Micheál Martin, to put pressure on the health board to supply information about Rose, he said. Patricia was amazed. Rose's story was going straight to the top. If the minister for health couldn't get answers, who could?

Patricia thought of the number of times she had heard 'there are no records for this period'. A health-board spokesperson had said that there may be anecdotal evidence of patients from the hospital being buried there but there are no records.

She had visited the graveyard again that day, three weeks after the last visit, and was disappointed to see that nothing more had been done. Maybe things would start to move now.

And they did – the management must have been contacted by the minister's office. When the phone rang later that day it was a call from St Senan's hospital saying that a staff member had been appointed to do a record search. So they had records after all!

Now, every day dragged. The dáil question would be tabled in a week's time, 15 February. Patricia prayed that something would come of it.

She read the copy of Ivan Yates' written request again. He asked that 'a thorough investigation be carried out between the health board and the former county health committees of the hospital and death records relating to St Senan's Hospital, Enniscorthy, County Wexford, in order that persons who have deceased relatives buried in the unmarked graveyard at the hospital can obtain the maximum level of information'.

News of the reply came the following day. Patricia found it hard to conceal her disappointment. It was merely more of the same. The minister's reply stated: 'I understand from the SEHB that the Board has been investigating this matter and that it has no record of any burials taking place in the graveyard in question in the last 40 or 50 years. The graveyard in question is owned and maintained by the SEHB and the hospital authorities are continuing efforts to determine who might have been buried there in the earlier part of the century. The Board has suggested that the County Council may have some records relating to the graveyard and the Deputy may wish to contact the Council in this regard.'

The telephone call, however, changed everything. It came the following day. Hugo Kelly, the senior staff member appointed to do the research at the hospital, had found records of Rose's admission.

'When was she admitted?' Patricia asked.

'16 February 1907,' he said.

A shiver ran down Patricia's back. Rose had been admitted to the asylum on 16 February 1907. Patricia checked the calendar. Today was 16 February. It was also her son John's birthday – her first-born.

5

MATCHMAKING

I won't marry him,' said Rose after Pat Murphy had left.
'You will!'
'I won't!'

Saliva gathered at the corners of Patrick Quinn's mouth. 'You'll do as you're told, woman! You want to be a skivvy all your life, is that it?'

Mary came between her sister-in-law and her husband. 'I'll talk to her.'

'You'd better talk some sense into her then,' said Patrick.

Mary made Rose sit down and she put an arm around her. Rose shrugged it off.

'You're not getting any younger, you know. It's time you were thinking of taking a husband.'

'I won't wed him!' The thought revolted her. She couldn't bear the sight of him, the sound of him.

'You'll do what you're told!' said her brother. 'If our parents were still alive you'd do what they wanted you to. I'm in their place now. We've promised two pigs as a dowry for you – animals we can sorely spare ourselves – and you throw our generosity back in our faces? You're an ungrateful wretch!'

'Rose, we're only doing our best for you,' said Mary.

Rose moved her stool further back. 'I never asked you to make a match for me.'

'No, you'd rather go prancing around after English soldiers or making eyes at Protestants.'

So he'd heard the rumours. Was this why a husband was suddenly being found? 'I haven't done anything wrong.'

'No, not yet, but what'd happen you if there wasn't someone keeping an eye on you – answer me that?'

'I've paid the price for my wrong-doing.'

'And so have the rest of us. Not able to hold our heads up for people talking about you. You should be grateful we were able to find anyone to marry you with your history.'

Rose's hand shook.

'Murphy is prepared to overlook your past. There's many men who wouldn't.'

'Go easy, Pat,' Mary said, sitting down beside her. 'He's a good man, Rose, if you only gave him a chance.'

Patrick kicked the stool in front of him, making the children who had gathered at the window scatter rapidly. 'She thinks she's better than the rest of us. That she can pick and choose for herself.'

'Patrick!' Mary said. 'You'll get used to him, Rose. You'll be surprised how quick it'll happen and you'll have more than a lot of women have. Just think, your own kitchen. No more slaving for anyone but yourself. And children maybe, with the help of God.'

Rose started to sob.

'You can stop your snivelling,' her brother said, going toward the door. 'You'll wed him as soon as a date can be set. Make your mind up to it.'

*

Bridget Rowe ran out of the servants' quarters to greet Rose when she saw her coming. 'You'll never guess what. There's soldiers coming – thousands of them, to Bannow for training.'

Rose couldn't even hear her friend properly. 'What?'

Bridget gripped her shoulders and danced her round in a

circle. 'They'll be camped at Major Boyce's and doing training exercises at Barlough – making the horses cross the spit and all. Just imagine, 1,500 fine specimens of mankind all in uniform. The thought of it is making me go weak at the knees.'

Bridget stopped in her tracks as she noticed Rose's face. 'Have you seen a ghost or what? You're the colour of death!'

Rose walked towards the vegetable garden where they could be out of earshot of the rest of the staff.

'What's the matter?'

Rose sat down on a stone near the cabbage patch. 'They want me to marry him.'

'What? Who?' said Bridget, sitting down beside her.

'The man who was with Patrick at the show. They've matched me with him.'

Bridget's eyes saucered. 'Jesus, Mary and Joseph, they haven't! What are you going to do?'

'I can't marry him. I won't.'

'You'll go against your family? Jesus, Rose!'

Rose suddenly felt as if a band of steel was tightening around her head. There would be no chance of changing Patrick Quinn's mind – even Bridget knew that.

Bridget was clutching at straws. 'Maybe it wouldn't be so bad, Rose. Maybe we were judging the book by the cover. We're always saying we shouldn't do that.'

Rose wondered where Ted Jameson was – checking on the horses before he turned in or sitting under a tree somewhere whittling something out of wood, as he often did in his spare time? She wished she could talk to him, tell him what had happened, but she daren't.

Bridget sat there still asking questions. What had he said? Who was this man? What did she think of him tonight?

'Same as I did before. He sat there and said very little, a big

73

laugh out of him every time Patrick said anything at all.'

'It could have been nerves with him. No one's themself when they're nervous,' said Bridget.

'The two of them had drink on them, big brave men, the pair of them. To give them courage, no doubt.'

'Maybe he'd grow on you,' said Bridget quietly. 'They say that happens. You don't like someone at first and then your feelings change.'

Rose stood up, trying to quell the nausea she now felt.

'At least he has work,' said Bridget. 'That's more than a lot have. Maybe you'd be all right.'

Rose didn't answer, just looked instead at the neat, straight rows of cabbage. She'd have to tell Cook to put it on the menu more often – a lot of it was coming in together.

'At least they're prepared to give you a dowry. I've no one to give me one.'

'I don't want their dowry.'

'But what about when you can't work any more, when you get old and sick? That's what worries me sometimes. There's nothing for us then but the workhouse.'

Rose stood up to go back to the servants' quarters, silent.

'Don't fret too much. Maybe they won't force you …'

'You know what my brother is like.'

'Look, maybe it'll never happen. Maybe two of these soldiers that are coming to Bannow will set their caps at us and sweep us off to God knows where. Wouldn't that be a great day for Ireland? With so many of them coming we'll be spoilt for choice. Come on, cheer up!'

Rose smiled. Trust Bridget to try lifting her spirits. What would she do without such a friend if she ever had to leave Rosegarland?

Sleep did not come quickly that night. When it did it

brought dreams of pigs attacking her, of soldiers in their hundreds, all playing bagpipes. And the face of Pat Murphy – distant and grinning.

*

In her home in Clongeen Bridget Rowe twisted and turned in the settle bed she shared with her sisters. Sometimes she wished she could live in at Rosegarland but because her home was so close by this hadn't been mentioned. She moved to get out of the way of her sister's breath. How was she supposed to sleep, especially with what she had on her mind? How would she ever tell Rose?

She had cycled back to Rosegarland after the show because of what her aunt Maggie who lived near the workhouse in New Ross had told her. With Rose's child there, Bridget often asked her aunt to keep an eye out for him when the workhouse children were being taken out for a walk. Normally this happened once a fortnight.

Her news of the last two occasions hadn't been good though. She saw no fair-haired boy of six among them.

'Are you sure?' Bridget had asked her. 'Are you sure he wasn't wearing a cap and you just didn't notice his hair?'

'I'm sure,' Maggie said.

Bridget couldn't understand what had happened. Rose's boy wasn't old enough to be boarded out to farmers as a worker yet surely? He should be in the group. Rose loved hearing news of him, even if it was only someone viewing him from a distance.

Was he ill or worse? Bridget shivered in the bed. Deaths were common in that place. How would Rose take the news – especially when she had this other worry upon her? 'Maybe it would be better if Rose did marry this man,' she thought. 'That way she might have more children. That'd take her mind off the child she had already especially if he's …'

It wasn't fair, she thought. Rose had paid dearly for her mistake, stuck in the workhouse until her child was weaned. Luckily the Leighs had given her a job to come out to.

Still, Bridget knew how some of the men talked about her. The way they eyed her up and down, always nudging one another and making some lecherous comment. Most of them fancied their chances with her but they knew better than to annoy her. They didn't want to suffer the same fate as the man who had taken her honour six years before.

He had 'disappeared' suddenly, run out of the country when the size of Rose's belly made it obvious to her family that she was with child. Some said he was in Australia now – one beating wiser.

*

The official opening of the railway was the talk of the estate. Mr Leigh had gone by train to Rosslare, where the official opening of the Rosslare–Fishguard route was taking place, at seven o'clock in the morning, his top hat brushed and the silver top on his cane shining.

All the important people in the county, businesspeople and politicians were there, including the lord lieutenant, all the way from Dublin. Mr Leigh was there because he was local gentry and because the railway had gone through so much of Rosegarland land.

'I wouldn't mind going to London,' said Bridget, checking the glass in the top of the churn to see if the butter had 'cracked'. 'What would you think they'd have for breakfast over there, Rose?'

'A lot more than we have, that's for sure,' said Rose.

'I'll bet they have lashings of rashers and Indian tea out of china cups like the master and the mistress do,' Bridget said, still turning the churn handle.

'Maybe.'

'Come on, Rose, cheer up. You haven't seen your brother since. Maybe he has forgotten the matchmaking.'

Rose filled a bucket of scalding hot water from the boiler in the dairy to sterilise the butter table. She lifted the bucket, throwing the contents onto the table too fast.

'Aagh!' Some of it had splashed her, getting her in the face and on her hands. She screamed with the sudden pain.

'Jesus, Rose, are you all right?' said Bridget. 'Put your hands in the cold water quick!'

'Jesus!' Rose said, submerging her hands while Bridget soaked a cloth and, holding Rose's head back, squeezed ragfuls of cold water onto her face.

'It's not too bad. It'll be a bit red for a while but you'll be all right. The cold water'll stop it blistering.'

'Thanks. That'll teach me to keep my mind on my work,' said Rose, still grimacing with pain.

'You were a bit distracted, that's all,' said Bridget, now getting a clean teacloth to dab Rose's face dry.

'I'm not going to think about him or my brother or the whole lot of them. I've told him no,' Rose said as she looked at her reddened hands. 'Maybe he'll forget about it.'

'Best to think of other things,' said Bridget. 'Soldiers even.'

'You and your soldiers. You'd think you never saw a man in your life!'

'Not these kind of men. Cook says they'll be there for weeks. The whole village'll be turning out to see them pass through. We'll have to go, the whole lot of us.'

'That's if the mistress lets us,' said Rose.

'She'll let us all right. A big occasion like that? Course she would. If she doesn't I'm going anyway. Can you imagine the sight of it – thousands of horses and big motorcars and guns and officers with big moustaches parading themselves like turkey cocks at mating time!'

'Ah, will you stop.'

'You have to come, Rose.'

'If all the work is done.'

'Good,' said Bridget. 'You take it easy with those hands.'

'It'd take worse than that to kill me. They're throbbing a bit now, that's all. Come on, we have to get this butter into blocks.'

'Right.'

Rose worked away, trying to forget about the discomfort of her hands. At least the dairy was cool – she loved the coolness of it on a hot day and the smell of the butter as it was slated and washed to make the little lumps gather together. Even though her arms often ached from long periods spent churning, she was happy with a job well done.

It would be nine o'clock tonight before they'd finish. More of the gooseberries had to be picked, and more of the loganberries and raspberries too, before rain came and spoiled them.

Then there would be many trips to the kitchen, where steam rose day after day from Cook's giant jam saucepan and where, if you were lucky, she would let you run your finger through the small quantity that she left to cool on a saucer to see if it was setting properly.

Rose crossed the dairy yard to the walled vegetable garden. Five women were already working there. They stopped their talk when they saw her coming.

'I hear your brother has found a husband for you, Rose,' said one.

'You'd be better occupied getting on with your own work than minding other people's business.'

'Oh, pardon me for speaking,' the woman replied, turning to grin at the others before putting a hand to another berry.

Going back to the house, Rose looked around her. She could not imagine life without Rosegarland – the size and the shape of it, the big fields that ran down to the Corach river, the view of the estuary where the Corach met the Owenduff.

As a child she used to list off the names of the fields – the keeper's field, the horse field, the canal field, rabbit hill, the pigeon field, Curry's Hill – she knew them all like the back of her hand. Then there were the marshes that lay under the farmyard road, the gardens that took up acres of ground, the lake, the orchards and the woods.

She loved the woods most of all – the greenness of them, the shade of them, the Big Wood where guests of the family rode horses along specially laid-out paths, the trees that turned all colours in the autumn and gave shade on hot days like this.

Often, in childish dreams, she had imagined herself lady of the manor, wearing fine clothes and eating fine food with servants to wait on her, but that was only in her dreams.

'There is no harm in dreaming,' her mother had said, 'as long as you remember your station. No good comes of wanting what you can't have.'

In real life you stayed at a distance from your employer and did nothing to draw attention to yourself. You didn't go where you weren't supposed to go, like around the front of the main house; you didn't steal game or firewood lest you be caught and sacked. Still, many's the time she remembered accompanying her father into the woods with a storm lantern where he sawed or chopped branches off trees. She held the lantern and helped cover the cut parts with wet soil so they wouldn't be noticed afterwards.

She had reason to be thankful to the mistress, too – she was aware of that. Only for her she might have been left in the workhouse after having the child. Having a job to go to had been her ticket out. She'd been luckier than most. She had promised to guard her chastity from then on. And she had.

The mistress would be worried if she heard the rumours of her and Ted Jameson, though, but that's all they were – rumours. They had done nothing wrong, unless smiles and the odd kind word were something to be guilty about, but then it didn't take much to set tongues wagging.

'She would think he was associating with someone beneath his station,' Rose thought.

Ted had come to work there as a groomsman a year before from another estate in Meath. He'd been shy at first but her brother Jack had befriended him and there was no doubting his knowledge of horses.

There would be no future in it, even if Ted did ask her to marry him. No Quinn had ever married one of *them*. Rose wondered if he had heard that a match had been made for her, though. If he had, he had said nothing as yet. Still, Patrick hadn't come looking for her since. She prayed that he'd changed his mind. It was easier to think that. That way she didn't feel paralysed with the fright of it.

*

Rose was afraid she'd be late. She'd promised Bridget she'd meet her in the village to see the soldiers turning for Bannow. A cat had got into the dairy and overturned one of the buckets of milk and she had to clean the mess up before she went anywhere.

'Just like what would happen when you're in a hurry,' she said to herself as she swept out the rinsing water.

Now she ran the length of the avenue, pausing to catch her breath before crossing the railway bridge. In the village the crowds had already gathered. Bridget shouted at her from the front of the crowd and Rose squeezed through.

'What kept you? They're coming! Can't you hear them?'

Rose listened. Yes, sure enough, she could hear the clop of thousands of horses' hooves and the murmur of engines.

'Ted says the cavalry'll be first,' Bridget said.

Ted – was he here? Rose's eyes scanned the crowd. No, no sign. Maybe just as well. If her brother saw her talking to him … She scanned the crowd again. No, no Patrick or Mary or the children. Patrick here? Was she stupid or what? He wouldn't come out to see English soldiers going anywhere.

'What are they going to be doing exactly when they get to Barlough?'

'Building bridges and competing with one another to cross the creek – training the horses and all. It's the best place for doing it, apparently.'

'That should test their mettle all right,' said Rose, knowing that the currents in Ballyteigue Bay were renowned for being dangerous.

'I'm going down there on Sunday to see what they're at and you're coming too.'

'Is that so?' said Rose as the crowd strained forward and the first horses appeared.

'What a sight!' Ted Jameson was beside her now, staring at the spectacle as rows of four horses appeared, soldiers sitting erect on their backs, the coats of the horses glistening in the sunshine.

Ted stood between Rose and Bridget. 'Takes the cavalry to have first-class horses,' he said, never taking his eyes off them as they turned for Bannow up Green Road.

'Who needs horses when there's men to look at?' said Bridget.

'Bridget!'

'Ah, will you stop, that's what you're here to look at yourself only you won't admit it!'

Rose tried to stop herself blushing to no avail as Ted turned to grin at her. She wished he wouldn't stand so close. It was unsettling her.

'There's the officers!' someone shouted.

Here they were, soldiers with peaked caps and fancy badges transported in cars like Rose had never seen before. They were sitting prim and erect in their seats, looking straight ahead, moustaches trimmed and uniforms immaculate.

'They must have pokers stuck up their backsides,' said Bridget. 'Either that or they're awful constipated.'

Telling Bridget to be quiet, Rose craned her neck to get a better look. The strange smell of petrol from the motorcars got up her nose – it was a different smell altogether from that of the steam lorry Patrick drove. Now she watched more and more of the soldiers on horseback turn for Bannow. The Third Dragoon Guards, the Eleventh Hussars, the Nineteenth Hussars. Some had come from England, some from the Curragh.

There were engines pulling heavy trailers full of equipment – fifteen of them, sixteen, twenty.

Two big guns. It was as if the area was being invaded but everyone had come out to watch.

Rose could see a photographer with his camera set up on the other side of the road disappearing under a black cloth, again and again. Some big shop in Dublin called Easons was publishing postcards to mark the event, someone said.

'Jesus, look at those animals!' Ted said again.

'Well, if the army can't have good horses who can?'

'What would I give to try out one or two of them?' said Ted, more to himself than anyone else.

'Maybe they'll let you if you ask them nicely,' said Rose. 'You never know.'

'Maybe,' said Ted.

Eventually, the last of them turned for Bannow. Rose had never seen such a spectacle in her life. She wished her nephews and nieces had seen it. They would have remembered it for the rest of their lives. 'That wouldn't be Patrick's way, though,' she said to herself.

'Back to the grindstone,' said Bridget as they made their way back to Rosegarland. 'Did you see the way one of them soldiers winked at me? The big fella with the brown moustache and the single stripe on his arm?'

'Which fella?'

'The one I'll be keeping an eye out for on Sunday,' said Bridget grinning.

*

It was unusual to see Mary Quinn in the yard at Rosegarland. She was there when they returned, waiting with the two younger children, Willie and John, and looking uneasy. Rose went over reluctantly, glad that Ted had parted company with herself and Bridget to walk back with the other estate workmen.

'Patrick wants to see you when you next have a half day,' said Mary. 'He says there's things to arrange.'

Rose's heart sank. 'I said I wasn't doing it.'

'You have no choice. The decision is made and well you know it. We thought you'd have seen the sense of it by now,' Mary said.

Rose said nothing, making a fuss of the boys.

'It might be the only offer of marriage you'll get. Beggars can't be choosers'.

Rose glanced over at the two boys, who were now climbing up on the doors of the stables to see what was in them.

'Patrick is going to see the priest to arrange the date. He has to do it soon.'

Rose turned away, tears of vexation filling her eyes.

'It was all organised for me, too, Rose, don't forget.'

Rose swallowed hard. She wouldn't give Mary the satisfaction of seeing her cry. 'At least you had some sort of fancy for your husband to be.'

'It'll come with time. You'll see.'

Mary saw Rose glance towards the stable yard where Ted was now putting the tackling on one of the farm horses. 'Thinking of him'll do you no good,' she said. 'You've to do your duty.'

Rose swallowed hard again.

'You're to come over when you next have time off, without fail. Patrick'll be expecting you. Come on, children.'

Rose bid her nephews goodbye, young John silent, knowing that something was wrong. Giving a final wave, she turned and walked to the potato house to boil the remainder of last year's spuds for the pigs. They would be fed them whole and unwashed, brown scum traces on some of them from the boiling.

When Bridget came in Rose was bucketing them into the boiler with a vengeance.

'You trying to mash them before they're even cooked?'

'I would if I was able this minute.'

'It wouldn't have anything to do with herself being here, would it?'

'Patrick's going to talk to the priest.'

'Jesus! What did you say?'

'What say have I got? I might as well be a beast being brought to the fair.'

'Rose …' Bridget put her arm around Rose to try comforting her. 'They're only thinking of what's best for you.'

'They're thinking of what's best for themselves. Get me married off so there'll be no danger of me making a show of them again. I don't need to get married. Another few years and I'll have saved enough to go to England or America. I can bring the child with me when he's old enough to work. We'd manage somehow.'

'Rose, you're dreaming. The two of you'd die of starvation! How would you work and care for a child?' said Bridget, her fear for her friend sharpening her tongue. 'The only people that get away from here is them that has relatives to send them the fare and help them out when they get there. You don't have anyone.'

'I'd work hard and save hard.'

Bridget swallowed. 'It wouldn't be enough – you know it wouldn't! How could you work and mind a child?'

'There must be some way.'

Bridget sat Rose down on an upturned bucket. 'Look, Rose … what if he's not in the workhouse when you go looking for him? What … what if he's gone?'

'Gone? I'll get him back, that's what, even if I have to steal him from wherever he is.'

There was no talking to Rose when she was like this. There was no point telling her yet either, Bridget thought. Not until she was sure something had happened to the child. Her aunt Maggie was still keeping her eyes open, watching for him every day.

Rose left the potato house to get more water.

'If he was sick maybe he's better now,' Bridget thought. It wasn't much of a hope but it was the only one she had. At least it was summertime – he was more likely to survive than if he was sick in the winter. A prayer might do some good. The Virgin Mary was a mother herself. Surely she'd take pity on Rose?

The whisper broke the silence of the potato house. 'Hail

holy Queen, Mother of Mercy, our life, our sweetness and our hope, to thee do we cry, poor banished children of Eve, to thee do we send up our sighs, mourning and weeping in this valley of tears ...'

*

Patrick Quinn closed the door of the priest's house in Clongeen and crossed the road to the pub. The meeting had gone well. He deserved a drop of porter after it. The priest, Father Lyng, had congratulated him on finding his sister a husband. He was a good brother, taking his role of head of the family seriously, he had said. Father Lyng would marry Rose Quinn and Pat Murphy on Tuesday 6 November after first mass and be pleased to do so.

It was a good date to choose, Patrick felt. They would have plenty of time to make the arrangements – twelve weeks. The wedding would cost a few shillings but Rose would have money to buy her own clothes – she'd have to pay for as much as she could herself. The neighbours would help out too, contributing food for the festivities afterwards. As long as he had money for drink he'd be all right and Murphy had agreed to help out with that. Patrick wouldn't like to be shown up by running short.

He sat down on a stool and sipped his stout, his lower lip pulling down the valuable froth that stuck to his untrimmed moustache. The stout tasted good. Didn't a man deserve a pint or two after breaking his back working all week? The match had been done here, like many's a match before it. He'd picked his moment, having known Pat from working on the railway for long enough. He'd brought the chat round to Pat needing a wife. What man didn't? Life was difficult enough without a few home comforts.

He'd handled the whole thing very well, he felt. Got away

without much of a dowry too, saying that Rose was a hard worker and would contribute well to the running of the house.

'She'll stop her stubbornness soon enough,' he thought.
'She knows it's the best chance she has.'

Putting back his head he let the dark liquid find its way to
the back of his throat.

6

RECORDS SEEN

The hospital grounds certainly look well in the spring sunshine,' Patricia said to herself as she drove up the avenue to the main door of St Senan's hospital. She was looking forward to seeing, for the first time, the register that contained details of Rose's admission to the asylum.

Although she already knew the main details of what was there she was still anxious to see the book itself. What would it look like? Would it be typed or handwritten? Would there be some item of information that would come as a surprise?

Looking back down the avenue where some patients were now walking she couldn't help thinking again what Rose's experience had been arriving here on 16 February 1907. What horror and dread would she have felt, knowing where she was going, being transported in a locked carriage, perhaps with her hands tied? Newspaper reports said that the week of 16 February 1907 was bitterly cold, with occasional snow.

'Raw weather for a raw deal in life,' thought Patricia.

The manager, Jeanne Hendrick, showed her to the office where the ancient-looking register was already open on a table. She introduced her to Hugh – Hugo Kelly – the senior nurse who had been given the research task and who had found the record of Rose's admission.

The register was bound, she saw, and the information typed. She handled the page gently – it was like tissue paper. She looked at the entry pointed out to her.

Rose Murphy had been admitted suffering from melancholia.

'That would equate with depression nowadays, wouldn't it?' she asked.

'Yes,' she was told.

There was mention of anaemia and some chest ailment also since before admission.

The fact that Rose had come from New Ross workhouse was something of a shock. Patricia had presumed she had gone straight to the asylum after she had refused to live with her husband. That had been her father's story. When exactly had Rose gone to the workhouse and why?

Patricia's library research offered up a possibility. Workhouses were also pauper hospitals at that time and contained wards for 'lunatics and imbeciles'. The harshness of the two words upset her. Lunatic ... Imbecile ... Tags applied so easily.

New Ross workhouse would have been the closest pauper infirmary to Clongeen. Was Rose committed to the lunatic ward there while awaiting a place in Enniscorthy asylum? Perhaps eventually Patricia would find out for sure if she could get access to the workhouse admission records for the period. 'That's a task for the future,' she said to herself.

She asked about doctors' casebooks. Were any records kept by the resident medical superintendent (RMS), Dr Thomas Drapes, at the time? Doctors' notes would surely yield more information.

The answer was no. Such records couldn't be found. She wondered were they really sitting in some attic or storeroom covered in dust – but what could she do if she was told they weren't available?

She knew some asylums had released their records to historians doing research – Ballinasloe, for instance, and Belfast.

The staff at other hospitals had written books to mark their anniversaries – St Mary's in Castlebar and St Fintan's in Portlaoise, the former Maryborough asylum, for instance. She wished someone from Enniscorthy had written up the history of this place. It would be a sign that the secrecy of times past was ending.

The way she felt this minute she wouldn't mind searching through dusty rooms herself but that would be impossible. She wondered, though, were there other people anxious to know details of their relatives who had died in the hospital? Perhaps if there were others it would help initiate a more comprehensive search. By her asking would it mean that other people might have easier access?

How many families in the county had had someone committed here over the years, she wondered? She guessed that many had skeletons in the cupboard just like the Quinn family – people not spoken about, people not visited, people left there to die and be buried there or brought back to their home parishes to be buried quietly after a lifetime of incarceration.

Even now how many elderly residents or patients were there, unable to fit into the world when the 'walls came down' in the 1970s?

Before going home she drove up the back lane that came out on the road near the graveyard entrance. Farm sheds, now disused, stood close by. Was there a walkway to the graveyards, she wondered, a well-worn track that represented the last journey of so many inmates, including Rose? Had a horse and cart, or human and cart even, brought her on her final journey along that headland?

She looked at the fields that stretched down to the main road. Good tillage land farmed by patients – some for their lifetime. If they had been mad how would they have done the work? Depressed even, how would they have done it?

'Dealt a cruel hand ...'

She thought especially of the people who had ploughed the fields under the graveyard. What was the psychological effect on them of knowing that's where they would be buried unless their families came up with the money for their funeral? It would be enough to drive anyone mad, even if they weren't ill beforehand.

She tried to imagine Rose's burial. Had she been buried the day she died, 4 May, or was it days later? How many days? Did the RMS contact her family and wait to see if someone would claim her? It made Patricia sad to think that she probably hadn't had a priest to see her into the next world.

Rose's life before she died was still preoccupying Patricia too.

The newspaper reports that told her what the weather had been like that year gave insights into what was going on in Rose's locality the summer before Rose married. Fifteen hundred soldiers had come to nearby Bannow for training exercises in July 1906. They came from England and the Curragh to train their horses in crossing the spit at Barlough. She had seen the pictures, commissioned by Easons at the time.

She tried to imagine the excitement of such an event in a small area in the days before radio and television. 'It must have been a spectacle – the soldiers on horseback, the cannon, the trucks, the commanding officers in their cars, the brightly coloured uniforms.' She bet they had pipers too. Some of the regiments, she knew, were Highlanders. It stood to reason. Yet again, she felt her love of piping was also something that Rose shared.

She stopped at the graveyard to visit it once again before returning home. It wasn't quite as it was marked on the ordnance survey map of the area that she had found. She had been anxious to know if it was marked as such or was simply an afterthought, a piece of the field marked off.

On the map it appeared to have three solid walls. Here now, though, there was only a ditch on the lower side. Did this mean that they had run out of room for burying people and the wall had been removed to allow some burials in the adjoining field, then a ditch put in position later?

She tried to calculate how many people could have been buried in this graveyard over the years. Burials stopped in the 1940s. The asylum was built in 1868. That meant burials could have taken place over seventy years at, say, one person a month. That's seventy multiplied by twelve: 840 people – a very conservative estimate, given disease levels at the time.

*

Over time the picture of Rose's era was building up – books, maps, even talk of speaking to an historian who had done primary research on the asylum era. Rose would be proud of her, going to all this trouble.

Before then, however, she would have to talk to Margaret, the radio researcher. How would she take the news about Catherine's ability, about the experience in Spain that had made them sure that there was a graveyard behind the hospital?

Would she take flight or, worse still, check under the table for a broom? In Rose's time, after all, people were put in asylums for less.

Still, Patricia was not frightened by what Catherine could do. It was a gift of connection with the after life that few had. Someday, she felt, her daughter, Catherine, would have the courage to speak openly about it.

7

SOLDIERS AND SPECTACLE

Rose's dress was stuck to her with sweat having cycled the five miles to Cullenstown. Bridget was ahead of her as they came within sight of the sea, the Saltee and the Keeragh Islands, the ribbon on her straw hat bobbing with each push of the pedal. The road was busy with people making their way to the coastguard station, same as they were, to see the soldiers at their training exercises.

Rose wiped her brow with the sleeve of her white blouse. All week Bridget had talked of nothing except the soldiers down in the bay and especially the one who had winked at her. Rose wondered how she would pick him out of so many and what ridicule she would expose herself to if she did.

'Come on, slowcoach,' Bridget called. 'We'll soon be there.'

They turned left now, past the small round tower that stood in someone's garden. To the right she could see the sea and the soldiers down at Barlough.

Rose turned right off the narrow road down to the coast-guard station. The place was thronged with people, over a hundred, the gentry taking up the seats by the whitewashed walls from where they had a good vantage point. Other well-dressed ladies and gentlemen stood overlooking the bay, picnic baskets beside them.

Rose leaned her bicycle against the ditch with all the others and followed Bridget, who was heading down to the beach to see what was going on.

The soldiers were building two bridges, two teams battling it out to be finished first, with officers shouting orders at them. Rose could see more officers with their clipboards watching the proceedings and writing things down. The Royal Engineers, someone said. A welcome breeze coming in off the sea tempered the summer heat.

'They must be roasting,' said Bridget. 'Look at them.'

Many of the soldiers had taken off their shirts and were riding around on horses, ready to take their turn crossing.

'Jesus! It's Ted!' Bridget shouted.

'Where?'

Bridget pointed. 'The one without the uniform. I'm sure it's him.'

Ted Jameson was speaking to one of the officers below them on the beach.

'What's he doing?'

They watched as the officer hailed one of the soldiers on horseback and the rider dismounted. Then they saw Ted strip off his coat and shirt and mount the horse.

'He's going to cross!'

Rose was terrified. 'He'll drown!'

'No, he won't. He knows all there is to know about horses, you'll see. Ted!'

'Bridget! Stop waving. There are people looking at us.'

'Spoilsport!'

Ted saw the two of them and waved back before joining the line of horses awaiting the signal to go. Three of them would go at a time. In a war a water-shy horse would be no use so they had to be given try-outs.

'The currents!' said Rose.

'He'll be all right. Shush,' said Bridget, shading her eyes from the sun to get a better view.

The horses were uneasy, probably picking up the tension of the riders. And they were off! Two of the horses went headlong into the water but Ted's horse showed reluctance. They watched him turn the horse and gallop up the beach, then turn sharp again and head the horse to the water at speed.

The soldiers in the small boat on the water were watching Ted and his horse closely. If the horse wouldn't cross, its reins would be tied to the boat and the men would row, forcing the horse to swim to lessen the strain on the reins. But Ted had no need of them. Rose watched as he sat forward on the horse, urging him to the other side.

Within minutes he was on the burrow and turning to come back. As soon as they reached the sand Ted and the other soldiers galloped the horses back to their starting point, water spraying everywhere and dripping from the cropped cavalry tails of the horses.

Ted waved at Rose and Bridget, his hair plastered against his head, his trousers stuck to him.

'Told you he'd do it,' said Bridget. 'He's been riding horses since he was three. Doesn't he look great stripped off?'

'Shush!'

Rose wiped the perspiration from her face and neck. The two women clapped along with the rest of the crowd for a deed well done. Again the photographers were on the beach, headless under black cloths as they took their pictures.

'I'll have to get some souvenir postcards when they come out. Maybe Ted will be in one of them,' said Rose, wishing she could take off her boots and paddle to cool her feet. A lot of the men were already doing it, their trouser legs rolled up.

'It's some world when women can't even bare their ankles,' she thought.

*

It had been a good day. They'd stayed until hunger drove them back to Rosegarland, where they had jobs to do before nightfall. Rose filled her pockets with seashells that she found on the strand before she left. She'd give them to young John to add to his collection. She'd given him lots of others she had found, picked up whenever she was at the beach. He liked the look of them and the feel of them, he said. And thinking that they were once fish's houses.

*

It was August and the harvest had finally started. All day the men and women worked in the fields after the binder, stooking sheaves of barley or wheat in case the rain came unexpectedly again before the horses and carts could take the corn into the haggard to be made into a rick.

It was a difficult harvest. The weather had broken and day after day it was difficult to know if the harvest would be saved at all. A lot of the fruit had been spoiled too and Rose and the other women in charge of picking it had tried to salvage what they could.

Word had it that the soldiers were being washed out of their tents in the last few nights before they broke camp to return to the Curragh.

Bridget wasn't in great form. Maybe it was Rose's imagination but it was as if she was trying to avoid her these days. 'Have you a puss on you because the soldiers are going?' she asked her, finding her in the laundry house, stuffing a letter into her pocket when she saw Rose enter.

'The soldiers?'

'Yes. Them leaving soon.'

'No,' Bridget said, picking up a bar of soap and rubbing it hard on the collar of her uniform.

'You got post?'

'Yes, my aunt Maggie in Ross.'

'Is she all right?'

'Yes.'

'Is there something troubling you then?'

Bridget looked away. 'No. No. Nothing at all.'

'You would tell me if there was, wouldn't you? I tell you my troubles,' said Rose. 'It's only right you should do the same.'

'Yes. I'm all right, honestly.'

'If you're sure …'

Rose felt worried leaving Bridget. Her friend looked as if she had the weight of the world upon her but she knew better than to pry. Bridget would tell her in her own good time.

She searched the stables for her brother Jack and eventually found him in the tack room.

'What ails you?' he asked, seeing her coming in.

'I need to talk to you. About what Patrick's planning.'

Jack took a bridle from its nail for cleaning. 'The decision's been made, girl,' he said, taking down another.

'How would you like to be told to marry someone you didn't like?'

'You're too particular – headstrong. You don't see the good in him because you don't want to see it.'

'I want to emigrate,' she said quietly. 'I can get a boat from Ross.'

Jack threw the bridle on the ground. 'That's madwoman's talk,' he said, ceasing what he was doing. 'How would you manage?'

'I'd get work like thousands before me have,' she said, quietly.

'And with not a friend in the world to help you in some foreign country?'

'If I had some money to start me off I'd be all right – if you could lend me a bit. I'd send it back to you as soon as I could, as God is my witness.'

'Have you taken leave of your senses? I've no money to be giving you or anyone else.'

'It wouldn't have to be much.'

'The only person you think of is yourself, same as always. Never what's good for you in the long run. Patrick's found someone suitable for you and you want to run away to die on some street somewhere!'

So Jack had been in on the planning as well. Rose's heart sunk to her boots. He'd been her only hope. What could she do if he was against her as well?

His voice softened slightly. 'Even if I did have the money I'd never hear the end of it. Murphy has been chosen for you and there'll be no going back on it now. You're getting wed and that's it.'

Rose turned on her heel and ran out through the door.

'And you can forget any notions of Jameson too. He's not for a Quinn,' he called after her.

Neither Rose, in her hurry, nor Jack, in his anger, saw Ted Jameson retreat from the stables where he'd been drawn by the raised voices and angry words.

*

The kitchen was in a frenzy. The Leighs had invited some of the commanding officers to dinner at Rosegarland, including General Rimmington and Lord Grenfell. The mistress had spent an hour deep in discussion with Cook about the menu and now Cook and her kitchen maids were busily preparing for what would be a grand occasion.

Duck, chicken, game – Rose had wrung the necks of several pullets in preparation for the feasting. They would be served in fancy sauces to suit the palettes of the officers.

If Cook had her way, they would be comparing her work with the best cooks in London. Rose and Bridget were given strict instructions to search the garden for the nicest vegetables – carrots, cabbage, onions and broccoli. The most even-sized potatoes for the roast too and the flouriest for the dinner plates. No trouble would be spared for the guests who would arrive at seven.

Rose watched for the first signs of the soldiers arriving. Then she saw them, some driven in cars, others in carriages, their silver buttons glinting in the evening sunlight. General Rimmington, head buck cat, had the car door opened for him by the driver. Then Lord Grenfell, second in command, stepped out, his white peaked cap setting him apart from the rest. The house would be busy all evening.

Rose left the kitchen as quickly as she could having delivered more coal for the range. Cook's face was crimson as she oversaw all her pots and pans bubbling on the stove. The butler was shouting orders at all and sundry, speeding the dining-room staff to their posts in readiness for dinner starting. 'Anyone who is not required in this room please leave *now*!'

Rose sought the refuge of the dairy yard where all was quiet now, the day's work done. At seven in the morning it would come to life again. She went to close the apple-house door. Young Martha again – you couldn't trust her to close a door after her. God knows what would get in and disturb the shelves of apples that were being stored for the winter.

Seeing her from where he was stabling one of the horses, Ted Jameson led the horse over to the apple-house door, glancing around as he did so.

'I have to talk to you. Meet me in the back lane in a few minutes – please.'

'I can't.'

'Please. No one'll see us. You go now and I'll follow on in a few minutes when I've finished this. They're all busy working – they'll never notice us.'

'Jack?'

'He's having a drink with the army drivers. Please.'

Rose knew she shouldn't but temptation won out over her reluctance. 'Just a few minutes,' she said, glancing this way and that to see they weren't being watched.

Ten minutes later Ted had arrived and they walked together in the woods out of sight.

'I can't bear the thought of them marrying you off! Could you not refuse? Tell them you won't do it!'

'I've already tried. You don't know my brother when he gets a notion in his head.'

'You should be able to choose.'

'Maybe some day women will. I hope so anyway.'

'Rose …'

He stood closer to her. Rose's heart beat faster.

'I wish I could offer you a life. We could leave – get work somewhere else. I know I haven't much but it'd be better.'

'No.'

'My religion – is that it?'

Rose said nothing.

'Why should a different way of praying come between people? It's the one God we're praying to!'

'It's the way we're brought up.'

'Well, your teaching is wrong!'

Rose blessed herself, fearing she would be struck down dead for listening to this talk. Blasphemy, her brothers would call it. She held on tightly to the rosary beads in her pocket. 'I'd better get back. There'll be trouble if anyone finds out we're here.'

Ted held her by the shoulders. 'Rose, promise me you won't forget that I'm your friend. If I can't be your husband then that's the least I can be. If I can ever help you I will.'

'We must get back.'

'You can't marry him, Rose.'

'What choice do I have? They say it's my duty to welcome the match.'

'Duty! Jesus!'

'Hush! I have to believe it will turn out all right. There's no way out of it.'

'Rose …'

He tried to put his arms around her and she panicked.

'No! We must get back. The gate'll be locked if we don't,' she said, walking away.

He checked his pocket watch. Rose was already retreating up the lane.

'Rose! There's plenty of time, honest.'

'No. You stay there for a few minutes,' she called, 'so no one sees us together.'

'Rose! Wait!'

Within a few minutes Rose had reached the big yard gate. It was locked! Surely it wasn't yet ten? Her heart almost stopped. The chain and padlock was on it – she couldn't budge it. It had been locked early. Had someone seen her and Ted leave and guessed they'd planned to meet?

Perspiration broke out on her brow as she tried to figure out what she could do. The gate was too high to climb by herself. With a long skirt to hamper her movements she would have no chance, but with a helping hand maybe she could do it. She had no choice but to wait until Ted arrived.

'What about going round the front of the house?'

'No! If we're seen we'll be sacked.'

'Right. I'll go first then give you a hand getting down the other side.'

'Be careful.'

'I've climbed higher things than this.'

Quickly he put his foot on one of the gate's bars and hoisted himself up, swinging his leg over the top and carefully easing himself down until he was able to jump clear. He landed on his feet.

'Ted!'

'I'm all right. Now you climb. Quickly. I'll catch you on the other side.'

Rose was in a quandary. She could not get across the gate without exposing her bare legs but what choice did she have? Quickly she grabbed a rail and pulled herself up. With great difficulty she hoisted her skirt and swung her leg across the gate. Ted caught hold of her as she climbed down the other side. Rose was flustered by the nearness of him as he prevented her from falling.

'Thank you. I must go. If someone sees –'

'Rose …'

'Goodnight.'

Suddenly she felt his lips brush her cheek.

'A friend – remember.'

Rose broke away, hurrying towards the servants' quarters. In her hurry she didn't see her brother Jack watching from the stable boys' quarters.

Jack Quinn's jaw hardened as he watched Ted Jameson and Rose go their separate ways. This wedding would have to happen soon.

8

REVELATION

The coffee went cold. Sitting in the Paris Café in Redmond Square, Wexford town, I found it difficult to take in what Patricia was saying.

When she had asked to meet for a chat after work I hadn't thought anything of it. Research was ongoing in my own time and we met every week or so to compare notes. If I had found out something I told her; if she had unearthed another snippet of useful information she told me.

I was at that time ploughing through all the information available in Wexford library. One day I had unearthed a treasure – a pioneering book on the asylum era written by Mark Finnane, now a professor of history in Australia. By e-mail he had pointed me in the direction of a colleague, Elizabeth Malcolm, at the Institute of Irish Studies in Liverpool. She had also done primary research on Irish asylums and yes, I'd found out, she would be amenable to an interview.

'I have something to tell you,' Patricia said. 'I think I trust you enough at this stage to tell you. Only a few people know about this.'

I hadn't yet met Catherine, her daughter, but by this stage I felt I knew her just from listening to Patricia speak about her.

'It's something about the holiday I told you about in Spain – the one Catherine and I went on together,' she said.

'That was just before you went to look for the graveyard, wasn't it?' I said.

'That was *why* we went to look for the graveyard.'

'How do you mean? The hospital hadn't replied to you then – how could you know there was one?'

'Because Catherine can … well, she can … see things.'

'See things? You mean dead people?'

'Yes.'

'She saw Rose?'

'Yes!'

'Oh!'

'Have I shocked you?'

'A bit,' I said, trying to take it in.

'I wanted to tell you so that you'd know the full story.'

'Catherine's psychic?'

'Yes. I'm not sure if psychic is the right word – clairvoyant maybe, a medium; she doesn't put words on it.'

'I see. Well, it would make sense – all the coincidences and that. There had to be some kind of spiritual connection between you and Rose but I didn't suspect anything about Catherine.'

I struggled to find the right words to cover my uneasiness. This was foreign – and scary – territory. 'I don't know a lot about that kind of thing, to be honest. If I was being really truthful I'd say I'm a sceptic but it would explain a lot with this story. You'd better tell me exactly what happened.'

I sat there for the next three-quarters of an hour listening to the details of what Catherine had seen the night she connected with Rose – Rose in Rosegarland, Rose in the graveyard, the walls, the description of it. Now a lot of things made sense – why Patricia had placed a plant on a particular spot on the ground in the graveyard, for instance. There had been flowers on that spot near the pathway the first time I visited. 'That was where Catherine saw her stand, wasn't it?'

Patricia smiled. 'Yes.'

'And the wall – that's why you kept drawing attention to it the first day I went there with you when all the briars and ivy had been cut away. You could see that it had been raised. It would have been possible to see one of the hospital towers over it before then. You just weren't able to say it at the time!'

'Yes.'

'I always wondered what the trigger was for your going to the hospital,' I said. 'There had to be some reason why you went straight after the holiday.'

'How do you feel about what I've just told you?'

'Amazed. A bit uncomfortable but fascinated at the same time.'

'You don't think we're mad – that you should stay away from the pair of us?'

'No, of course not,' I said, hoping I sounded convincing.

Privately I wondered what I was getting myself mixed up with. Mediums, séances, psychics, fortune-tellers – I shied away from them all. Somewhere along the line I had picked up a notion that it was better to keep my distance from them. Weren't they people who preyed on others' desperation, loneliness or unhappiness, making things up as they went along or getting clues from a person's words or body language?

Was it a faith upbringing with me – don't mess with things you don't understand because you might find yourself out of your depth? Anything between life and death was cloudy country and better not to mess with. Yet the psychic connection here was totally understandable.

Rose had suffered injustice in the days when the individual had few rights – criminals, lunatics, children, women. Being in two of these categories, what chance had she? If I had been her I wouldn't have rested easy either. I'd have wanted to settle the score and make the world remember that I, and maybe hundreds of thousands like me, existed.

'I believe what Catherine has is a gift,' said Patricia. 'I believe Rose is in heaven but that she has some unfinished business on this earth. She wants the wrong done to her righted.'

'She's a restless spirit,' I said. 'She won't find peace until that happens.'

'I don't think so.'

*

Sleep didn't come easily that night. What was I getting mixed up in, I wondered? Would it be too much to handle? Where exactly would it lead? There was frustration too at not being able to tell the real story for the radio documentary.

Still, it made sense. Catherine had been right about the graveyard. I had never experienced anything like the urge to tell this story either – was someone pulling my strings from another world? Some relative or relatives of my own that I never knew who had also died in that place? Right now anything was possible.

Also the more I studied the period, the more I was annoyed by the injustices, especially in relation to women. The census of 1901 records for the asylum had given an insight into the reasons people were there. Mania and melancholia were the two great classifications. Women were also committed for 'moral insanity', for being pregnant, even for being likely to become pregnant. They were put in too for postnatal depression – a condition no one understood at the time. The census painted a bleak picture.

We began to make preparations for our trip to Liverpool. Historian Elizabeth Malcolm would be an excellent interviewee. Already she had commented briefly by e-mail on Rose's story.

It would have been far from rare in nineteenth- and early twentieth-century Ireland, she said. Paupers' graveyards would not have had headstones or priests to say prayers. Many people at that time were committed as 'dangerous lunatics', which meant that the asylum could not force their families to take them back or pay for their funeral if they died.

'Dangerous lunatic' – how would Patricia feel when she heard that term used in relation to Rose? Even if Rose had become hysterical when it came time to go home with her new husband she would have been far from a lunatic by today's standards.

Melancholia, as a category, meant very little, Elizabeth Malcolm said. How could it when the doctors involved had no training in mental illness?

Rose's dying of TB would have meant stigma for the family too. It was almost more of a stigma than having a relative suffering from mental illness. Perhaps that added to why she wasn't mentioned in the family.

'If she had gone on to die in an asylum, she would have been written out of the family history. This may sound a bit brutal, but this is how people thought at the time.' It wasn't a good idea to condemn the past according to the moral standards of the present, she added.

Was that what we were in danger of doing? I was in no doubt that we were appalled by what had happened to Rose but it was important to record how things were. Yes, the visit to Liverpool would be short, a straightforward interview that might upset Patricia.

Portraying Rose as a victim would not dignify Rose, Elizabeth Malcolm said. In women's-history circles recently, she said, there had been a reaction against portraying women only as victims. 'Victimhood diminishes them. A lot of them fought back as best they could,' she said.

That line in the e-mail irked me. Rose had fought back but where had it got her – into an asylum.

How would Patricia react to hearing this in Liverpool? We'd have to wait until the June bank holiday weekend to find out.

9

THE CHILD

Rose had no sooner entered Jack's house in Rospile the next evening under orders from Jack when Patrick arrived, fire spitting in his eyes.

'Nothing'd do you now but to consort with a Proddie, is that it?' he said, grabbing her arm.

'Go easy,' said Jack, coming between them.

Rose retreated into a corner.

'I've a good mind to thrash you.'

'I've done nothing wrong!'

'Nothing wrong and you going down in the woods with that fella – do you think I'm daft or what?'

'We did nothing – we just talked, I swear.' Rose slumped down on a chair. 'You can't talk to me like this. I'm a grown woman, not a child!'

'A grown woman without a tither of sense!' said Patrick, coming towards her again.

Jack blocked his path. 'Leave her be! Talk to her civil or get out of here, I'm telling you.'

Jack being the taller, Patrick backed off.

'I've heard about you, down in Cullenstown, sporting your figure and gawking at that fella stripped to the waist. Do you like being the talk of the parish? Do you want your parents turning in their graves with the way you're going on? Are you wanting to bring more shame on this family?'

He was so close she feared he was going to strike her.

'Pat. Leave it!'

Rose struggled to find words. 'I only spoke to him.'

'So you weren't revelling in his attentions like you did with that other fella?'

'No!'

'I don't believe you!'

'Leave her be, Pat,' said Jack.

Rose huddled in the corner, covering her ears.

Patrick paced back and forth in the small kitchen. 'You're taken in by their good manners and their fancy clothes and their posh way of talking. Well, it was their forefathers who took our land from us and no Quinn is going to get mixed up with them.'

'Ted isn't from around here!'

'No, but he's the seed of them that took the land off people like us.'

'Your bitterness is rotting your soul,' she screeched.

'Better rotting my soul than getting mixed up with the likes of them. You'll stick to your own kind and you'll marry the man we've matched you with. One of your own, do you hear?'

Rose wrapped her arms around herself as he bent over her. 'Yes. Yes,' she sobbed, praying he'd leave her alone.

'Good. The date is set, 6 November before eight o'clock mass, so start making your plans. The missus'll help you.' Patrick had his hand on the door latch. 'Go near that fella again and I'll sort him out the same way I sorted out that other fella who made a fool of you.'

Rose felt almost too weak to stand. So what she'd suspected was true. The man who had fathered her child six years before had left the country suddenly after her shame became known. They didn't even give him the chance to marry her. She had no doubt now but that he had been persuaded to go.

Next morning in the dairy she told Bridget what had happened. Bridget said very little. 'Maybe – maybe it'll be for the best if you marry him. Most women get used to their husbands over time.'

Rose saw Bridget's troubled face. 'What is it? You look burdened by troubles yourself. Would you not tell me …'

Bridget sat down on a milking stool and placed one beside it for Rose. 'It's the child …'

'The child?'

'Your child.'

Rose grabbed Bridget by the shoulders. 'Tell me!'

'Rose – you mustn't fret. Maybe he's just sick, with the help of God.'

'What are you talking about? Tell me!'

'Aunt Maggie hasn't seen him out with the rest of the workhouse children for months.'

'But she must have! He's easy to pick out.'

'There's no child of his size with fair hair there any more. She saw them out walking again the other day.'

'There has to be!' Rose desperately tried to think of an explanation. 'Maybe they've put him out to work early. Maybe someone has taken pity on him and brought him home to rear him.'

'Three of the children died a few weeks ago. They say it was consumption. Aunt Maggie heard from the porter. I'm so sorry, Rose.'

Rose felt a wave of weakness pass over her. 'He's not dead!' She stood up and headed for the door.

'Rose – where are you going?' Bridget said, following her.

'I'm going to find him. He'll be in the yard with the rest of them, you'll see. If I watch out for him long enough he'll be there.'

'You can't go there, Rose. They won't let you in. You can't go!'

Rose had already run out into the rain, heading toward the shed where the bicycles were kept.

Bridget called after her. 'You'll be sacked if they find out you've gone. Rose, listen to me,' she said, grabbing her by the shoulders, 'there's nothing you can do!'

'Tell them I'm sick. Tell them anything until I get back.'

'Rose, you'll catch your death. You can't go!'

*

Rose was drenched and exhausted by the time she had cycled the fourteen miles to Ross. Summoning up what strength she could muster, she made her way uphill towards the workhouse from the Foulksmills road.

She knew where to go. If she went round the side and up the hill she could see through the hedge into the yard where the children played. He would be there. They'd let them out when the rain stopped so the dormitories could be cleaned.

As she passed the entrance gate of the workhouse a two-horse carriage came out with two policemen and another man in it. It was the asylum car. She'd seen it when she was in the workhouse having her child. It was the one with locks on the door.

'Gee up, there!' The driver slapped the reins against the horses' rumps and turned the carriage for Enniscorthy. Rose saw the terrified face of the man who was tied up inside.

'He doesn't look like a dangerous lunatic,' she thought.

That didn't surprise her. She'd heard the stories of how some people were gotten rid of. Their families told the doctors and the magistrates that they were a danger to themselves or to someone else and the form was signed. That way the family had to pay nothing.

Rose shivered as she hurried round the corner and up the hill. 'It's not right,' she said. 'Like a lot of things in this world.' She knew of several people who'd been put in the asylum, most of them far from madness. The farmer's son from the next parish who stood in the way of his brother inheriting; the neighbour who had tried to drown himself in the river, driven out of his mind by the loss of his animals in a fire. Women had ended up there too. Fallen women. They'd never been seen again. Rose blessed herself, glad that had not been her fate.

She threw her bike against the ditch and climbed up to try to get a look through the hedging on top. The rain had eased; the children would be let out after their dinner. 'If you could call it dinner,' she thought, knowing the lump of dry bread and half pint of milk that would be measured out and fought over. She was weak from lack of food herself now and the dampness of her clothes was making her body ache.

After what seemed like half an hour she heard the noise of children. She crawled onto her hands and knees and peered through. Her eyes scanned the group, desperately searching for a fair-haired child. 'Sacred Heart of Jesus, let him be here.'

There was no sign of him. Her eyes desperately scanned the group of sixteen or twenty ragged-looking children moping around the yard. 'Sacred Heart of Jesus, help me!' She collapsed on the pathway, her body shaking.

'You! Get away from here!' It was the workhouse porter. 'You can't loiter around here. Get away or I'll have the police on you.' Seeing that she did not move, he drew closer.

'The child – is he … is he?'

'Who? What child are you talking about? Speak up, girl.'

'My son. He's six.'

'How the hell do I know? There's hundreds of them come and go in there.'

'He has fair hair.'

The porter thought for a minute. 'Your bastard, was he? Child with that colour hair died a few months ago. Consumption. Rotten with it.'

Rose felt faint.

'No good you pining over him. He's better off where he's gone than in this place. You hear me?'

*

Rose woke three days later in her bed in Rosegarland. Bridget was holding her hand. The porter had eventually got her to say her name and he told the parish priest in New Ross. She had been transported back to Rosegarland in the sexton's pony and trap. Bridget had looked after her until her fever broke.

'Rose! Thank God,' Bridget said when her eyes eventually opened.

As the recollection of what had happened hit her Rose turned her head to the wall. What was there to thank God for? It didn't matter what happened to her any more. She had done wrong, bringing a child into the world out of wedlock. God was punishing her for her sin now. Who was she to go against her family's wishes? She would have to marry the man they'd chosen for her. She closed her eyes again and began to pray. 'O my God, I am sorry and beg pardon for all my sins and detest them above all things because they deserve Thy dreadful punishments because they have crucified my loving Saviour Jesus Christ and most of all because they offend Thine infinite goodness ...'

She closed her eyes tighter, hoping sleep would come quickly. Right now all she wanted to do was shut out the world.

10

LIVERPOOL BOUND

Interview with historian Elizabeth Malcolm at the Liverpool Institute of Irish Studies, 5 June 2000

R ose was buried in an unmarked grave in the grounds of the former asylum – was this usual at that time?

Yes, these were pauper asylums and a lot of pauper institutions buried people in the grounds. Workhouses and hospitals did the same thing because it was cheap.

If you were a pauper, funeral and burial plots and headstones were expensive and if you wanted to be buried in the churchyard in sanctified ground it cost money. If you were a pauper, by definition you didn't have money. The ground beside the asylum would not have been consecrated.

What were the criteria for commital in Rose's time?

People were usually committed at the instigation of their families. Sometimes it was a complaint from a neighbour but in the main it was a member of the family, the immediate family, who would have gone to the police and would have said that a person was being violent or threatening violence, either violence against themselves – suicide – or violence against other members of the family.

A lot of women were committed at that time with what we would now call postnatal depression. That wasn't understood at the time.

Could a husband have committed her?

Husband, brother … From my work I've come across a lot of instances where mothers, widows, would have a son committed but, yes, brothers especially. I found a lot of brothers committing brothers or sisters.

If a member of Rose's family had wanted to take her out of the asylum would that have been possible?

Yes. If the medical superintendent who was answerable to the board of governors had gone to the board and said she is fit for discharge, she would have been discharged.

However, you would have had to have someone who was prepared to take her and of course under the Irish legislation, the way it was framed, committing someone as a dangerous lunatic meant the family was freed of all responsibility for taking them back and often didn't want to take them back.

So what you get were more people dying in Irish asylums than were being discharged. Families could commit people and have no responsibility so it was difficult to discharge people.

I did notice a pattern where men would be committed and then the family would take them back, usually because they were needed to work on farms. Women, though, were more likely to be left in.

With males, with a family, the man was the breadwinner. Sometimes with women, and I think Rose is a case, the family had no particular advantage in having her back.

If Rose herself had demanded her release would she have been listened to?

Probably not. In casebooks from several institutions that I have seen, if a patient said that they wanted to appeal for release to the governors – local gentry from the area – this was regarded as confirmation of their insanity.

I've come across cases where in doctors' notes 'is demanding release' is written repeatedly and then you'll get a note 'is not demanding release', then some time later 'is released'.

We can take that to mean that if the patient stopped demanding release it meant that they were getting better. Demanding release might ensure that you never got out.

Rose's refusal to marry this man – would that have caused a lot of problems for the Quinn family?

Yes, it would. A lot of Irish marriages at this period were arranged between families so if a woman refused to go along with this, or after she'd gone through the marriage refused to go live with the husband, this would create big problems for the family. The husband could demand compensation, in fact.

Rose went to the asylum after a three-month stay in the workhouse – could she have been sent there because there wasn't room at that time in the asylum?

Yes, if Wexford asylum was overcrowded at the time they may have been reluctant to accept new patients.

The easiest option, then, would have been to commit her to the workhouse as a lunatic.

The workhouses at this time were major pauper hospitals both for the mentally and physically ill. Twenty per cent of lunatics at this period were in workhouses.

What was the procedure for having her committed?

A medical certificate would have been required. This would have been given by a dispensary doctor. These were the doctors who were employed throughout Ireland in what was a very basic health system. Dispensary doctors were not trained in mental illness. They dealt with the illnesses and diseases of the poor and were paid by the government for doing this.

They weren't very well paid but committing lunatics was quite lucrative. The fees varied from one to two guineas so the doctor would simply sign the form saying he considered the person a dangerous lunatic.

If the family said 'this person is dangerous or difficult' the police concurred.

After getting the medical certificate the person was taken to the magistrate, who pretty well automatically committed people.

Would the permission of Rose's husband or family have been needed to transfer her from the workhouse ward to the asylum?

Oh, no. The family were out of it now. By committing her to the workhouse as a dangerous lunatic the family had abrogated all responsibility.

Rose died of phthisis – TB. How prevalent was that at the time?

TB was rife in 1907 – it had reached epidemic proportions by then.

That Rose had TB before she went in wouldn't have surprised me but in institutions like workhouses and asylums TB was rife. She could have got it there and died within a very short time.

If Rose had had TB and her family knew she was ill and considered her a (future) burden on the family when she couldn't work as a servant any more they may have tried to marry her off. Thirty-six is quite late to get married even though people got married late in that era. Obviously the husband would be looking for children – at thirty-six it was getting a bit late.

What if Rose had had a child before she was married off?

Rose could have been committed for this alone. You could become a social outcast by giving birth to an illegitimate child at that time. The child would be taken away and put in an orphanage. In England too there was this category of 'moral insanity'. This was used particularly in relation to women. Yes, if Rose had a child it would have added to her personal problems and to the family's desire to get rid of her.

How many asylums were there in Ireland at this time?

There were about twenty-five, built from the 1820s on. By 1900 you had asylums accommodating 600 to 1,000 patients. There were 20,000 people in asylums at that time in Ireland.

How were they funded?

The government paid a proportion of the cost of the maintenance of patients but a lot of the cost had to be paid by local ratepayers.

By 1900 a lot of ratepayers weren't too happy at the cost of the system and you get the system being starved of money at this period.

There are various descriptions from the 1890s on of the very poor state of these hospitals, that they are extremely run down and that they are dilapidated. A lot of them had been built sixty or seventy years earlier and not properly maintained so their facilities and accommodation would have been out of date.

Did patients work in the asylum?

Yes, men would have worked on the farm and women would have done a lot of cleaning and sewing and laundering. A lot of the clothes for the patients were made in the institutions themselves and laundry was often taken into asylums as a money-making enterprise. There was a notion at the time that if you were mentally ill work was therapeutic.

Were doctors trained at that time?

There wasn't training at this period. Some doctors developed an interest in mental illness and read up on it themselves but there was no formal training.

What were the chief reasons for committal?

The two big categories at the time were mania and melancholia. If someone was quiet and withdrawn they might be seen as melancholic – if they were going around shouting or screaming they might be classed as maniacal.

Mental illness was at that time considered hereditary. This meant that doctors didn't make much effort to cure people. You get figures at the time saying that 80 per cent of those committed were considered incurable. Doctors didn't have anything much in the way of medicines at this time. It was considered that the most you could do, therefore, was just look after these people.

Because mental illness was considered hereditary you just had this warehousing of people. There was the notion that the mentally ill should be taken out of the community, because you didn't want them marrying and reproducing because if mental illness was hereditary then if you left them in the community you were only going to increase the problem.

Because there was very little that could be done for them, asylums ceased to be therapeutic institutions and became custodial ones. By 1900 they were just institutions to confine people. After the 1950s, when mood-controlling drugs came in, this changed. This development and the decline of these institutions go hand in hand.

Should we measure people from that era by modern moral standards?

I think you can demonise Rose's family and you can see her as a victim of an oppressive family, you can see her as a victim of the asylum, of doctors and of magistrates, but I am uneasy about doing that. They had certain attitudes that we don't share today but their attitudes reflected views and attitudes of their time.

It is so easy to condemn them for not having our attitudes. We can see them as more prejudiced and more bigoted and more intolerant but you can't ask people a hundred years ago to have our attitudes.

I think Rose herself, just seeing her as a woman who is pushed around by family, by males particularly, and by professionals with no say of her own, I think that dehumanises her.

Okay, I don't doubt she suffered but I think she was a woman with a mind of her own … I think that the fact that she wasn't married at thirty-six does suggest someone with a strong mind of her own.

*

Patricia said very little on the few-hundred-yards walk from the Institute of Irish Studies to the Feathers Hotel where we had stayed the night before.

Halfway through the interview she had gone quiet, no longer asking questions of the historian. Gone was the jovial spirit when we had talked about the taxi driver calling the very modern-looking Roman Catholic cathedral in the city centre 'Paddy's Wigwam'. We were no longer laughing either about the waiter who had to enquire from the chef who the singer Charlie Landsborough was when Patricia said she was a fan. He wasn't a Liverpudlian, the chef had pronounced, but a 'plastic Scouser', meaning he was from Birkenhead.

In the hotel room, microphone switched on, Patricia's upset was obvious.

'Rose was not insane. Rose was never a lunatic. I've listened to what I felt was her being classified as insane or a lunatic. She was a victim of circumstances. I feel that she stood up for her rights. She did not want to live with this man and she said so. It was because family and her husband walked away from her and turned their backs on her that she ended up first in the workhouse, a victim, and from there into the asylum.'

But would Patricia accept that they were different times, that there was a different understanding of the word 'lunatic'?

Yes, she said, she understood the difference between now and then but she still thought it was so unfair. 'I feel that she was so let down by family,' she said. 'I have strong feelings about family, that you stand by your own family regardless of what they do, that you're there for them as support. It comes across to me now that her family wasn't there to help. If Rose's family — my family — had supported her she would not have ended up in the asylum and possibly might have had a longer, happier life.'

Patricia was very glad, she said, that she lived in this century. 'There is more love and understanding among people now. Society is much more open. Some people say some of the changes are not for the better but there are so many that *are* for the better.'

The Quinn family had lessened in her estimation now, she said. 'I had them on a bit of a pedestal and it's difficult for me to accept that they've slid a bit. Initially I blamed the husband, I had him down as the big baddie, but that for me has changed now. I see him as being an ordinary man now; again maybe he was a victim of circumstance. He got a wife who wasn't a wife but blood ties should have been stronger than that.

'In the first place Rose shouldn't have been forced into a marriage against her will, and when she refused to go live with him, family should have stood around her regardless of circumstances. They shouldn't have shunned her, excluded her, made her a victim – this is what I feel she was, a victim – because she stood up for, a little bit too late maybe, but she stood up for her rights. It was the cause of her death, I think.'

Within an hour we were on the plane back to Dublin, the two of us silent and Patricia's sadness palpable.

Michael, Patricia's husband, had said he'd be at the airport to collect us. Going out to the arrivals lounge, Patricia stopped in her tracks. 'I hear piping!' she said, striding immediately in the direction of the sound.

A lone piper was standing at one of the front doors, close to a bus where French tourists were being greeted. 'Rose has sent him,' Patricia said, smiling now from ear to ear. 'She knew I needed cheering up.'

11

CLAY GAME

Mary Quinn sewed another square of fabric onto the half-made patchwork quilt. She couldn't help but feel pleased with herself. Another few weeks and she would be done, well in time for Rose's wedding. Neighbours had helped out, too, contributing cloth scraps or old garments that they could spare to be cut up for the quilt.

A woman getting married needed a few things for her bottom drawer. Rose would have as much as she had had. Already Mary had made her a nightdress and some underwear, working late into the night by candlelight while her children slept close by.

Thank goodness Rose had finally agreed to the wedding. There was a bit of peace in the house now. Patrick was more cheerful and they weren't feeling the brunt of his temper so much. If he'd had to go back on his word to Pat Murphy they'd all have suffered for it but, thank God, things had worked out well. She'd never doubt the power of a novena again.

'Rose will be glad she's married after a while,' Mary thought. Although Rose wasn't saying much about it, she was no longer saying anything against it. That was a good start. Rose was all right – just occasionally she had notions above her station.

And she had at least been civil to Pat Murphy. She had been in the house a couple of times at the same time as him and she had passed herself. It wasn't easy settling down to talk when you knew everyone was listening to you. Hadn't she felt that way herself when her own marriage was arranged? But there would be plenty of time for Rose and Pat to get to know one another after the wedding.

At least Rose was able to work a full day again, after her illness. She was lucky she hadn't died after that wetting she got going to Ross. What had possessed her to do such a thing? How did she think she could change anything that had happened? Perhaps it was better if the child was gone. It would be preferable to his being farmed out as a labourer as soon as he was old enough. Mary had seen children like that. Ragged, bags of bones, treated no better than animals. Anything was better than that.

At least with Rose working again she would be able to contribute to the cost of the wedding. Patrick couldn't be expected to pay for clothes – Rose would have to spend her own money on those. Hadn't they already done enough promising their two pigs as a dowry for her?

*

'Won't be long till your big day now, Rose,' said the man she'd brought the bucket of water and a mug to at the threshing. 'We'll soon be toasting your health,' he said, wiping his mouth with the back of his hand as he got down off the rick of straw that a group of them was making. The other men stopped what they were doing and stared at Rose.

'Yes,' she said, looking away. She hated this job, the men gawking at her as she went about her work. Next time the younger women could do it. Young Martha, for one, wouldn't mind this sort of attention.

'Doesn't seem too happy about the idea of getting wed,' he said as they watched her return to the yard. 'She's a stubborn one, that. The marriage bed'll tame her, though. It's tamed many's the filly.'

The other men laughed.

'That's if Murphy is up to it.'

She could still hear them laughing as she returned to the dairy yard where Bridget was washing potatoes for the men's dinner. Bridget knew by Rose's face what had happened.

'They've been saying things to you?'

Rose nodded.

'Don't let them upset you. It's only men's talk. They're all the same.'

Rose sat on the stool by the door and put her head in her hands. 'What ...what if I can't get used to it – him ...'

'Of course you will. Maybe not at first but after a while. Some say it's enjoyable.'

'Not if you've no feeling for the man, it isn't. You might as well be animals if there's no love in it ... or if it's against your will.'

'It wouldn't be as bad as that. Try not to think about it, that's probably the best thing.'

Rose busied herself at her work. If she was busy she had less time to think – that was the best way, she'd found. Shut it out of your mind as much as you can and that way you could get through the day. There was certainly no shortage of work to keep her occupied from early until late – feeding poultry and pigs, milking cows, making butter, cleaning utensils, picking vegetables, cleaning out henhouses. The list was endless.

'At least if you're married you'll be looking after your own hens and making your own butter and you can sit down when you want and not be afraid of the steward shouting at you for slacking. I wish my family'd find a man for me. I fancy being my own boss.'

'He'd be the boss, not you,' said Rose, scrubbing down the butter table.

'I'd have my say too. Just like you will.'

'Women are like cattle. They're traded off in pubs, same as the animals.'

'Try not to think of it so harshly, Rose. You'll only torment yourself. If matches weren't made no one would get married and the world would come to a full stop. If your father and mother were still alive they would have tried to make a match for you too. You couldn't have gone against their wishes.'

'The hens need feeding.'

Rose left the dairy with Bridget watching her. Bridget was worried about her friend. Rose was so pale now. And thin. She'd seen her sew another button onto the waistband of her skirt because it was now far too big for her.

Bridget sighed, at a loss to know what to do to help her friend.

*

Rose wished she had been able to go to a different mass – nine o'clock, maybe. Anything rather than hear her own marriage banns read. Neither did she want to see Patrick or Mary grinning at everyone, looking so pleased with themselves.

They were there now, Mary with the children on the right-hand side of the church, Patrick on the other side of the chapel with the men.

The words she had dreaded hearing came halfway through the mass. Father Lyng cleared his throat and looked down at the congregation before he began the banns, checking to see if she was there. 'The banns are hereby read.'

Rose felt an inclination to cover her ears but instead she concentrated on the floor, studying the grain of the wood between the seats, while the priest's voice droned on.

'… marriage between Rose Quinn, spinster of this parish, and Patrick Murphy …'

The grain was running eastwards. How many trees did it take to make the pews, she wondered? How long did it take to cut and plane them?

'If anyone knows of just cause why these two should not be joined in matrimony ...'

Rose felt the eyes of the congregation bore into her back. She dug her nails into her two palms. She could see young John turn his head to look at her and smile before Mary glanced over and made him sit properly. The children would be at the wedding. They were all excited about it. It wasn't every day that such a thing happened.

As mass ended she left the church as quickly as she could.

'Hello, Rose.'

It was Bridget's mother, Mrs Rowe.

'Good morning,' Rose said, hurrying away. As quickly as she could she walked down the hill and back towards the village, Mrs Rowe looking after her.

'God love her,' she said before joining a group of neighbours for a chat.

'Rose didn't stay to talk,' Mary said, seeing Rose disappear.

'Odd as two left feet that one, sometimes,' said Patrick, spitting in the grass that ran along the edge of the roadway.

*

The streets of New Ross were thronged. With the harvest over and the grain paid for, the farmers of the district and their wives were in town with money to spend.

'Wish I was one of them,' said Patrick Quinn to another Clongeen man who had stopped to bid him the time of day. Mary and Rose were inside Power's shop on the main street doing the clothes shopping for the wedding. 'If the landlords were forced to sell to us like they're supposed to we'd have land back by now. Leigh'll have to do it in the end, same as the rest

128

of them. If they don't do something for us soon we'll starve over the winter.'

'Three years is a long time waiting all right,' said the other man, a labourer himself and the son of an evicted tenant. 'It's time it was done.'

'They want to hold onto what they've got. What they took.'

'Aye.'

Patrick wished the women would hurry up. He hated hanging around on the street like this, especially when he hadn't got a few pence to buy a drink, but nothing could be spared at the moment. Mary was keeping a tight hold on what they had. He knew she would get the best value too.

With Rose's wages the wedding would be taken care of. He was looking forward to the spree after the ceremony. It would be a long time before there would be as much drink in the house again. He could feel the thirst coming on him already.

Inside Power's shop, where a 'great cheap sale' was taking place, Rose was fitting on a costume. Tweed. Ten shillings. Two weeks' wages.

'It's the best you'll get for the money,' said Mary, telling her to turn around. 'And it suits you. Makes you look a bit more robust. You're fading away these days. You'll have to eat a bit more. A husband doesn't want a skeleton for a wife.'

'He'll have to take me as I am,' Rose said.

Mary was now fingering the display of hats on the counter. Two shillings each. 'The hat you have will have to do. We can't afford to be extravagant,' said Mary.

Mary was pleased with what they had purchased. Cheap cotton to make sheets, a few remnants at eleven pence halfpenny a yard to make a couple of blouses. If Rose could hold onto her Rosegarland uniform skirt it would bulk her wardrobe out for a while and her wedding costume would do her for mass for many years to come. Mary still had her own.

'What did your employers give you as a present?'

'Blankets.'

'Good. You'll need them with the winter upon us. And you'll have the quilt I've made for you. You'll be well away. Come on, cheer up. Some thread now and we're finished.'

Returning to Clongeen, the cart shook as it travelled over the rough road. Rose prayed silently. The Memorare – that was the one when you wanted intercession. Her lips shaped the words as they turned at Ballinaboola. 'Oh Mother of the Word incarnate, despise not my petitions but graciously hear and answer me, O clement, O loving, O sweet Virgin Mary …'

The donkey stumbled slightly as it walked slowly toward the cross of Newbawn.

Maybe Mary, mother of Jesus, had already answered her prayer, making her not care what happened any more. Would not caring bring her through what was before her? The marriage would be her redemption, Father Lyng said. She could hold her head high again as a married woman. Rose looked at the road ahead of her. It seemed to stretch for miles.

*

Bridget came into the servants' quarters that evening to look at the purchases. Rose said nothing while she took one item at a time out of the parcel, lifting the clothes and the fabric to her nose to breathe in their newness.

'They're all lovely,' she said, before handing Rose a small brown paper package. 'It's not much, I know, but I wanted to give you something.'

Rose untied the twine. It was a present of two small handkerchiefs trimmed very neatly with lace.

'The house-parlourmaid gave me the material. Just a few scraps from the mistress's sewing box.'

'I'll treasure them,' said Rose. 'They're the nicest I've ever had.'

That night Rose slept fitfully and woke agitated. She'd seen her own child in a dream but his face was a blank.

*

Autumn had arrived at Rosegarland. Everywhere the trees were shedding their leaves, golden, russet, swept off the branches by the winterish winds. Everyone on the estate was talking of the shoot. The woods were full of pheasant and soon the shooting season would open.

Friends of the Leighs were coming for All Souls' and there was much work to be done.

Already small shoots had taken place and Rose and Bridget had had the job of cleaning the game and dressing it. Dozens of birds hung in a shed awaiting their time on the kitchen table.

Rose was glad of a break late on All Souls' Eve to go see her nieces and nephews in Rochestown. All Souls' was a special time, especially if you were a child.

It was seven o'clock by the time she reached the house, barely a mile away. In a bag she had apples that she had taken from the apple-house. She had been careful to pick one here and there and move others to fill the spaces so that no one would notice. And she had a bit of butter from the dairy. No one would miss it. She didn't like stealing but right now what did it matter? She would be leaving Leighs' soon. And her employers well had their value out of her. Her hands bore testimony to that.

Rose was delighted with the welcome she received from the children.

'It's a frosty night to be out, Rose, but they've been waiting for you.'

'I knew you'd come,' said young John, pulling at her skirt.

'We're going to play games like last year.'

Inside the kitchen was warm. On the table was a loaf of bread and some potatoes for supper. Patrick was sitting in the corner smoking a pipe of tobacco. 'Rose.'

'Patrick.' Rose looked quickly round, half expecting to see Pat Murphy there and relieved to find he wasn't.

'He was here last night,' said Mary, as if reading her mind. 'He's looking forward to the wedding. He's fixing up a room for you. You'll be in grand style altogether.'

'Oh.'

'Aunt Rose, come and play with us.'

'What do you want me to do?'

'Put this on.' John handed her a rag to blindfold herself.

'Now what?' she said, tying it behind her head.

'Turn around three times and then you have to pick something from the saucers on the table.'

'We know which ones you're going to pick, Rose.'

Rose knew the game. She'd played it herself as a child.

Slowly they turned her round, the children's voices excited as they pleaded with her not to look.

'Put your hand out and touch something on the table,' they said. 'Whichever one you like. Go on.'

The giggles rose from the children again. She moved her hand away from its first place of lingering. 'I choose this one,' she said, putting her hand forward.

The silence in the room made her remove her blindfold quickly.

'You were supposed to pick the ring,' John said, his lip quivering.

Rose looked at the four saucers in front of her. One had a ring placed on it meaning marriage. One contained water, signifying emigration. The one with straw meant the chooser

132

would be wealthy. Rose had picked the last one. Clay. Early death.

'It's only a silly game,' said Mary. 'Pagan nonsense, the lot of it. Lizzie, go get some pieces of string and I'll thread them through the apples that Rose brought. You can tie them up and have a go at eating them.'

'You were going to pick the ring, I saw you,' said young John, still looking unsure. 'You're not going to die, are you, Rose?'

She gave him a hug. 'No. Not till you're twice married and once a widower.'

*

On the way home, the carbide lamp showing her the way, Rose felt unsettled. It was only a game. Still, some people put a lot of store by such superstition. Maybe she would die young. 'What matter? I feel like part of me is dead already.'

Reaching the end of the Auk Road, she screamed. A man had stepped out in front of her.

'It's me, Rose. You're all right.' Ted Jameson was standing beside her.

'You frightened the life out of me!'

'I'm sorry. That was the last thing I wanted to do but I had to see you. I knew you'd be coming back soon so I waited for you. I wanted to give you this. As a wedding present, since you've made up your mind you're going through with it.'

'I don't need presents.'

'I'd like you to have it, something just for yourself. It's only small but I know how much you liked the music that day ...'

Rose held her hand near the beam of the lamp so that she could see the tiny wooden object that he had laid on the palm of her hand. It was a tiny set of bagpipes, the wood of the drones and chanter whittled expertly and sticking out of a tiny tartan-cloth goose bag.

Rose closed her fingers on her present as a lump formed in her throat. 'Thank you. Thank you very much.'

*

The last week had passed very slowly and Rose had clung to every moment. Every small job she did, every part of her daily routine, was important because it was the last time she would do it. Even jobs that she had often complained of, like cleaning out the pigs, no longer seemed so onerous. She wished she would be there to do those jobs next week and the week after.

Her days in Rosegarland were nearly over – she had to reconcile herself to that. Panic rose in her chest at the thoughts of having to live in a small, strange house with a man she barely knew.

It was as if she was looking at everything from a distance now, from outside herself. All this was happening to someone else. Even Bridget was no longer making any pretence at joviality. After tomorrow nothing would be the same.

When her day's work finally finished she stood for a long time in the dairy. Tomorrow someone else would do her work. Someone from the village, probably, who'd be glad to step into her place. Early tomorrow morning she would leave here to get married in Clongeen church. Some time during the next day or two her brother Jack would deliver what little possessions she had to her new home and that would be the last Rosegarland would see of her.

Another flood of panic made her search her pocket. *Maybe* … She counted the money she had there. Four, five, six shillings. That was all she had in the world. She could make no life somewhere else. Tomorrow she would be wed. Closing the dairy door, Rose felt more desolate than she had ever felt before in her life.

12

PATTERN AT ST SENAN'S

It was July 2000 and the pattern day had come at last. Patricia was glad she'd been invited. At least some sort of service was held in this graveyard once a year – she had been so glad to hear that. She was pleased, also, to have been asked to read a prayer during the service.

She parked in the field beside the graveyard. The mini-bus from the hospital drove in behind her. Ten, maybe twelve, people got out – patients and nurses. The nurses took care of their elderly charges, helping them down the steps.

Patricia's eye was drawn to one woman wearing a headscarf. Where was that woman in her mind, Patricia wondered? What was the story behind her? What was the story behind each patient here? How long had each one been here? If the world had been different would they have spent their lives in a psychiatric hospital? So many questions …

Blue flowers! Patricia spotted them as soon as she walked through the gateway. A little tingle ran down her spine. Catherine had seen blue flowers when she connected with Rose! Bluebells, not blue hydrangeas as were here now, but still blue. Who had put them there, she wondered? Was it someone from the hospital? A kind-hearted local resident? Who had Rose guided to put them there?

Did Rose know that today her name would be mentioned in prayer – the first time a priest had spoken it in this place? Were the blue flowers a sign from Rose that her goal was on its way to being achieved? Were they a thank you from the next life and encouragement to complete the task? Patricia decided they were. She couldn't wait to ring Catherine.

She looked around at the now tidier graveyard again. She hoped the next time she was here it would be for the special service to erect a monument to everyone buried there. She laughed to herself. 'Me ordering a granite headstone and not a penny to pay for it – I must be mad,' she thought. Ordering it that day had been a huge leap of faith. She had picked it out, a simple granite one at Hughes' memorial works opposite the railway station in Wexford.

No matter, if no county or borough councillors could spare any of their amenity grant funds she would pay for the head-stone herself. Seven hundred pounds. Still, it would be worth it. She would find the money somewhere. She wished she had known about the councillors' discretionary funds earlier. She hoped she wouldn't be too late and that the funds wouldn't be all used up already.

Father Jason O'Donoghue was beginning the prayers.

In the trees a few crows squawked. A butterfly fluttered on the ditch behind.

'Lord, hear our prayer. And we pray for all who have died, and we remember Rose Quinn who is buried in this cemetery, and for all retired members of staff who may have died during the year. We remember also the residents of St Senan's who died throughout the year.'

Patricia listened while he read out the names.

'May they all rest in peace. Let us pray to the Lord.'

'God, our Father, we believe that those we have known and loved and who have died are now alive and living in Your kingdom. May their memory be for us a continuing source of strength and inspiration, we ask this through Christ our Lord.

And now we ask the Lord to send His blessing upon all these graves here today.

'Lord, You are the author and sustainer of our lives. We commend the memory of all who are buried here who we gather to remember today with Your loving care, trusting in Your mercy and Your embracing love, we pray that You give us happiness forever.

'Turn also to us, those who may have suffered loss, strengthen the bonds of our families and communities, confirm us in faith and in hope and in love so that we may bear Your peace to one another and one day stand together in heaven to praise You for Your saving help. We ask this in the name of Jesus the Lord. Amen.'

The priest now moved around the graveyard, sprinkling holy water from a bottle. Patricia willed him to put some on the spot where Catherine believed Rose was buried but he didn't.

*

In the following few weeks Patricia felt as if a calm had settled. She had felt it in the graveyard after the pattern, a great feeling of being at peace. Catherine felt it too, she knew. Rose had left her now, she said, as if her job was done for the moment. It was down to Patricia to do the rest. But would Rose ever connect with Catherine again, she wondered?

As far as the feeling of peace went, was it her own peace having heard Rose's name finally mentioned? She believed it was more. Rose had been recognised.

She would come to the pattern every year from now on, and on her and Rose's birthday – 11 July – and at Christmas and any time she felt the need. It was right that this graveyard should be a prayerful place. She couldn't get complacent, though. There was still work to be done – the crooked steps needed straightening, the weeds needed sorting, the paths needed to be scuffed. Kerbing would be nice too. She would have to keep the pressure on.

Maybe when she met Joe Casey, the chief nursing officer, in a few weeks' time they could talk about the improvements. The fact that the bishop of Ferns, Brendan Comiskey, had agreed to help with the cost of the memorial stone and also say the blessing at the unveiling would work in her favour.

A date would have to be agreed. The stone would be ready by mid-September, Hughes' said.

October, then, for the special service? She hoped so. October was always a lovely time in Wexford. With the opera festival in full swing, it was a time of celebration. For Patricia it would be another kind of celebration.

13

WEDDING DAY

Rose woke to find Bridget shaking her. 'It's nearly six o'clock, Rose. Time to get up.'

As the realisation of what day it was hit her, Rose sank her head back into her pillow again, dreading the thought of getting out of the warm bed where she had had very little sleep.

Bridget was blowing her fingers to heat them up in the cold room. Two other servants, Martha and Ruth, turned over in their beds, glad they had another hour of rest.

'Quick. Get dressed,' Bridget said as Rose finally stirred. 'Cook has promised to have a big mug of sweet tea ready for you before you go. She does it for everyone who's getting married.'

'I don't want any.'

'Just a few mouthfuls.'

'I might be sick.'

Bridget sat down on the bed beside her friend. 'It's only nerves. Everyone feels like that but Cook says you have to have something to line your stomach.'

Rose reluctantly got out of bed.

'Rose – you will be all right?' asked Bridget, fetching her friend's wedding clothes.

Rose shrugged her shoulders and looked away.

'I wish you could come with me after the wedding – to Patrick's.'

'So do I but I can only get time off to go to the wedding itself. Still, I'll be there at the church: that's the important bit.'

Bridget said a silent prayer that Rose would be happy as she watched her lace up her new boots. With her hair brushed and pinned up Rose looked well. She was thin and not what anyone would call a beauty but she walked tall and had a dignity that many didn't have. Bridget wished her eyes were not so sad, though, on her wedding day.

Cook slipped Rose a shilling before she left the kitchen. 'You'll be needing a little something for yourself later on. May God look after you.'

'Thank you.'

'Remember it's not your execution you're going to, girl. There's lots of us women who would have liked to have married but were never blessed with the means nor the opportunity so cheer up.'

'Yes,' said Rose, forcing a smile.

'That's more like it.'

Bridget placed Rose's hat on her head and checked to see that it was properly positioned. 'There you are – your house is thatched! Time to go.'

Rose had difficulty controlling her emotions as she walked away from Rosegarland for the last time. Would she ever come back to the place that had been part of her life for so long? Even to visit the people she knew there? And was that Ted Jameson she saw at the top of the lane watching her go?

'We'd best get a move on, Rose,' said Bridget, following her friend's gaze. 'They'll be waiting for us at the church.'

*

Patrick and Mary and the children were already there when Rose and Bridget walked up the hill towards Clongeen church. The ground was covered in a blanket of frost, making massgoers watch their horses' steps on the road.

Jack was at the pub door a few yards across from the church door, trying to beat the frost out of his feet, by keeping them moving. 'It's for the best, Rose,' he said, seeing his sister's pale face and haunted eyes.

Rose looked at the ground, unable to speak.

The children, including young John, ran around breaking the ice on the puddles of water, their warm breath visible in the cold air.

'A drop of whiskey wouldn't go astray this minute,' Patrick said to Jack, casting longing glances at the closed pub door.

'Aye.'

'Rose. You look very well.'

Mary was there, fixing Rose's lapels and telling the children not to maul her clothes as it was her wedding day and she needed to look her best.

'Pat's already in there. He's a reliable man – we told you that.'

Rose felt her chest heave as the enormity of what was happening hit her.

Bridget put her arm around her. 'Rose! Rose! Don't cry.'

Mary took Rose's other arm. 'We'll look after her. You go into the church. It's family she needs now.'

Bridget flinched, dropping her arm.

'She'll be in there in a few minutes.'

'Rose?'

Rose didn't answer. Huge sobs were building up inside her, looking for release.

'Go into the church – now!' Mary's voice was sharp, seeing Bridget's delay. 'You're only making matters worse. I told you, it's family she needs.'

'But …'

Bridget reluctantly did as she was told. Jack silently went

inside, unable to bear looking at his sister any more. Patrick ushered most of the children towards the door. Mary would do what had to be done. This was women's business.

Young John lingered near his mother, his eyes saucering at the sight of his aunt Rose crying. His mother's voice cut the frosty air like a knife.

'Pull yourself together, for Almighty's sake. It's only nerves with you, Rose – you'll feel better in a few minutes, honest you will. Here, blow your nose again.'

Rose did as she was told.

'Do you want to let us all down, your parents in that grave there looking down on you as well?'

'No …'

'Well, then, stop making such a fuss. You've a whole life to look forward to. There's women that'd give their eye teeth to be where you are today.'

'I can't!'

'You can and you will! Everybody feels like this before a wedding – do you think I didn't? But it all turned out for the best. I've a fine family now and you will have too some day. A few months from now you'll be thanking us for finding you a husband. Come on, you're upsetting the child.'

'What's she crying for, Mammy?' asked John.

'Hush, child. Get inside with your father.'

Putting her arm around Rose, Mary half-guided, half-supported Rose into the church where Patrick was waiting at the door. At the top of the church sat Pat Murphy. Rose felt a wave of weakness pass over her.

'Steady. It'll all be over soon.'

Rose could see the children's eyes staring up at her as she walked up the aisle. The altar, the big window, the smell of incense, it was as if she was in a church she had never been in before. She was outside herself again. This was happening to someone else.

Father Lyng stood at the foot of the altar. 'In nomine Patris et Filii et Spiritus Sancti. Amen. Introibo ad altare Dei, ad Deum qui laetificat juventutem meam …'

Later, the sound of the priest's words came in waves.

'Rose, will you take this man …'

Not a sound was heard in the church.

'I … will.'

The words were barely audible except to the priest. Rose could see the man's hands shake as he placed the ring on her finger.

'I now pronounce you man and wife.'

Outside the church faces were coming at Rose, one after another. Hands shaking hers, Bridget's face a blur among the rest of them.

Patrick was slapping Pat Murphy on the back. 'That's it. Your bachelor days are over now.'

'By God, they are,' Pat said, grinning from ear to ear.

'Come on, let's go to our place and get a drink down you.'

Bridget hugged her friend tightly before she left to go back to work. Rose was as cold as ice.

'I'll be thinking about you,' Bridget said. 'I'll come see you in Carrig next time I get a day off. You can depend on it.'

Bridget turned quickly so that Rose wouldn't see that she was upset. Already the neighbours were getting into ponies and traps or setting off on foot or bicycles for the short journey to Rochestown. Jack turned for home. He couldn't stand the thought of a party.

Smoke was rising from the house in Rochestown when the wedding party arrived. Neighbours who hadn't gone to the wedding had the place warm and welcoming for the guests. Rose's hands were so cold she could not feel them.

'Come in to the heat, love. You look frozen to the bone.'

It was Bridget Rowe's mother. She handed Rose a cup of very hot tea.

'She could do with something stronger, I think,' said Mrs Rowe to the woman beside her.

'Aye. God love her.'

*

The day passed in a blur. Rose ate very little, just played with the food on her plate.

When the tables were moved back to make room for the dancing Rose refused to dance. Pat, the groom, stood there embarrassed until Mary told him Rose wasn't feeling well and that she'd dance with him later. Very soon the first half set had started and the awkward moment had passed. Rose stayed in the corner tending to John, who was tired now from his early start.

She listened to the storytellers, to the singing where old faces with closed eyes sang songs of motherly love, of injustice and invasion and the gallant rebels of '98. Her brother contributed a long poem about Parnell and the bravery of the land leaguers.

'Landlords be damned!' he said to finish up.

'Aye,' came the shouts from others in the room.

The crowd was in the middle of singing a Thomas Moore air when Rose eventually got up and went up to the bedroom. She couldn't stand the noise any more. There she covered her ears to shut out the sound and huddled in a corner.

Mary was standing at the door. 'Rose, you should be down there with your husband. Jesus, Mary and Joseph, what's up with you now?'

Rose tightened her arms around her knees. 'I won't go home with him.'

Sadness at Cemetery

Dear Sir,
Recently while trying to trace my family tree I discovered I had a grand-aunt, Rose Quinn. Rose was born in Clongeen in 1870. Forced into an arranged marriage, she refused to live with her new husband and soon after the wedding was committed by him to St. Senan's Hospital in November 1906. She died there on 4th May 1907, and was buried in the hospital cemetery.

And so the purpose of this letter. I have recently paid a visit to this cemetery, and I was deeply saddened at what I saw. There is not one word inscribed anywhere to say who is buried there, indeed not even to say anyone is buried there. A lone cement cross stands in the centre of the plot. The entrance from the hospital grounds has been blocked up and the only access now is from a side road at the rear of the hospital. It is quite difficult to find. I came away feeling sad and guilty that my aunt, and I'm sure many more unfortunate people, are buried there. Up to now these people seem to have been forgotten.

My dream is that the cemetery would be turned into a garden of remembrance, with a suitably inscribed monument, to give due recognition to all those buried there. The cost would not be prohibitive, and as we enter a new millennium it would be a wonderful gesture to remember all those who have been forgotten for so long.

I would be very grateful if you could use your influence in any way to make this dream come true.
Yours sincerely
Patricia Murphy (nee Quinn)

Clockwise from top left: John Quinn (1900–94), Rose's nephew and Patricia's father © PJ Browne; Catherine Murphy © Ger Hore; Patricia Quinn-Murphy © PJ Browne; the letter that started it all, *The Wexford Echo*, November 1999.

Top: Enniscorthy District Asylum for the Insane Poor; built in 1868.
Bottom: The graveyard behind St Senan's Psychiatric Hospital, formerly the Enniscorthy District Asylum for the Insane Poor. Photograph taken in January 2000.

Top: Rose's birth certificate; her year of birth was stated, incorrectly, as 1875. Note the correct year of registration - 1870. This may explain the error in age in the asylum admissions register.
Bottom: Rose's baptismal record; courtesy of Wexford County Council Archive.

Top: Clongeen parish church where Rose, and later her grand-niece, Patricia, married men with the same name, Murphy, from the same parish, Carrig-on-Bannow.
Bottom: Clongeen church - interior.

Top: Pub across from Clongeen church where the match was probably made.
Bottom: The cottage Rose moved to on the Rosegarland estate after her family was evicted from the farm at Newcastle no longer exists. The cottage pictured above was occupied by Patricia's youngest uncle, Willie Quinn, and is situated 100 yards further up the lane. This cottage was the first image shown to Catherine in her initial spiritual connection with Rose.

Top: Graveyard at the hospital in 2000. The cement cross was erected in the 1960s.
Bottom: Graveyard from hospital entrance side (doorway now built up).

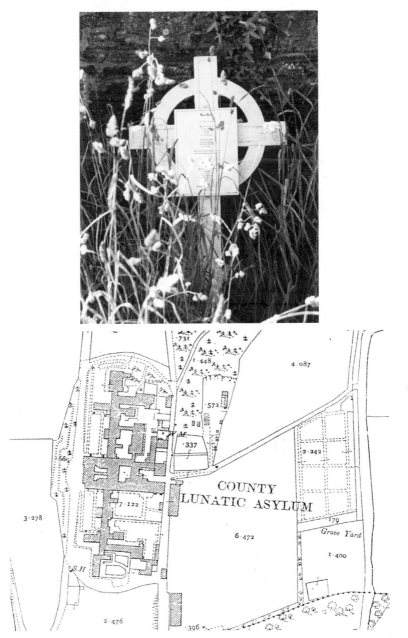

Top: Plaque with poem written by Patricia which she put in graveyard in January 2000.
Bottom: Map of County Asylum showing graveyard.

Top: View of raised wall on one side of cemetery. *Bottom left*: Clongeen graveyard where Patrick and Mary Quinn (Rose's brother and sister-in-law and Patricia's grandparents) are buried. *Bottom right*: Rose's name was put on her brother, Jack's, headstone in the new cemetery in Clongeen – Patricia's way of 'bringing her home'.

Top: Road from Clongeen to the parish church - the one Rose would have travelled on 6 November 1906. The entrance to the old graveyard where her parents are buried is on the right of picture. *Bottom*: Marriage certificate for Rose Quinn and Patrick Murphy. Rose may have added 'anna' to her name at her confirmation.

ROSS UNION.

Population in 1901— *30,795*   Present Net Annual Value, £ *106,303*

STATE of the Workhouse for the Week ending Saturday, the *24th* day of *November* 1906.

A total of 197 were admitted that week, 1 child was born and 1 person died there. It also gives figures for the number of lunatics and idiots in the workhouse at the above date - 36 - some of whom were in separate wards and some in wards with other inmates.

RETURN of Destitute Persons relieved out of the Workhouse, as by Relief Lists, for the last Week ended Saturday, the *24th* day of *November* 1906 authenticated and laid before the Board of Guardians at this Meeting.

COPY OF MINUTES of Proceedings of the Board of Guardians, at a Meeting held on *Saturday* the *1st* day of *December* 1906.

PRESENT—In the Chair,

9   **581**

The Reports of the Master ~~and other Officers~~ were read, and Orders made thereon, as follows:—

1. The Schoolchildren were out for exercise since last Meeting, the boys once, the girls once.

2. Mary Butler was sent to the Mater Misericordiae Hospital Dublin on the 12th inst., and Pat F and Rose Murphy to Enniscorthy L. Asylum on 16th.

3. I sold 8 fats pigs on 11th instant for £35.16.0 and bought 8 store pigs on 12th. for £18.10.0.

Orders thereon

Nos. 1. 2 & 3 Read.

Top: The above shows the numbers given relief in New Ross workhouse in the week ending Saturday, 24 November 1906.

Bottom: Page 581 of New Ross Union minute book for February 1907. The entry includes mention of Rose Murphy being transferred to Enniscorthy Asylum on 16 February.

POOR-LAW COMMISSION.

Recommend Sweeping Reforms.

Abolish Workhouses.

Almshouses for Aged and Infirm.

Children in Nurseries or Boarded-Out.

Time and Labour for Tramps.

Hospitals, Home Nursing and State Medical Service.

The Present Workhouse System Should be Abolished.

and the various classes of inmates, except children, should be segregated into separate institutions; the existing hospitals, whether poor law or county, should, except in a few cases, be retained in their present localities, but all should be placed under the management of County and District Committees. Such hospitals should, as far as possible, be used only for the acute sick. A sufficient number of

Consumptive Sanatoria

should be established. Additional cottage hospitals should be established at certain places in Ireland, and the system of home nursing for the poor extended.

A State of Medical Service should be established, and the cost thereof defrayed out of money voted by Parliament. Right of admission should be given to the district hospital nearest to a patient's residence. The "aged and infirm" of all the workhouses within a convenient area should be placed in a disused workhouse to be known as the County or District "Almshouse," in which proper classification can be carried out. The Insane

should be removed from Poor Law Institutions, and be detained in auxiliary or other asylums under the control of the Lunatic Asylum Authorities. Sane epileptics should be placed in separate institutions, for which purpose disused workhouses will be available.

Unmarried Mothers

should be sent to institutions under religious or philanthropic management, or to "labour-houses" and be kept apart from other classes. The question should be considered whether a law ought not to be passed enabling mothers to proceed in their own name against the putative fathers of their children, and to obtain affiliation orders. Infants should be placed in "Nurseries," either under religious and philanthropic management, or, when disused workhouses are used, under Poor Law control. All children between infancy and maximum limit of age should be boarded out. Certain cases might be temporarily placed in certified, or industrial, schools. The Poor Law District Schools of Glin and Trim should be dissolved as Poor Law Schools.

Casuals and Vagrants

should be detained for long periods under magistrates' warrant in "labour houses," under the control of the General Prisons Board, and be maintained out of imperial funds. Genuine workingmen about to travel to seek employment should be provided with satisfactory documentary authorisation for obtaining from relieving officers food and lodgings during their journey. Two disused workhouses should be handed over to the War Department for the accommodation of pensioners, ex-soldiers, reservists, and militiamen, who claim support owing to destitution. Special Casual Wards should be established in Dublin, Belfast, and Cork, and possibly in Limerick and Waterford. Destitute respectable widows with only one legitimate child should be eligible for outdoor relief. Clauses prohibiting the granting of outdoor relief to be afforded to the occupier of more than a quarter of an acre of land should be repealed. The area of charge for outdoor relief and for children sent temporarily to industrial and certified schools should be the electoral division, with an adequate rate-in-aid as regards outdoor relief for towns. Guardians should be empowered to strike and collect a special rate for outdoor relief. The cost and maintenance of boarded-out children between infancy and maximum limit of age should be a union charge. The expenditure on

The Sick, Aged and Infirm,

epileptic, lunatics, infants, and unmarried mothers in institutions should be defrayed out of a county at large rate. Vagrants, casuals, and other classes sent by a Court of Justice for detention in "labour houses" should be maintained out of money voted by the House of Commons for prisons. Those remitted by guardians for "test" purposes, or who enter voluntarily, to be paid for out of the County rate. All existing officers should be compensated for loss of office and be entitled to receive pensions.

Free Press newspaper item from 3 November 1906: the Poor Law Commission recommended sweeping reforms including the removal of all 'lunatics' to lunatic asylums.

The seventh annual show, which was held under the auspices of the New Ross Agricultural Society on yesterday, was favoured with the most ideal summerlike weather. Since early morning the town wore the appearance of the bustle and traffic, and everything augured that its success would not be in doubt for a moment. The advent of the Cameron Highlanders, who came from Dublin by the mail, was looked forward to with some interest, and not a little excitement, as a considerable portion of popular opinion was fiercely opposed to the engagement of a military band. The Camerons played some enspiriting airs from the station en route to the grounds.

MILITARY MOVEMENTS IN

WEXFORD.

In the course of a few days Bannow will be the scene of some camp training operations. The participants will almost entirely belong to the cavalry arm of the forces, Barlough being considered a suitable venue for accustoming horses to ford water. A contingent from across the channel will travel via Waterford and Dublin, and Dublin and the Curragh will also contribute detachments. A number of Wexford victuallers tendered for 1,300 lbs of meat per diem, but we understand the tender of a Waterford flesher has been accepted. The troops, during the course of the operations, will move as far as Kilmore.

ENNISCORTHY DISTRICT ASYLUM.

WANTED a Female Attendant at Wages commencing at £13 per annum with good service pay, and allowances.

Applicants must be healthy and robust, able to read and write, must be single, or widow without children, age 20 to 35, proof by certificate required.

Application to be made to the Resident Medical Superintendent between the hours of 10 a.m. and 12 noon. Applicant should bring copies of their testimonial with them.

THOMAS DRAPES, R.M.S.
31st January, 1907.   155

Enniscorthy Asylum Board.

WEDNESDAY.

CONTRACTS.

THE POSITION OF BANDMASTER

Mr John Cullin presided, and there were also present—Rev Canon Sheil, P.P., Bree; Messrs John Sinnott, J.P; Jas Codd, J.P; John J. Kehoe and Ald. Doyle.

Superintendent's Report.

Dr Thomas Drapes. R.M.S., reported as follows—Eight patients were admitted since the last meeting of the committee; two were discharged; and two died; leaving under care at present 265 males, 263 females, total, 528. The condition of the institution generally, and the health of the patients, is satisfactory. I lay before you my annual report for the yead 1906. We commenced boring operations on our own account on the 15th inst., at a point near our motor pumps, where Mr Jones was of opinion that spring water was flowing. We have gone down to a depth of 37 feet, and water comes into the bore hole at about a gallon per minute. It is not improbable that we may succeed in getting a more abundant supply at a greater depth.

Top left: Item in *Free Press* of 13 July 1906 detailing the presence of the military band, the Cameron Highlanders, at the New Ross Agricultural Show - an event not welcomed by some.

Centre: 1,500 soldiers spent from 28 July to 18 August 1906 in Bannow on training exercises. Three regiments were represented: the 3rd Dragoon Guards, the 11th Hussars and the 19th Hussars. Postcards were published by Eason & Co. to mark this event.

Bottom: Advertisement in the *Free Press* for female attendant wanted by Enniscorthy District Asylum. Dated 31 January 1907.

Top right: A section of the minutes of the asylum published in the *Free Press* on 18 May 1907. It states that two people died in the asylum that month. Rose Quinn was one of them.

ENNISCORTHY DISTRICT ASYLUM.

SCHEDULE No. 10.

I Hereby Give Notice that Rose Murphy a patient admitted to this Asylum on the 16th day of February 1907 died therein on the 4th day of May 1907 and I certify that attendant, Kate O'Connor was present at the death of Rose Murphy that the apparent cause of death (as ascertained by post mortem examination) was Pulmonary Phthisis and that the disease existed since before admission

TO ALTER THIS DOCUMENT OR TO UTTER IT SO ALTERED IS A SERIOUS OFFENCE

Top: Entry in doctor's notes showing that Rose died at noon on 4 May of pulmonary phthisis. There was no entry between 27 April and that date.

Centre: The entry in the asylum records that recorded Rose's death.

Bottom: Rose's death certificate. Her death was registered by an inmate.

Top: Another view of the graveyard after it had been tidied up in 2000.
Bottom: Memorial erected in October 2000 in memory of Rose and all those buried in the cemetery behind St Senan's Hospital (the former asylum) © Tony Murphy.

Top: At the unveiling of the memorial. Left to right: Joe Casey, Chief Nursing Officer, St Senan's Hospital, Fr Jason O'Donoghue, chaplain, Fr Brian Broaders, Jeanne Hendrick, manager, St Senan's Hospital, Ivan Yates TD, Bishop of Ferns, Brendan Comiskey, Archdeacon Wilkinson and Patricia Quinn-Murphy © Tony Murphy.
Bottom: Death certificate of Patrick Whelan, grandfather of Mary Farndon. Patrick died in the asylum in 1926. Mary did not find out where he was buried until 2000.

Top: Mary Whelan-Farndon with her cousins Kathleen Murphy and Breda Shiels at their grandfather, Patrick Whelan's, grave. He was buried in St Mary's graveyard, Enniscorthy © Jack Caffrey. *Bottom*: Hugo Kelly, St Senan's researcher.

'Hmph! We'll have none of your defiance. If you don't stop talking like this people'll be saying you're cracked. You're married to him now. You have to go.'

Rose stared at the pattern on the bed cover.

Mary stood in front of her, hands on hips. 'What in the name of God am I going to do with you at all? You're flying in the face of God and His plans for you, you know that?'

'They're not God's plans.'

'And who are you to say that? You think you know better than your brothers and the dead parents that have gone before you who would have counted themselves lucky to have made as good a match for you?'

Young John came in, looking frightened.

'Go downstairs and get some whiskey, quick!'

'What's wrong with Aunt Rose?'

'Hush! There's nothing wrong with her all. Just get the bottle and say nothing to nobody.'

The child fled to the kitchen.

Mary sat down beside Rose and put an arm around her. 'It's the way of the world, do you not see that? You just have to accept it.'

'No.'

Mary turned Rose to face her. 'Now you listen to me, Rose Quinn. You're not going to make a show of us this day. You're going home with your husband like any other married woman would. You've no choice, do you hear?'

The child arrived back with the whiskey. Mary held the mug to Rose's mouth. Rose spluttered as the fiery liquid hit her throat.

'You'll be all right in a few minutes. It's only nerves with you.'

'She doesn't like it, Mammy!'

'Go back into the kitchen and stay there! Now!'

The child fled again.

Rose now appeared a bit calmer.

'There, you'll feel better in a few minutes. Tomorrow you'll wonder what you were making such a fuss about.'

*

At nine o'clock Patrick announced that it was time for the happy couple to depart. Unsteadier on his feet than the groom, he announced that Redmonds' donkey and cart was ready to take them home. Mary helped Rose into it outside the door.

Rose's head felt a bit dizzy from the whiskey. As the crowd of neighbours gathered round her to say goodbye she said nothing.

'You look after her, Pat,' Mary said to the grinning groom. 'She'll need gentle handling.'

'That I will,' he said. 'Nothing surer.'

Noticing Rose's silence the crowd quietened. Mrs Rowe, Bridget's mother, shook her head as she watched her go. 'I've never seen a bride look so unhappy. It'll be a long month for her before she can visit anyone again.'

'It'll be bad luck if she doesn't stay away,' said another neighbour. 'It was hard for all of us but we all had to make a life for ourselves. She'll have got accustomed to it in a month.'

'Please God,' said Mrs Rowe, saying a prayer for Rose as the couple turned the bend on the lane.

*

Her new husband's attempts at conversation fell on deaf ears. Rose stood as far away from him as possible in the small kitchen.

'The women tidied the place for you.'

It was obvious somebody had been busy. The fire was lit and the table set for a cup of tea. Rose placed her clothes parcel and the patchwork quilt on the table beside the lamp.

Pat stoked the fire and put the kettle on to boil. Looking nervous, he gestured towards the small room that opened off the kitchen. 'I fixed up the room inside too.'

Rose clenched her fists.

'I told your brother I would keep my end of the bargain. Do my best for you. He said you would too.' He came closer.

'Don't come near me – please!'

Rose saw amazement register in the man's eyes. 'That's a fine thing to say on your wedding night.'

Rose backed further away.

'The bed's clean, if that's what you're worried about. I changed the hulls in the palliasse myself – honest to God. Like I said, I'll always do my best for you …'

He steadied himself at the table. Rose could smell the porter on his breath.

Suddenly loud noises were heard outside, in the fields behind the house. Pat went to the window a bit unsteadily.

'Bastards!'

Rose was shaking. 'What is it?'

'The blowers. Out to torment us.'

Rose had heard of the blowers before. Neighbours and guests at a wedding joined together to disturb newlyweds' coupling on their first night by making continual noise, blowing horns, clattering pans, beating drums – anything they could find to make a din.

Rose felt as if the roof was coming in on top of her – the pandemonium outside, the size of the room, the unaccustomed smell of it, of him, so close she felt suffocated.

'They'll clear off after a while, never fear.' He came closer again. 'Are you not going to talk to me? It wouldn't do any harm to be a bit friendly?' He made a half-hearted grab for her, catching her arm. 'We're wed, after all.'

'No!' Rose broke his hold, moving round the other side of the table.

He moved round the table after her. 'There's more spark in you than I thought. What has you so reluctant now? You weren't always reluctant, from what I heard.'

Rose grabbed the lamp as he made a move after her again. As he tried to take it from her she suddenly let go and the lamp smashed on the edge of the table.

'Jesus Christ!'

Flames had already caught the fabric of the patchwork quilt as the shade broke and the wick fell directly against it.

Pat Murphy staggered back from it, unsure what to do.

Rose froze momentarily then ran for the bucket of water in the corner and threw it at the burning blanket. The flames fizzled out and the two of them stamped out the last of the flames with their feet.

'You're a mad one,' he said, wiping his mouth with the back of his hand.

Rose picked up a stick from the pile by the fire.

'You'll wave no sticks at me,' he said, making another lunge at her.

The whack hit him on the shoulder. With all the drink he had taken he fell heavily, hitting his head on the floor. Rose ran for the door. The winter cold cut through her as she stumbled down the lane in the dark, glancing back again and again to see if he was following her. No …

Sobbing, she came to the road. Where could she go? She turned in the direction of Clongeen, the moon giving her light, not sure where she was going. She couldn't go back to her brother's house or to Jack's. They would only send her back again. Rosegarland? Would they take her in?

Oblivious of the cold she ran as fast as she could. Luckily, there was no one on the road. Frozen and exhausted she eventually knocked on a door she recognised.

'Holy Mary, mother of God, help me ...'

Bridget Rowe and her mother could see no one when they first opened the door of their cottage. 'Who is it?' they called out into the darkness as they held a lamp aloft.

Then Bridget saw Rose on the doorstep and screamed. 'Rose!'

'Mother of God, what's happened to you, child?' Mrs Rowe said, helping her daughter support Rose as they led her into the kitchen. 'Get her some dry clothes. Quick.'

'Rose – what happened?'

'I can't go back there. I can't. Please let me stay here – just for tonight.' Rose was clutching her friend's arm so tight it hurt.

'Beat up an egg in hot milk, Bridget. It might stop her getting a chill.'

'What'll we do if he comes looking for her?' said Bridget, who was as pale as a ghost.

'We'll cross that bridge when we come to it. Until then, she needs looking after. They'll come soon enough.'

14

RESPONSE

Summary of a radio interview given by Joe Casey, chief nursing officer at St Senan's hospital, to South East Radio in August 2000 following a request to comment on this particular matter.

Patricia had a lot of questions for Joe Casey, chief nursing officer at St Senan's hospital. She would now get a chance to put them to him in a recorded interview situation.

She wondered if he felt as uneasy as she did. She had been very critical of the hospital management initially. Now she felt more positive. There are two sides to every story – she knew that. Besides, what happened in Enniscorthy asylum would have happened in asylums all over the country.

To Joe Casey's knowledge there had been no burials in the hospital graveyard since 1944. One had to put the graveyard associated with the hospital into context, he said.

St Senan's had opened in the 1860s. At that time many patients were admitted to the hospital from the countryside, where the standard of housing and their living conditions was often very poor. They were sometimes poorly clad, he said, had little to eat and were surviving mainly on charity. Others were in workhouses and it was accepted that the mentally ill at that time were not treated for their mental illness. There was very little treatment in the workhouses for mental illness at that time so in that sort of situation people came into the asylums from the countryside. Many of them remained there for most of their lives.

'When it came to the final stage of their lives in many instances there were no relatives available to see to their needs at the end of their lives, or who were interested in making personal contact with them. For those patients who hadn't relatives to see to their burial arrangements, the hospital graveyard was used for their interment.

But were people committed who were not mentally ill?

Well, it is difficult to say that people were committed who had no symptoms of psychiatric pathology. The standards of judgement and diagnosis of mental illness were so much different in those times. Records would also show that there were social reasons why people were admitted to asylums in the latter half of the nineteenth century.

It is probably also true that recording procedures by today's standards were relatively low key at that time, so that people with what would be today considered relatively minor mental illnesses, found themselves in asylums, because this was society's way of dealing with individuals who somehow behaved differently to what was deemed at that time to be normal behaviour.

Of course the mythology and prejudice that was associated with mental illness in those times resulted in a deep rooted fear and prejudice which was held by society. Their answer to these questions was to institutionalise patients and to isolate them from normal society. That is a core reason why a network of asylums were built throughout Ireland, simply to house people whose behaviour at a personal and social level was considered by society to be abnormal.

But why was it so difficult to get information from the hospital?

Well, I very much regret if you found some difficulty in finding accurate information. The fact is that there are very few records relating to this period on the precise location of burials in the hospital graveyard. One has to recognise that the management of hospitals has changed a number of times along the way.

In the early days hospitals such as St Senan's were managed by a board of governors. Later on that accountability transferred to the county council and the county manager had a key role.

Then in 1970 the Health Act came into being and health boards were established so that was around the period when I came to Wexford to work for the South Eastern Health Board as a chief nursing officer. The health board itself began to operate around 1971 and I took up my post in 1974.

It is true to say that there are few accurate records pertaining to the precise location of burials in the hospital graveyard. It is my understanding that the difficulty in finding accurate records for patients who are buried in the graveyard is not different to that which exists in many other psychiatric hospitals around the country.

The information we have is rather basic, perhaps a name, a date of death, the reason for the patient's death certified by a registered medical officer and some other personal details, but there is no record of the precise location of where that person is, or was, buried in the hospital graveyard, and that is the basic fact as I understand it.

The primary reason for the building of a network of asylums throughout Ireland in the latter half of the nineteenth century mainly was to house persons considered as unsuitable or unfit to live in ordinary society and to label them as persons of unsound mind so that they could be admitted to the asylums, thereby isolating them from society.

These institutions were relatively secure and the patients were isolated from society. They had little ordinary interaction with the local people in the neighbourhood and this perpetuated the culture and mythology associated with the stigma surrounding these people down through the years.

Regrettably in these times records of precise burials were not deemed essential for recording and there was no political, administrative or social pressure at the time to ensure the maintenance of such precise information regarding the burial of persons whose mere existence as human beings was sometimes not accepted by families and neighbours.

Patients were well treated at a subsistence level at that time and one has to pay tribute to the staff who worked in these institutions at that time. They did the best they could with the resources they had and the information, knowledge and expertise available to them.

Who is responsible for upkeep of the graveyard?

Well, the responsibility lies with the hospital management, the graveyard is hospital property and we recognise the sacredness of it. In 1970 an annual pattern was begun and the chaplain of the hospital who is a priest in St Senan's parish ensures that this pattern is held each summer and that is a very good thing.

The maintenance of the graveyard is a function of the hospital maintenance programme. What we had in the graveyard were small white crosses with no names or numbers. When the graveyard ceased to be used for burials it became overgrown and it was difficult to maintain.

The decision was taken in the 1940s to remove the crosses

and place them alongside the wall so that the grass could be mown and kept in a reasonable state of maintenance. Now that is not dissimilar to what happened in other similar graveyards throughout the country. To maintain the graveyard at a higher level would of course require more resources.

Since you took an interest in the graveyard yourself, and indeed it is something that is welcomed by all of us, both management and staff, there is an interest expressed in forming what might be regarded as a cemetery maintenance committee that will maintain the graveyard into the future at an acceptable level.

The voluntary principle in doing this type of work is probably the best approach and there are many members of the staff and some local neighbours and people who have retired from the hospital who have a special interest in the graveyard and some have expressed a willingness to be part of that process.

Would it be easier for other relatives now to get information?

Yes. We're all becoming more aware of openness and transparency and the culture of treatment and recovery from mental illness is now accepted as a matter not just for the professionals but also for society itself.

There is a general move towards community mental health services and all of this has to be welcomed. We are beginning to witness the demise of the traditional institutional psychiatric hospitals and as I speak, a number of psychiatric hospitals in the country are either closed or near closure and this would be the objective for St Senan's over the next decade or so.

15

COMMITTAL

Pat Murphy woke on the kitchen floor just before eight o'clock the morning after the wedding. He'd slept where he'd fallen. He felt his head for the small cut as he pulled himself up by the table. His head pained, although he wasn't sure if it was from the cut or the whiskey.

What day was it? What had happened? How much had he drunk? Slowly the events of last night came back to him. She had hit him with something. He staggered to his feet and looked around. The blackened edges of the patchwork quilt lay on the floor, the bucket beside it.

'Mad woman!' he muttered.

He opened the door of the bedroom. No one had slept there. He grabbed his cap. He'd go to Patrick Quinn's. He'd hear what had happened. He wouldn't be codded by anyone. All Patrick's talk about how good a wife she'd be – agreeable, biddable … He put his hands over his eyes as the brightness hit him when he opened the door.

*

Patrick eventually appeared having been roused by the children. 'What do you mean she's gone?'

'Is she here?'

'What would she be doing here? She went with you last night and that's the last we saw of her. What are you talking about?'

Mary appeared behind her husband.

'Gather your wits, man. You're not making sense.'

Pat Murphy eventually told them the whole story – or what

he remembered of it. 'Like a madwoman, she was, when I went near her.'

'Glory be to God! Where is she now?'

'I don't know. That's why I came here.'

'If she's been out all night she could be dead in a ditch somewhere. Mother of God!' said Mary.

'She'll be dead in no ditch,' said Patrick, pulling his braces up over his shoulders. 'She can't have gone far. If a few of us search we'll find her.'

'The woman's not right in the head.'

'I'll run down to Rosegarland and tell Jack. Maybe she went back there.'

'Get the children to check the outhouses – go on, quick!'

'Sacred Heart of Jesus, what have we driven her to?' said Mary.

Patrick grabbed his coat. 'We've done nothing wrong, woman. It's her own stubbornness that's done it. Come on. We'll find her soon enough but I'll never forgive her for this.'

Two hours later they had found nothing. Jack arrived on horseback to say he'd been to Rosegarland but no one had seen her. A shiver had run down his back thinking of all the places she could have hidden and of the Corach river that was running high at this time of year.

'There's only one place she can be. Bridget Rowe's. Come on,' said Patrick.

'If she's there, keep a civil tongue in your head,' said Mary. 'Losing your temper'll serve no purpose.'

'I'll say whatever needs saying. She'll go back to her husband as any decent married woman would.'

Patrick headed off on the bike, the iron wheels making a loud clatter on the frosty ground.

*

Rose refused to come out.

'Let her rest a few days,' said Bridget, who had stayed away from work. 'She's not well. She nearly caught her death of cold last night. She's too weak to eat even.'

'It's not food she needs. It's to go back where she belongs,' Patrick shouted.

Mrs Rowe stood at the door with her daughter, blocking the entrance. 'You haven't heard the last of this. You'd think you'd have enough to do to keep yourselves alive without harbouring people who don't need harbouring.'

Inside the house Rose covered her head to block out the shouts. She might as well be dead. What would happen to her when the Rowes put her out? They couldn't keep her forever. Maybe she could get her job back in Rosegarland. 'I won't go back to him,' she said as the two women returned to her. 'I'd rather die.'

*

Two days later Rose was physically able to get up. She remained low in spirits, however, staying in the corner of the room and saying very little.

When Bridget returned from work that night Rose could see she was uneasy.

'I asked about your employment.'

'What did they say?'

'The butler asked the master and mistress and they said they had engaged someone else, given that you were getting married, and that was that.'

Rose turned her face to the wall.

'What are you going to do?'

Mrs Rowe shouted anxiously from the window, 'The priest's coming! Jesus, Mary and Joseph!'

Father Lyng stood in the doorway.

'I believe you have Mrs Rose Murphy in your dwelling?'

'Yes, Father.'

'Then I would speak to her please.'

Reluctantly Rose stood up, using a chair for support. She struggled to raise her head to meet his angry stare.

'You've gone against the law of God, Rose Quinn. Leaving the man that God in His wisdom joined you to. I have just one question to ask – will you return to him this very night?'

Rose lifted her head. 'I will not.'

'They said you weren't in your senses. I can see that they are right. May God have mercy on your soul. You no longer have the support of your family, who have done everything they could to give you a start in life. It is up to your husband to decide what's to be done with you. Good night.'

The three women stood shaking long after the sound of the horse's hooves died away.

'Maybe Mary and Patrick will see sense and help you.'

Rose tightened the blanket around her. 'They've made their decision. Who do you think sent the priest?'

*

'You want to have her committed?'

'Yes, doctor.'

The dispensary doctor sat down in his chair and removed a form from a ledger. 'And why exactly is that?'

'She's not … not right in her mind, doctor,' said Pat Murphy.

Patrick Quinn swallowed hard. 'She got married four days ago, doctor, but when she went to her home with her husband, Pat here, she … wouldn't act as a married woman should.'

'Was she in any way violent?'

'Yes,' said Pat, 'she tried to hit me with a stick and she knocked over a lamp and nearly set the place on fire.'

'I see.' The doctor made some notes. 'And how is she since?'

'Won't talk, sir. Just lies in the bed. Or else she has bursts of anger and defiance.'

'I see.'

'We can bring her to see you if you want to see her yourself,' said Patrick.

'That won't be necessary in the circumstances.' The doctor finished filling in the form. 'You must bring this to the magistrate. He will take it from there.'

'Thank you, doctor.'

Patrick Quinn turned his cap round and round in his hand, glancing at Pat.

'And will there be anything to pay, doctor?' said Pat, who knew what he had to ask.

'Not since she is being committed as a dangerous lunatic. Since she is a danger to herself and others, that is the case.'

'Yes, sir. Thank you, sir.'

'She will go to the lunatic ward in New Ross workhouse and to the district asylum when necessary.'

The two men thanked him and left.

The doctor closed his notebook. Really, these people were to be sorely pitied. Poverty, disease, lunacy – he had seen so much of it. He scribbled down Rose Murphy's name. He wondered how she would fare. The lunatic wards in the workhouse were not pleasant places to be but it would be for her own good until she could be transferred to the asylum. Maybe the doctors there could cure her.

He finished his entry. There would be no questions from the magistrate. He would commit her immediately once he had the form. That sort of behaviour wasn't acceptable in society. A woman refusing to live with her husband was not the action of a sane woman.

The doctor made a final note in his accounts book – certification for committal, Rose Murphy, two guineas.

He totted up the committal amount for the month so far. Yes, he could claim a considerable sum for certifications this time. He was lucky to be in an asylum district. Other doctors had to survive on half the income.

*

'Rose!' Mrs Rowe's face was stricken with fear.

Two RIC men from Wellingtonbridge station were outside with a two-horse carriage.

'We've come to take Mrs Rose Murphy to New Ross Union,' the first officer said. 'She has been committed as a dangerous lunatic.'

'Dear sweet Jesus!'

'Where is the woman?'

Rose stood up, not believing what she had heard, her pulse beating in her ears.

The two officers came inside and grabbed her as if she was going to lash out at them.

'Leave her alone – she's no lunatic! You know she's not!'

'Mrs Rose Murphy, by order of the magistrate we are to remove you to the lunatic ward of New Ross workhouse.'

'No!'

'Jesus, she's fainted!'

The two officers picked her up, Mrs Rowe trying to push them away from her. 'Leave her be!' She sat Rose on a chair and put her head between her knees. 'Who has committed her? Tell me!'

One of the officers checked the form he had in his pocket. 'Two signatures. Two Patricks. Murphy and Quinn.'

'Sacred Heart of Jesus!'

'Out of the way, missus,' said one of the officers.

'But you can't take her to that place –'

'Whisht, woman, you'd best stay out of it or we'll be coming back for you.'

The other officer held Rose's hands together while he tied them with a piece of rope.

'You can't tie her up!'

Rose's head was pounding. She was outside herself again.

One officer held her still while the other finished the tying.

'You don't have to do that – she's as weak as a kitten, for God's sake!'

'We never take any chances. Out of our way, missus.'

'Lunatic …' Rose repeated the word, her head spinning. She felt herself being half shoved, half lifted towards the door and into the carriage.

Mrs Rowe was sobbing. 'You can't do this.'

Rose tried to prevent herself being lifted into the carriage. The man's grip on her upper body was like steel.

'You behave yourself and there'll be no trouble,' the second officer said as he squashed into the carriage beside her. 'We know how to deal with the troublesome ones.'

Everything blurred in front of Rose as she fainted again.

'Ah, no! She's gone again.'

'Put her head down. She'll come to in a minute. Drive on.'

'Thanks be to God we'll be off duty after this,' the officer said as the carriage headed for Clongeen. 'I hope she doesn't vomit on us. Took me a week to get the stink out of my uniform after the last one we took. Desperate job this, sometimes.'

'That it is.'

16

WORKHOUSE

T he size of his manhood frighten you off, then?' The
female attendant with the rotten teeth laughed as she
and a second attendant shoved Rose along the corridors of New Ross workhouse's admissions building.

'That why you threw a fit and got yourself locked up?' said
the other woman.

'Maybe it was too small and she was mortally disappointed!'
said the porter who was carrying the lamp and walking ahead
of them.

The women laughed again. 'Aye, that'll be it! She threw such
a fit she lost her mind! Cat's got her tongue now, though.'

One of them suddenly yanked Rose's head back, pulling her
hair hard. Rose cried out with the pain of it.

'Hasn't lost her voice yet, though! Come on – we haven't
got all night.' The women repositioned their hands on her el-
bows, almost lifting her off her feet again. They were out in
the cold now – the raw November wind stinging Rose's face,
the sound of the porter's hobnail boots clattering on the flagstones.

She felt ill, distanced from what was going on. Where were
they? They had left the admissions building – now they must
be on the path to the main building where the women's and
men's wings and the kitchens were. That was it. This part of
the workhouse she knew.

'Holy Mary, Mother of God, pray for us sinners now and at

the hour of our death, Amen … Please let me be kept here, merciful Lord, let me be kept here …'

She had been there to have her child and had survived. Beyond the women's exercise yard was fear and terror.

Looking up, the building ahead of her towered over her like a giant grey crow trying to smother her in its wings. Darkness had fallen on the drive from Clongeen. The two policemen had handed her over once they reached the workhouse.

'Married, single, widowed or bastard?' The master of the workhouse's opening question had stung her brain as he looked at her from behind a distant desk.

She received a whack from one of the attendants when she wouldn't answer.

'You're married, you bitch, or is your memory gone too?'

Rose felt her body shake uncontrollably now at the memory of it. Suddenly she slipped on the frosty path, almost bringing one of the attendants down with her.

'Get up!' they shouted when they steadied themselves. 'God-damn lunatics – can't even walk straight!'

She was pulled to her feet and her arms grabbed again. The fumes from the paraffin lamp were now making her feel physically sick. Her mouth tried the shape of words. 'Hail Mary, full of grace, the Lord is with thee …'

'Praying'll do you no good here, missus,' said the porter, hearing her mutter.

'God pays no attention to mad people,' said one of the women. 'It's the devil you're in league with now, did you not know that?'

Rose closed her eyes again, trying not to hear the women's cackles.

Shape the words, shape the words but let no sound come out …

'Blessed art thou amongst women, blessed is the fruit of thy womb, Jesus ...'

Panic rose in her throat when she realised they weren't going into the main building. The porter was now leading the way round the back.

'Let me stay here, please. Dear God, let me stay here.'

'Oh, picking and choosing now, are you? You'll go where you're sent, my girl!'

'I'm not mad ...'

Her jailers laughed again.

Rose's stomach turned and the hairs on the back of her neck stood up as memories flooded through her of the screeches and the screams in the dead of night from the infirmary building where the lunatics and imbeciles were housed.

'You're insane if they say you are – and they've said it so stop your snivelling.'

'Wants special treatment, if you don't mind. Thinks she's too good for where she's going. Ha!'

The porter joined in the laughter.

Rose felt weak again.

'Stand up, for feck's sake. We're not getting paid for lifting the likes of you!'

Rose closed her eyes, not wanting to see. She couldn't stop the smells telling her where she was, though – near the kitchens and the laundry. She could smell the stacks of soiled linen and the cesspits in the far yard. The heavy aroma of boiling ox heads enveloped her too – she could see the skulls, the bone white now and holes where the eyes should have been.

'Walk!'

She almost tripped as she was shoved forward again. 'Lord have mercy on my soul ...'

'Stand up, I'm telling you!'

Rose tried to. At the same time the two women tightened their holds on her arms and yanked her up. One of her arms was held so tightly she screamed.

Their footsteps clattered on the flagstones as they reached the main door of the infirmary wing. The smells were heavier now – poverty, squalor, ether, carbolic.

'There'll be a nice bed for you here,' said the older attendant. 'Fit for a bride.'

'Aye. Feather pillows and a horsehair mattress, no less!'

God in Your Mercy, let me wake now and be in Rosegarland with Martha snoring in the bed across the room …

'Anyone say anything about giving her any food before she's locked up?'

Rose's stomach heaved.

'No.'

'Then we know nothing about it. She can starve till morning. Nothing like a bit of starvation to quieten 'em down,' said one of the women.

Rose felt as if she was outside herself again. 'Pray for us sinners now and at the hour of our death …'

The porter rapped the big door ahead of them several times. A nun answered.

'New guest for you, Sister,' said the porter. 'Murphy. Clongeen. Dangerous lunatic. Isolation cell for observation. Paperwork's all here, Sister.'

He handed her a copy of the committal warrant.

'Thank you, Martin,' said the nun, ushering them in. 'Hold her securely, please.'

In the gaslight of the hallway the nun roughly lifted Rose's chin and looked into her eyes while the two women restrained her. 'Do you know where you are, Mrs Murphy?'

Rose felt her pulse pound in her ears. She looked down,

away from the nun's steel eyes.

'What day is it today, Mrs Murphy?'

Rose tried to think. All the hours had run together, blurring the edges of the days.

'Answer me.'

Rose tried to moisten her cracked lips. 'I don't know.'

The nun let go. She rechecked the documentation. 'Right. Follow me.'

Rose was lifted again. The large keys that hung from the nun's belt jangled, the noise almost exploding in Rose's ears. They came to another heavy door.

The huge key grated in the lock. The two women held her tightly as the nun locked the door behind them.

God Almighty, not here … She wanted to run, break through the locked door, but her legs wouldn't move.

'Whisht with your moaning!'

The noise was deafening – shouts, screeching, banging. The two women holding her had suddenly gone quiet. Was it fear she sensed from them too?

'Come along,' said the nun, leading the way through the long corridor with wards on either side.

Rose opened her eyes and strange faces filled them – distorted faces, childish faces, faces making strange noises and dribbling as she passed. The clatter of noise, the smell of stale urine was overpowering.

A woman suddenly came towards her from a doorway ahead, smiling like a child, wanting to touch her, saying something indecipherable. 'Uum-pah!'

'Back to your cell now!' the nun shouted. The woman with the awkward gait scurried back to a doorway like a chastened child.

'Jesus, Mary and Joseph …' It was the imbecile ward. Rose

tried to remember that they were harmless. *Daoine le Dia*, that's what they called them.

They came to a second set of doors, the two women beside her holding her tighter now. The nun chose another large key from the belt ring and put it into the lock on the reinforced door. The noise from the lunatic wards was deafening. Rose felt a cold sweat break out on her body as the big door was locked behind her. Shouts, screeches of pain, tin mugs being banged, raucous laughing, shouting, the clatter of tin plates being banged against tables.

The porter and the two attendants were quiet now, anxiously glancing each way as they followed the nun.

'Keep those people under control,' the nun said to the warders who came out to see who was going by.

'Yes, Sister. Of course, Sister,' said the women with the hard faces.

A sudden scream made them all jump.

The nun stopped momentarily to look round then continued on. 'This way.'

Eventually they stopped at a door near the nun's desk. Rose felt outside of herself again. Foul curses from the cell next door offended Rose's ears.

'Put her in here. Don't untie her hands until I tell you to.' The nun's words cut the air. 'There is water here, Mrs Murphy. You will be here until we have decided upon the nature of your insanity.'

Nature of your insanity …

'No!' Rose felt as if her insides had collapsed.

'You must pray for release from the devil's hold on you.'

Rose didn't speak, her body shaking in shock.

'Let her rest now,' said the nun, stepping outside the door. 'Untie her hands and leave the cell immediately.'

The attendants pushed her onto an iron bed in the tiny room. Rose could feel the rope being loosened on her wrists. Within seconds the attendants were outside the cell and the door slammed behind them.

Rose ran to the door. It couldn't be locked … 'Jesus, Mary and Joseph.'

The cursing from another cell started again. A woman was cursing her forefathers, her children, her Maker.

Rose pulled at the handle on the door, a wave of weakness making her hold it to steady herself. This wasn't happening … Staggering, she reached the iron bed and sat down. She had to think.

The room was dark except for the small amount of gaslight coming in through the observation panel in the door. The walls were high with one half-shuttered window close to the ceiling. Half of it was open to the elements. Rose shivered. The room stank, the bedclothes stank, the blackness tried to choke her. Feeling as if she was going to vomit, she made her way to the bucket in the corner.

Her body heaved again and again as she got sick, the substance that left her mouth disturbing the rank contents of the half-full bucket. When it was over she dragged herself back to the bed, trying to ignore the dampness from the wet clay floor coming in through her too-small shoes. They had forced them onto her feet having washed her with carbolic soap and dressing her in the workhouse uniform when she was admitted.

Rose tried not to think of it, of where she was. She wished now that she had thrown herself in the Corach river. Blessed Mary, protect her, she shouldn't wish such things. Her mind struggled to come up with the name of the man in Clongeen who had tried that, been rescued and taken to the asylum. Alfie … Alfie someone. He had never been seen again.

She lay down on the bedstead now, wrapping herself in the blankets. The smell of previous occupants clung to the uncovered mattress.

How could they have done this to her? Who had committed her? Him? Patrick? What could she do? Another bloodcurdling screech came down the corridor and made her jump.

Warders shouted now, threats included.

As the noise continued she covered her ears with her hands, trying to block out the sound. She hummed to herself in the darkness, rocking to stop the thoughts from coming. She wished she were in her mother's arms being rocked to sleep. Sleep would be an escape. She tried to think of a way forward, even though her mind felt slow and unclear and her head throbbed.

She had survived in the workhouse for six months when she was having her child – she could do it again. She had never been in this part of it, though. She had never been locked in like this before. She must try to think, keep hold of hope. What would happen to her?

'Patrick will let me stew in here for a few days then he'll take me out. Then I'll get a job somewhere and pay my way.'

Dangerous lunatic, dangerous lunatic – the words of the policemen pounded in her brain. Was she really that?

Show us Thy mercy, O Lord. *Ostende nobis, Dominae, misericordiam tuam* ... She tried to remember the words of the priest in Clongeen.

'God above, I lost my temper. I was distraught. If I was wrong I ask Your forgiveness. I am penitent, Lord. If they see my penitence I will be released. Holy Mary, Mother of God, pray for us sinners now and at the hour of our death ... Oh, God in heaven, help me!'

*

The master of the workhouse, David Meany, in his admissions-building office, scratched his signature on his weekly report and carefully blotted the ink. A total of 403 admissions this week including three to the lunatic ward.

He had added up the names including that last woman, Rose Murphy. At least she was tractable, not like some of them. Often it took several to restrain them.

It was a side of his employment that he did not savour but at least the Sisters of Mercy had taken over charge of the lunatics for the past few years. Thank God he didn't have to go near them other than to register them on admission.

Good, he was finished.

'Just as well I like paperwork – there's so much of it in this job,' he said to himself. Still, he was very efficient – the board of guardians couldn't fault him on that. Everything had to be in proper order before they arrived for the monthly meeting. At least there was more of an attendance now, since tenant farmers had been elected to the board.

'Not like when the gentry were on it,' he said to himself. 'Bunch of wasters, the lot of them. Rather be out prancing about on their estates giving orders than coming to meetings here, helping to run this place.'

The tenant farmers were more interested – too interested sometimes, he decided, in saving the ratepayers' money. 'You'd think it was their own the way they ration it,' he muttered, putting on his best coat.

The meeting would be held in the boardroom on the second floor, up a stairs away from the admissions office. There was a separate entrance for the guardians. He must remind Martin Ryan, the porter, to keep all relief-seekers away from it.

He checked his appearance in the small mirror that he kept behind a cupboard door. Having checked his face for missed stubble he closed the cupboard door. He always made an effort to shave better on meeting day.

Still he'd seen them all, at one time or another, moving away slightly from him when he entered the boardroom, afraid they'd catch germs off him – but what did he care? He had a job, standing in the community. People looked up to the master of the workhouse. In the town people saluted him – tradesmen, suppliers, shopkeepers all treated him with respect, knowing the business he could bring their way.

And the guardians couldn't accuse him of not doing his job properly. Wasn't he always coming up with ideas to improve matters for the ratepayers? Today at the meeting, for instance, he would bring up the issue of tramps. Cold baths every morning – that's what he'd recommend for them. That'd stop them turning up in their hundreds on the eves of fair days and demanding a night's lodging.

*

'Where's Aunt Rose?' young John Quinn asked as he walked with his mother to the village of Clongeen.

'Whisht with your questions, child!' said his mother.

Neighbours were watching them from the door of the village shop, going silent as they approached.

Mary wouldn't have gone to the village only that she had to. Since Rose's wedding everything had been in turmoil. The friends and neighbours who had come to the wedding and eaten at their table now looked away when they met her. They were blaming them, saying they'd mishandled the match, but they'd have done nothing different themselves.

Hypocrites the whole lot of them! They all had their secrets – scratch the surface of any family's life and the secrets were there. She felt like reminding a few of them. She would if this continued much longer.

Didn't the whole parish know about the family who had a child, deformed at birth, hid in a shed for fear the world would see him? Didn't she know that Finnertys had TB in the house but were trying to keep it a secret? Didn't she know too that young Annie Keane's belly was getting bigger by the day?

Why should they blame her and Patrick for what his sister had done? She had gone against the law of God. Even the priest couldn't talk sense into her. She should have gone back to her husband, not carried on going against everyone.

'She's made her bed, now she must lie in it.'

Mary hurried on, the child running to keep up.

Hadn't they enough to worry about, six children on the brink of hunger, no regular work yet and no sign of getting a few acres of their own? Patrick was spending hour after hour in the forge in Foulksmills, plotting and planning and ráiméising about Land Acts and the landlord and how he should be forced to give up the land that the law said he had to sell to the tenants. In the meantime, how would they manage?

*

'How many days have you been here now, Mrs Murphy?' said the nun who was standing by Rose's bed with Dr Hickey. 'Sit up and answer the question, Mrs Murphy.'

Rose felt the two attendants grab her and push her to her feet.

Rose looked at the ground, trying to think. 'Four days? Five?'

'How do you feel?' the doctor asked, signalling to the attendants to hold her tightly.

'Ill. I need air. Exercise.'

The nun wrote something down.

The doctor, who wore gloves, tested her vital signs, expressionless as he pulled down her eyelids. 'Anaemic. You have not been eating well for many months?'

'Answer!'

'I have not felt like it.'

The nun wrote something else down.

The doctor took her pulse then told the attendants to bare her back while he listened to her chest.

'Cough, please.'

The cough came easily, drily.

'Hmm. Has she been fractious?'

The words went out over Rose's head, disappearing into the air.

'No. Says little. Melancholic, I'd say.'

'Yes, well, since she is not intractable she can be placed in the women's wing rather than here. She should be constantly supervised, however, until we see if she is prone to any more violent outbursts or hysteria.'

'Yes, doctor.'

The nun wrote down something else having glanced at the doctor and then at Rose, who now stood looking at the floor.

The doctor washed his hands in the bowl of water provided by another servant, then left the cell.

'You can let go of her now,' said the nun. 'She is passive.'

The two attendants dropped Rose's arms.

'Following our observation of you, Mrs Murphy, we have decided that you may join those in the women's wing for the present. You will, however, be supervised at all times and re-strained at the slightest sign of violence – do you understand?'

Rose tried to speak. Her own voice seemed miles away from her. 'Yes.'

'Yes, Sister!'

Rose forced the words out again. 'Yes … Sister.'

'You will be expected to work as hard as you are able. Tasks will be assigned to you in due course. Come.'

Where were they taking her?

She felt herself being shoved out through the door, back along the corridor where the screeches spilled out of doors.

The nun, Sister Aloysius, watched the new admission as she walked ahead of her. She did not appear violent but Sister Aloysius knew enough to know that lunatics were unpredictable. She'd learned that to her cost last night.

It had taken her and Dr Hickey half an hour to stitch the wound Statia Dolan had inflicted on herself with a blade stolen from the supplies cupboard. She would never trust her again. Nor this new inmate. Calm one minute, violent the next, that's the way they were. How many times had she seen it, suffered personal injury because of her mistaken trust even? Lack of time had made it impossible to offer such patients any treatment. Mrs Murphy had been uncommunicative.

'It will ease your soul if you forgive those whom you have wronged,' Sister Aloysius had told her.

The woman had looked at her, eyes full of sadness. 'I have not wronged them. They have wronged me.'

The examination had ended there. There was no point in continuing. The woman had no awareness of her insanity. Unless she realised her illness of the mind and asked for forgiveness she would be destined for damnation.

'Move on,' she shouted at Rose as she paused at the open door of one of the other wards on the corridor.

One of the inmates was being fed, her hands tied and a dribble of bread-and-milk mush trickling down her chin. Suddenly the woman spat out the food, splattering the face of the warder who fed her.

Whack! The inmate fell backwards with the force of the blow and screams and shouts broke out in the room as the chair hit the floor.

'Move!'

The door into the imbecile ward was unlocked and locked again behind them.

As on the day she had been brought here, people with childish faces stared at her from doorways as she passed. Rose looked away, trying not to be repulsed by their deformities, trying not to be fearful of their distorted faces or wary of the childish smiles on those who pranced around as if being pulled by strings from another world.

As soon as the big door that led out of the building was opened Rose inhaled deeply. Fresh air – she'd thought she would never breathe it again. Her heart was beating too fast, though, her head felt light and a sweat had broken out on her.

The breath was useless. Beside her another woman in the line, hair matted and with dark circles under her eyes, began to cough. Forced to stand beside her, Rose couldn't escape. She could feel the mist of the woman's cough hit her. The woman continued to cough, eventually covering her mouth with her skirt.

The nun held a handkerchief to her face. 'This way,' she said, going ahead of them.

Rose's arm was gripped again as the attendant hurried her along. 'You behave or it'll be the worse for you. I've left bruises on ten women already this week and I'm not afraid to leave some on you,' whispered the woman.

To the right Rose could hear the noise of footsteps – hundreds of them leaving the high-walled exercise yard for the women. Rose looked at the sky. It was as grey as the clothes on everyone around her. Was it dinner-time? All the inmates were heading for the dining hall.

Rose thanked God for releasing her from the dungeon she had been in. Nothing could be worse than that.

The matron of the workhouse's voice rang out from the top of the huge hall. 'Form a line, now! Silence or it'll be the worse for you. Collect your food then sit down. Do not touch your food until I say so.'

Rose walked slowly behind the rest of the women, trying to keep her head up. More coughs rang out all over the hall with the bare rafters and the huge, bare tables. Many people looked ill but how could it be any different in a place like this in the middle of winter?

Her eyes took in the single turf fire and the sodden wooden floor, the walls unplastered but once whitewashed, now a dirty shade of grey.

Rose felt faint as she sat through the roll call. The attendant gave her a dig in the ribs when her name had been called three times. 'It's you, for God's sake! Shout!'

'Here,' Rose said, trying to concentrate.

She could feel the hundreds of eyes on her as she spoke. Were they wondering who she was, where she was from and why she was here? Rose felt weighed down by a great sense of shame. What had she done to bring her to this place?

'Move, mad bitch – that's my place!'

The attendant gave the woman who had pushed Rose a shove backwards.

'Over there, Cuddihy. She's sitting here.'

'No, she's not!'

The attendant grabbed the woman's arm and twisted it behind her back. The black-haired woman squealed with pain.

'I said get back over there – now!'

The matron's voice rang out. 'Silence down there – immediately!'

When the place had fallen silent, the matron read out the rules and regulations for all new inmates. Rose had heard them every day when she had been there before – so many rules. No noise, no bad language, assaults would be punished, no insults or refusals to work. No feigning sickness or no attempting to break out of the workhouse. Rose wished she could escape but knew she wouldn't have a chance.

The soup was only lukewarm yet she was glad of it. She devoured the bread quickly, eager to calm the hunger pangs in her stomach. Somewhere in the hall a row broke out. Bread had been stolen again, probably. She tried to concentrate on the tin plate and banish thoughts of the soup's origins. She had to eat if she was ever to get out of here. She tried to console herself that she wouldn't be here long. She would get out. They would sign her out.

She tried to imagine what was happening in Rosegarland now. What time of day was it? Three o'clock, four o'clock? Darkness was coming in. Bridget would be lining up the pounds of butter she'd made in the dairy and stamping each one with the special Rosegarland stamp.

The matron's voice boomed again. 'Pans and mugs back where you got them. Rose Murphy, up here now.'

The crowd now queuing to return their vessels turned their heads to gawk at her as she made her way to the top of the dining hall.

'That's your one from Clongeen. Came in two nights ago. Refused to live with the husband,' said one to another.

'She should have had more sense. She should have bided her time then poisoned him when no one was looking.'

'Silence!'

The matron referred to the ledger on the table in front of her. 'You're on cleaning duty in the infirmary. Step out of line and you'll be thrown into a cell so quick you won't know what's hit you.'

The rest of the day went by in a fog. The stench in the infirmary made her vomit. There were patients there with dysentery, consumption, sores – Rose had never seen so many hideous sights in her life. Everywhere there were women coughing and spluttering and others lying silent, close to death.

The cleaners had to empty the urine containers in the corners, mop up the vomit and wash the floor with cold water and carbolic soap.

Merciful Lord, spare me from this …

Rose's head ached, her hands stung and her stomach churned. She wondered how she could get word to Bridget. Bridget would surely come see her – maybe she would get a message out to Jack for her. Surely he could do something.

'Laundry with those clothes now,' shouted an attendant. 'Move.'

Rose wished she had been put on kitchen duties, even stone-breaking. She had been set to do that a few weeks after her baby was born. The work had been hard and tedious on an empty stomach but at least she had been out in the open air.

She stopped to catch her breath, the pile of stinking clothes heavy in her hands.

'Hurry up! This is no place for slackers!'

Reaching the laundry, she dropped the pile in a corner with the rest.

'Put those in the soaking tubs – now!'

Rose and the other women did as they were told.

'Now get over to those tubs and start washing.'

Rose transferred some of the items previously soaked from the soaking tub to one of the washtubs that another woman had filled with hot water. She put her hands into the water willingly, glad of the heat.

She felt water on the floor soak into the shoes that had

left sores on her feet. Looking down she saw that the floor was flooded. Why couldn't it have been angled to drain toward the corner? That would have solved the problem. She looked at all the other women with wet feet.

Who had designed these places, she wondered? 'No one who was ever going to live in them, that's for sure,' she decided, angling the scrubbing board so that she could begin to remove the vomit from the first of many rags.

*

The master of the workhouse locked the door of his office before pouring himself another glass of malt from his private supply. That clerk was too nosey altogether, keeping track – well he could keep his nose out. He was master of this house and if he fancied a glass of whiskey he would have it.

He lifted his pen to add the last items to the list of provisions required by the workhouse in the next two weeks:

16 ox heads (3 per 100 inmates)
1,080 lbs beef
2 tons flour
2 packets gilt coffin nails
1 pound of snuff
36 yards of habit material
4 gallons of oil for the bakery …

Thinking of bakery matters, he made a note of Francis Brown, the baker, wanting leave. He was getting married next month. 'The guardians won't like him wanting time off but they'll have to lump it.'

He made a note about employing a temporary baker. 'Fifteen shillings a week will have to do him,' he said to himself.

He made another note – replace milk ration with tea. What

else could he do when the farmers couldn't supply the correct quantity at this time of year?

He added more items to the list as he thought of them: 1 gross rosary beads, 5 tons oaten straw, 112 lbs of starch.

'More problems,' he said to himself, seeing a letter on his desk. The schoolmaster was looking for time off over Christmas. 'Christmas Day to Twelfth Day, if you don't mind.' Entering the dates in his diary, he then scribbled a single sentence beside them. 'Porter to take charge in his absence.' The workhouse children wouldn't learn much, he knew that, but they never learned much anyway.

The schoolmaster was lucky he had been kept on after that incident with that female pupil. If the board had believed her he would have been gone, bag and baggage, but they decided there was no case to answer.

Noise drew him to the window that looked out on the town. It was the coal merchant, the shafts of his cart creaking and the harness of his horses jingling as he came in through the trade entrance. The master watched as hooves stumbled on the uneven cobbles and the driver with the blackened face steadied his charges.

'Whoa! Easy there.'

Scotch coal, he'd ordered a ton of it – that was all. Still, it would be needed in the infirmary – the rest of the workhouse would have to make do with turf. Pity turf smokes so much, he thought. Makes the place look even more miserable than it is.

He read another note on his desk. It was from Dr Hickey. 'Gas jet required in hall,' he read. 'Both my colleagues and myself, along with the parish priest and minister of the town, request that you install a gas jet in the hall as it is most unpleasant to visit the workhouse at night. Your earliest attention is advised.'

That would have to be done immediately. He'd need one at the entrance gate as well. 'Too many tramps are getting in when the van comes in.'

That week 198 tramps had been admitted. 'Idlers, the lot of them. They don't deserve the charity of the county. If I had my way they could starve on the streets. That would teach them to get out and find work.'

Now, what else did he need to make a note of? Yes, check on the mental state of the new inmates – he would need to update his figures for lunatics in the lunatic wards and those among the general population of the workhouse. The nun in charge of the infirmary had decided to let a couple of the lunatic women stay in the ordinary female dormitories. She had better be right. There would be hell to pay if another woman threw herself out of a window. The free press had gone to town on that story.

*

'Whoa, girl! Easy now!' Jack Quinn was checking a horse's shoe for stones in one of the stables at Rosegarland.

He ran his hand down the mare's leg, lifted the hoof gently, knowing she was nervous. 'That's the girl!'

If he took it easy she wouldn't object. She had been limping a bit coming back from town earlier. With a bit of luck it wouldn't be anything worse than a stone.

A bucket clattered outside the door. The horse started. Jack jumped back quickly to avoid being hurt. 'Blast!' Jack looked out over the half door. 'Do you want to get me kicked?' he said, seeing Ted Jameson replacing the bucket by the wall.

Ted said nothing.

'Damn the man,' thought Jack.

Ted Jameson was seldom in good humour these days. If this kept up Jack wasn't sure how much longer he could tolerate it.

181

Ted was now reaching into his coat pocket and pulling out a newspaper. 'I'd let you read this if I knew you could but since you can't I'm going to tell you what it says.'

He turned to the fourth page. 'It might interest you and that brother of yours,' he said, his eyes cold.

Jack turned back to the horse.

Ted rested against the half-door as he told him what the paper said.

'You think you and your matchmaking ways are right, don't you? Well listen to this and see what one of your priests thinks of your bog methods!'

'What are you talking about?'

'It's something your Canon Whitty said at a meeting of … let me see … the Forth Agricultural Association.'

'What?'

'It's about the marriage industry, as he calls it.'

Jack turned back to the mare, trying to lift her foot again. Sensing his tension, she shifted to the right. 'There's the girl, easy now.'

'This man talks a lot of sense – just listen to this. "The prevailing system of matchmaking should be stamped out. It is a well-known fact that over fifty per cent of unhappy marriages are due to matrimonial negotiation in the public house tap room."'

Ted closed the newspaper. 'Do you hear that? He's saying it's wrong, do you hear? What you did to your sister is going to be outlawed by your church – your priests are even speaking out against it now.'

'I had no hand in it.'

Ted's face reddened. 'You did nothing to stop it, man! Rose would never have married him only she was pushed into it. You know she wouldn't.'

'Go about your work! I don't have to listen to the likes of you.'

Ted held the door to prevent Jack leaving the stable. 'No, you won't listen when someone gets too close to the truth. You wanted her married off in case she'd take up with me and her soul would be damned. Well you've damned her soul now where you've put her.'

'Shut your trap!'

'I don't know how you can live with yourself. If she dies in that place I hope she comes back and haunts the lot of you!'

Ted's anger had blown out, seeing the other man's unease and shame. He removed his hand from the door. Jack came out, walked a few feet across the yard. 'We were doing what we thought best for her.'

Ted turned away to tidy tackling that didn't need tidying. 'What help is that to her now?'

Jack climbed the steps to the hayloft. He would check the mare's feet later on when Ted had disappeared.

Rose ... How was it that she had caused so much trouble? 'If only she'd gone along with it! She'd have been all right.'

The stubborn Quinn streak, that's what did it. How much trouble had that got the family into over the years, he wondered? The last few weeks had been a nightmare. He hadn't been able to sleep properly. His brother hadn't either. Jack could see it in the dark circles under Patrick's eyes and his fondness for spending time in the pub.

Jack closed the loft door behind him, glad to be out of the stable boys' earshot. Had they heard everything? It would be round the estate like wildfire. When would the tongue clacking end?

He didn't know what he was supposed to do but there was no going back now – Patrick had told him that. Jack hadn't been with them at the magistrate's. He had no hand in it. Still, hardly anyone had spoken to him since the day of the wedding. If they did their greeting was cold and to the point or awkward with embarrassment.

A sister going against the law of God and family and then committed as a lunatic – how could he ever hold his head up in the parish again?

*

Rose tried to remember what day it was, what month it was even. December?

Scrubbing the floor of the dining hall, along with several other inmates of the workhouse, she wondered if her mind was going. Her health certainly was. She seemed to have a cold and cough all the time. She stopped her work now as the coughing began again – hard, dry, as if feathers were lodged in her neck.

'Shut up, will you, with your poxy coughing!' said the woman beside her. 'Get on with your work.'

Rose rested momentarily as the bout subsided. Her chest felt tight and perspiration had broken out on her forehead again. If only she could get out of here …

Every day she asked if there had been any communication for her from her family and if anybody had come to see her.

'Nobody's been to see you, madwoman. You're in the workhouse committed as a lunatic, for God's sake,' said the matron. 'Who do you think is going to come see you – the Almighty himself? Stop wasting my time and get back to your work!'

The woman was obviously mad, the matron thought as she proceeded to the girls' exercise yard to see that all was in order there. For that woman to think that anyone would bother about her from now on she had to be deluded. Matron would have to keep an extra eye on her. That cough of hers seemed to be lingering too, despite Dr Hickey's looking at her. Bad chests

– so many of these wretches had them. 'A weakness among the poor – I've always said it.'

With so many dying in this place it was hard to keep up with habit-making. She'd have to tell the inmates in the sewing-room to work harder – the master wouldn't be happy if there wasn't a proper supply.

She sometimes wondered why the dead weren't just buried naked – that would save on material – but what the board said went. She was surprised they weren't trying to cut back on fabric too.

Rose sat back on her haunches to catch her breath again. She didn't remember having flu like this since she had got a soaking after coming here to search for her son. How long ago was that? She couldn't remember. Her heart heaved as she realised that she didn't even know where her child was buried.

'He's better dead than in a place like this. Good Lord, look after him and give him a better home in heaven. He did nothing wrong, Lord, it was me, born in sin and sinning, that brought such hardship upon his head.'

'Stop your muttering and get on with your work, woman.'

Rose's hand moved the scrubbing brush around again. She wiped the sweat off her forehead with the sleeve of her jerkin. Last night she had woken in the night covered in sweat, her bed saturated. God knows how she would sleep tonight – her bedclothes would not be dry.

The weather was wet, too, rain blowing now against the high windows of the dining hall, the wind blowing up from the quay making the small panes rattle with the force of it.

How long was it to Christmas, she wondered? Weeks? Days? Maybe someone would take her out at Christmas. A whack in the side of the head put an end to her wondering.

'I said get on with your work. This is no place for slackers!'

Her head spun with the bang and another fit of coughing started.

'That one's not long for this world, if you ask me,' said one of the other inmates, emptying a bucket of water into a drain outside the door.

The woman beside her looked over at Rose and said nothing. Rose had now resumed her work at a slow pace, her shoulder blades almost visible under her workhouse jerkin. 'Death – there is too much of it in this place,' said the woman to herself, a sudden shiver going down her spine.

*

The master of the workhouse listened politely as the chairman of the board of guardians, Tobias Rossitor, Esquire, read out the communication from the Enniscorthy union on the subject of phthisis. A conference on consumption had been held there and unions throughout the county were being made aware of its findings.

'All inmates should cough into a handkerchief,' he read to the assembled meeting. 'Spitting among inmates and the general community should be stamped out too, as it is leading to the spread of the disease.'

Another rule to impose. David Meany sighed at the thought of it. He signalled his request to ask a question.

'Yes, Mr Meany?'

'Will the board be sanctioning the purchase of handkerchiefs for all inmates? I estimate, given a total of 400 at the moment, that we would need in the region of 1,000 handkerchiefs. This would necessitate the purchase of a considerable amount of cotton.'

'Can't you use rags?'

Another guardian gave a polite cough. 'Would that not add to the problem rather than improve it? The cloths would need to be regularly washed.'

'Perhaps we can bring this up at the next meeting,' said another guardian, taking out his pocket watch to look at it. 'Today's agenda is quite long enough.'

'All agreed.'

'Aye.'

'Please enter it on the agenda of the next meeting, secretary.'

'Next item for discussion – the half-yearly report of the local government board inspector,' said the chairman, taking it out to read the summary of findings. 'Let's see … absence of proper lavatory accommodation, well dry all summer, ambulances of old two-wheeled pattern – uncomfortable for patients – manure needs to be confined rather than spread carelessly around grounds, new piggery should be completed with concreted yards, laundry floor to be re-laid – water should fall towards drain trap.'

The master finished making his list. How long, he wondered, would it be before the money was available to do all these things?

The water supply had been a problem for several years, especially in the summer when water had to be drawn to the workhouse in carts. How could the place or the inmates be kept clean with very little water? Already he'd had to give instruction that the bath water should only be changed after thirty-five orphans had been washed – except, of course, if they had sores.

*

The cook at Rosegarland was in good humour. The mistress had complimented her on the wonderful selection of cakes she had provided for the afternoon's high tea when the Leighs had guests over.

Bridget Rowe liked it when Cook was in good form. It lifted the spirits of the whole servants' quarters.

'Pass me a slice of that currant bread, there's a good woman,' said Cook, 'while I have a look at this paper. Have a bit yourself as well.'

'Thank you, Cook,' said Bridget, pleased to be so honoured.

'Don't know about this vice-regal commission's notions,' said Cook, her mouth full.

'How do you mean?'

'They're saying the present workhouse system should be abolished.'

'Oh?' Bridget sat up straight. 'Are they going to be closed then and everyone let out?' Maybe Rose could come home …

'No, child,' said Cook softly, reading her mind. 'It's being suggested for the future. They want to separate out all the people – put the consumptives in san-a-tor-ia, whatever they are. Unmarried mothers are to be sent to institutions under religious or phil– phil-o-sophical management.'

Bridget blessed herself to fend off ill luck and wondered what those places would be like. 'Worse than the workhouse probably, with nuns screeching eternal damnation at you every hour of the day.'

Cook had now gone quiet.

'What else does it say? What's wrong?'

'I'm sorry, love, it … it says the insane are to be removed from the workhouses to asylums. There's a lot of them in the workhouses, you know.'

The asylum? For Rose? It was too unbearable to think about.

It was now almost six weeks since she had been taken away. Bridget and her mother had cried all night after the police had left. Now Bridget tried to block out the memory of Rose's screams as the carriage went up the road. How could they treat her like that? Tie her up like that? She wasn't dangerous.

Bridget shivered. Rose had been pushed beyond what she could bear, that's all. Bridget had told her to try to put up with him, that it might get better in time, but she wouldn't listen. Why hadn't she drunk more of the whiskey that Mary Quinn gave her? That way she'd have got over the first night and things might have worked out.

'I wish I knew how she was.'

'You might be better off not knowing, girl,' said Cook.

Bridget looked at the pots of mincemeat already made and standing on the table. 'But it'll soon be Christmas. I can't bear to think of her in there.'

Cook put her hand on Bridget's. 'It's best not to upset yourself about these things. No magistrate would commit her without a reason. Look, maybe there are things we don't know about her. The doctor would have had to sanction it.'

'That fella'd sign anything that was put in front of him if there was money in it – they all would.'

'Here, have another cup of tea and try not to think about it. It's got nothing to do with us.'

'Maybe the mistress would take her out ...'

'Stop wasting your time on foolish thoughts, girl. Start annoying her and it'll only mean trouble for you.'

'Maybe I could go there and ask to see her.'

'To the workhouse? Lord above, girl!'

'I could pretend I'm her sister so's they'd let me in. Maybe I could bring her something.'

'That's if she's still there, child ...'

Rose gone to the red brick already? She couldn't bear thinking about it.

Bridget stood up to clear the table. 'I'll have a few hours off on Christmas Eve. I'll go then. They'd hardly refuse her a visit on Christmas Eve.'

'I don't know,' said Cook, 'but take my advice – don't tell anyone you're going. The workhouse isn't a place for a respectable woman to be visiting.'

*

Rose tried to swallow a mouthful of potato.

'At home I wouldn't have given these a second look.'

The potatoes were small and dirty, a brown scum on them from being boiled without being washed properly.

'Scrills for the pigs – that's what they are,' she said.

'If you don't want them give them to me,' said the woman beside her, seeing Rose's delay in eating. Rose pushed them across. She could taste nothing. What was the point of eating?

She coughed again. The other woman continued to eat beside her, the potato cupped in her palm as she took ravenous bites out of its grey insides.

Coughing at mealtimes had caused problems. At first it was just people stopping to look at her or move away from her. Then it was her food being stolen while she coughed. Now she didn't care who took what.

She shivered as the hundreds of mugs in the dining hall clattered on and off the tables. The cold had gone into her bones. Work didn't even make her warm, yet at night she sweated profusely. How she wished the night sweats would stop – they sapped her of energy and left her trying to sleep in a wet bed.

'Christmas – look!' the woman beside her said, pointing.

Rose followed her gaze to one of the workhouse attendants who was sticking up holly on the window-sills of the dining hall. So Christmas must be close – next week? Tomorrow?

Rose didn't know. She struggled to remember Christmas the previous year.

She had had her dinner in Rosegarland and afterwards walked to Patrick and Mary's to give the children presents – sweets, apples and curranty bread that Cook had given her, knowing where Rose was going and how little they had. She thought of the girls and boys gathered round the table, all glad to see Aunt Rose, especially John, the youngest. She suddenly felt weak.

'No feigning illness,' said the worker, 'or it'll be the punishment book for you. Off the stool and get on with your work.'

Could she get out of here? Could she get up now and run her way through locked doors and high walls? Tears came as she thought of the two women who had tried it. They had been locked up for days, on water, everyone told about it so that an example would be set.

*

'Preparations for Christmas are satisfactorily in hand,' thought the master of the workhouse. He had done it so many times now that he scarcely had to look up the records.

Kill two pigs for the inmates over Christmas – if they didn't get much each day it would last over the festive season. Organise a party for the children, unanimously passed by the board with expenses not to exceed two pounds. He wouldn't go mad on that with the amount of children in the place. 'Still, it'll keep them in line, thinking they're getting a present.' Discipline always improved before Christmas with the threat of not receiving anything held over them. 'Lull before the storm usually,' he said.

The dark days of January were never something to look forward to. He had another task to do then, too. The numbers would need to be weeded out.

Why not start putting the commission's report into action and get rid of a few dozen inmates they could do without – some of the violent ones especially. He'd have no more people breaking furniture or tearing bedclothes. It was costing the union money to employ people to restrain them.

And the imbeciles – they'd never be able to go out to work so what use were they here? They weren't like the blind, who could be found something to do – within limits. No one else wanted these people – why should the county have to feed them?

It was a good decision to separate them all out. The loose women too. Traditionally they'd come to the workhouse to give birth to their bastards. Good enough for them to be shut up somewhere else where they wouldn't be in contact with other decent women.

Matron had told him that a few of the inmates were melancholic and not fit to work. He would ask her to make out a list.

Getting rid of the consumptives would be a blessing too. If that professor he'd heard speak was right the disease wasn't hereditary – it was fostered by overcrowding and bad air. The master laughed. Three thousand cubic feet of air per person was needed, Professor McWeeney had said at that lecture in New Ross. Three thousand! They'd be lucky if they had thirty each here.

*

New Ross was a cold but busy town on Christmas Eve. The gaslight from the shop windows shed a mellow glow on the frosty pavements. It illuminated too the well-plucked turkeys and geese that hung upside down, feet to attention, at shop doors. Bridget Rowe tightened her coat around her as she dodged their deadly stares.

'There's snow on that wind,' she thought as she crossed the

narrow main street, trying to avoid the piles of horse dung as she walked. She wished that the snow would come without the cold wind. Her cheeks were still smarting from it on the long journey from Rosegarland.

She had got a lift on the estate carriage, going to town to collect the Christmas provisions. It was a substantial order – flour, sugar, spices, confectionaries, spirits, beer for the staff, presents already ordered for the estate children's party that the mistress always organised. Her employers might not be renowned for their generosity but at Christmas there was always an extra few pence in their pay packet and a speech from the mistress thanking them for their good service during the year.

Bridget didn't have much time to waste. The steward had said he would be staying at least an hour and a half. If she wasn't back at the carriage by then he would go without her. She hadn't dared tell him where she was going. She had pretended instead that she was calling on her aunt Maggie.

The street was very busy. People were everywhere and horses and carriages and carts were struggling to pass each other, harnesses clanking with each movement of the horses' heads and the stamping of metal-shod feet.

Taking care that she didn't slip on the steep footpath, she left the centre of the town and walked up the hill toward the workhouse. Her heart beat faster as she approached it – even the look of it made her uneasy. Most people were one meal away from it much of the time.

She knocked on the door of the admissions building. A bell clanged inside. The porter eventually answered.

'What do you want?'

Bridget swallowed, hoping God wouldn't strike her dead for telling a lie. 'I wish to visit my … sister, Rose Quinn. Sorry, Rose … Murphy.'

'What is the purpose of your visit?'

Bridget swallowed. 'To ascertain that she is well and to bring her news of her family.'

'Hmph! "*To ascertain that she is well and ...*"' said the porter, mimicking her. 'Wait here. I'll have to ask matron. She might let you in if she's in a good humour or if ...'

Bridget looked at the man in front of her who was standing there grinning, his hand cupped in begging fashion. She fingered the money in her pocket. Would thruppence do? She proffered the money.

Looking at it with contempt, the porter sighed and left her sitting in the waiting-room.

Half an hour passed. Had he taken her money and not told anyone that Rose had a visitor? Anxiously she watched the minutes tick away on the clock overhead, blowing her fingers to banish the lingering frost. The turf fire in the waiting-room was small and emitted little heat. A family of five was huddled round it. By their dress and their demeanour Bridget knew that they were waiting to be admitted. Both parents and children looked ill and emaciated, the children too quiet because of their lack of sustenance.

What a dreadful place to have to go on Christmas Eve. If only they didn't split up families that came in here. She had heard stories of mothers not knowing their children had died in the children's wards, of fathers not knowing that they were widowed. 'Why can't they keep families together, at least mothers and their children – what harm would there be in that?' She couldn't even begin to imagine the grief she would have felt if she had been separated from her mother as a small child.

A tall, thin woman wearing two coats eventually arrived and beckoned to Bridget from the door. Because of the bunch of keys she had, Bridget knew she was the matron.

'This way. You can speak to Mrs Murphy for five minutes. In my presence.'

'Thank you, ma'am,' Bridget said, following her into a small room off the hall.

'Five minutes, remember,' said the matron, sitting down on a chair at the back.

Bridget saw a gaunt woman sitting on a chair, breathing heavily and looking flushed after her hurry. 'Rose?'

The woman looked at her briefly then looked away.

'Rose?'

'Answer!' said the matron, sharply.

'Yes.'

Bridget's heart pounded as she tried to hide her shock at her friend's appearance. 'Rose, it's good to see you. It's Bridget.'

Recognition flickered in Rose's eyes. 'Bridget!'

Rose was so thin, her eyes sunken into her head, dark circles under them. Her hair was unkempt and the dreadful uniform of the place was hanging on her bones.

'How are you? How have you been?' Bridget moved towards her.

'Stay where you are. Union policy,' the matron barked.

Bridget stepped back, rushing to fill the silence in the room, anxious to use the five minutes well. 'Everyone from Rosegarland is asking for you, Rose.'

Rose looked up and a thin smile came and went.

'Cook was just talking about you the other day,' Bridget went on, 'saying what a great worker you were. You'd make two of young Martha, she says. The butter isn't the same since you left either. Martha puts too much salt in it. And the cows aren't giving the same amount at all – it's as if they know you're not there. But you must tell me how you are …'

Rose began to cough – a cough that frightened Bridget. It

was dry, hard and took Rose several minutes to recover from. She saw the matron cover her mouth with her handkerchief. When the bout was over, Rose sat there, head down, breathing heavily.

Bridget took out the shawl she had hidden under her coat. 'I brought you this. I knit it myself. Something to keep you warm.'

'No presents for inmates. Union policy. Present-giving upsets those who get nothing. Leads to disciplinary problems and thieving,' said the matron in singsong fashion.

'Oh!' It had taken Bridget weeks to knit it. She looked at Rose – she wished she could have the shawl: she looked so cold.

'Rose – say something please …'

Rose seemed to have trouble concentrating.

'The child …' she said eventually.

'You … you mean young John?' Bridget said, a wave of panic going through her at the words. Was Rose talking about her dead son? 'All your family are well that I know of. John is getting taller all the time. He is doing well in school, I hear. The other children are looking forward to Christmas.'

'Time is up. Finish your conversation.'

'Young John still speaks of you,' said Bridget. 'All your brother's family are well, I think.'

Rose sat in the chair, her head down. Bridget could see a tear floating down her cheek as she spoke. 'I'm not insane.'

The matron guffawed behind her.

Bridget struggled for words. 'We'll have snow for New Year, they say.'

Rose looked confused. 'Snow?'

The matron stood up, walked to the door and opened it. 'Your time is up.'

Bridget turned to leave then whispered, 'Please – is she being well looked after?'

The matron's laugh filled the room. 'People don't come here to be well looked after! That one's sick. Can't do a tap these days and she seldom talks. An asylum case if you ask me.'

Bridget looked back at Rose, forcing herself to smile. 'I'll pray for you, Rose.'

Rose looked about to say something, then stopped, as if speech was pointless, and looked into the distance again.

'Happy Chr–' The words died in Bridget's throat. 'Goodbye, Rose.'

Going home, squashed between boxes in the Rosegarland carriage, Bridget cried for a long time. She couldn't get the change in Rose out of her mind. What had happened to her? Her cough was so bad. She was so thin. Bridget shivered. She'd heard that kind of cough before.

Once when she was a child she'd wanted to talk to a neighbour, Kathleen Dempsey. Seeing Bridget go over to the woman, her mother had run down the road and grabbed her, hauling her back into the house.

'That family's consumptive,' her mother had shouted, the fear in her eyes frightening Bridget. 'For Jesus' sake, stay away, child!'

17

MORE CONNECTION

I t was summer 2000 and, sitting in fold-up chairs in the glasshouse in their John Street back garden, Patricia Quinn-Murphy and her daughter, Catherine, were enjoying a mother and daughter chat.

It was Catherine's day off and the conversation turned to Rose, as it so often did these days. The research was going well – her mother was keeping her informed, adding each snippet of information as it arrived. The blue flowers at the pattern had given her a lift. So many details had been correct but the blue flowers hadn't come into it until now. When her mother had rung to tell her, Catherine had smiled – Rose was there, letting her know she was around.

The day she first visited the graveyard had been an emotional one. As she slumped on the spot where Rose had been buried she felt overcome with the grief that Rose had felt. She felt her pain, her despair, her shame and her isolation in her last days in the asylum, like vibrations in her body.

Rose hadn't connected with her since the night in Spain, however. 'Probably thinks I have enough to be going on with for the moment or that I've done what I'm supposed to do,' she said to herself.

'She must have suffered so much in the workhouse and in the asylum,' said her mother, who had been talking about the historical research into conditions of the time.

Suddenly Catherine felt the familiar woozy feeling come

over her. She looked to the side, away from her mother, tuned into the images now coming into her head.

Her mother knew instantly what was happening and watched her closely. 'What do you see?'

Catherine's voice was quiet. 'She's on a bed – an iron one. She's looking up at the ceiling. There's a naked bulb overhead…'

Still keeping eye contact, Patricia wondered about this detail. Electricity in St Senan's in 1907 – surely it was too early for that?

'She is very thin, very weak …'

Catherine was still looking away, into a distance that Patricia couldn't see. 'What is she feeling?' she asked.

'She has given up. She hasn't eaten for a long time. Despair. Utter depression.'

Catherine stayed silent for a few moments, Patricia also.

'She's showing me herself in a big room now. There are lots of other women there – a day ward, maybe.'

'What's it like?'

'High ceilings and white walls. Part of the room is divided off by some sort of partition.'

'What does she look like now?'

'She's sitting in a chair. She has her head down. She feels distant from everything, overcome with shame at being in the asylum.' Catherine moved slightly in the chair. 'Her hair – it's in a kind of figure-of-eight style, wisps of it falling down. Someone is trying to feed her bread and milk – "goody".'

'Forcing her?' Patricia asked.

'No – encouraging her, another woman in the ward, but she turns her head.'

The image saddened Patricia but she knew it was probably the case. Rose died seventy-one days after she was admitted

– roughly the same amount of days that someone who went on hunger strike would last.

'James … no, Jameson. A man.' Catherine was seeing a word now, as if Rose was communicating it to her.

'Who is he?' her mother asked.

'I'm getting warm feelings. He was someone who cared for her. Yes, she was fond of him too. I see him in the graveyard. He has blue flowers in his hand.'

'Was he a patient?'

'No.'

'Someone from Clongeen? Someone from Rosegarland?'

The sound of the doorbell made them both jump. The connection was broken. Patricia got up to answer the door, unable to stop herself feeling frustrated at the timing. What else would Rose have shown Catherine if they hadn't been disturbed?

Speaking again later, after the oblivious visitor had gone, they went back over the details Rose had given.

Jameson – it wasn't a common name in Wexford. Patricia had never heard of such a family in Clongeen. Perhaps it was someone who worked on the estate who had come from somewhere else? It pleased both of them to think that someone cared for Rose, that someone had bothered to go to the asylum to get news of her.

Patricia now had something else to do – research hairstyles of the time, look up the census records for a family of Jamesons, check out when electricity had come to St Senan's.

Catherine went back to her own house, tired but pleased. Rose was still with her. She would be, she felt now, until the job was done.

18

TRANSFER

It was New Year's Eve and Patrick Quinn had just reached the pub in Clongeen. It would soon be full with men coming in after their day's work, cold and thirsty. Patrick knocked the mud off his boots before entering.

He had spent the day cleaning out cattle sheds in Rose-garland and his hands were covered with welts after the heavy sprong work. Labouring wasn't easy. If things had been right, though, he would be a farmer, not a labourer living from day to day. He'd be cleaning out his own cattle sheds.

Sometimes the pain of the eviction burned in his belly. He could still see the bailiff and the RIC men arriving at Newcastle – the shouts, the terror, the fear, the realisation of what was happening. The only thing to banish the memory was pints of stout – the memory of the whole lot of them, with their belongings, being ordered to leave. Rose had called the policemen names until their mother silenced her. He'd admired his sister's courage at the time. Rose … The sooner he had a whiskey inside him the better.

At least the neighbours had started talking to them again. Father Lyng's sermon might have had something to do with that. Difficult decisions have to be made within families sometimes, he had said, and those who have to make them should not be ostracised but should be supported and comforted. That silenced them.

What else was he supposed to do? Leave her to continue

her mad-tempered ways, walking the roads with no job and a reputation that would prevent her ever getting a job? He couldn't support her – none of the family could – and the husband didn't want to know. He was trying to pretend the wedding had never happened.

Patrick took a last look at his boots. They'd do. With a bit of luck 1907 would be a better year for them. There was much talk of Leigh being forced to sell the land to his tenants at last. Those who had been evicted and their families would be given priority. He'd be the first one in the queue.

He fingered the coins in his pocket as he went into the heat of the snug. Mary would want most of it. Still he hadn't told her everything he had. Why should he – wasn't he entitled after a week's hard labour, up to his ankles in snow and slush and the hands falling off him with the cold? He could taste that first pint already.

*

The siren blasts from the vessels docked at New Ross harbour broke Rose's uneasy sleep. She tried to concentrate. What was the noise?

Shouts broke out around her in the women's ward.

'Happy New Year!' someone called at the top of her voice.

Rose could hear several women hammering on the locked dormitory door. 'Let us out of here. Jesus, let us out of here. Give us something to toast the New Year! Give us something, youse bastards!'

An answering bang came on the door, accompanied by a keeper's shout. 'Back to bed, the lot of youse, or it'll be the lock up for ye!'

Rose turned carefully in her bed, trying to avoid the wire sticking up from the broken mattress. She felt her clothes – the night sweats had happened again. She lay back down, freezing cold, her bones aching and her chest hurting. New Year's Eve – she tried to concentrate. What year was it now? 1907. Faces, dates were getting mixed up in her mind – where had she been this time last year? Where would she be this time next year?

'Hail Mary, full of grace, the Lord is with thee …'

'Shut up with your poxy praying or I'll throttle you, you mad bitch!'

Kate Cuddihy was standing over her. Rose closed her eyes, shutting the image of her out.

'We shouldn't have the likes of you in here with your moaning and your groaning and your goddamn silence. The asylum's the place for the likes of you. I'm going to tell that matron bitch that we're sick of your gibberish and hallucinations.'

Rose shrank down further under the clothes and said nothing. What was the point in saying anything about anything? Escape into the mind – that's all she could do.

She began to rock herself gently and started to hum the 'Derry Air'. She imagined herself safe in her mother's arms as she sang it to her as a child. Hadn't the piper at Rosegarland played it the night the soldiers came? Soldiers – she could see them – all colours, horses, guns, uniforms … they were tying her up, the uniforms were taking her away … *Dear sweet Lord save me.*

*

The master of the workhouse entered the total for the last week of January 1907 in the record book – 407 in the house. 'Up on last week's figures again,' he said to himself, checking the previous entry.

The number of tramps was up again, too – twenty-two last night alone. The master dipped his pen, preparing to vent his spleen on this subject once again to the board of guardians.

'The room set aside for them is thirty-four feet long and

203

nine feet wide and holds only eleven beds,' he wrote, 'so at present the tramps are sleeping two to a bed. I am not asking the board for more accommodation, however. Indeed I would prefer the place to be as uncomfortable as possible for tramps.'

That should convince them he wasn't going soft on the problem.

He checked the next item on his list of things to do. Deserted families – three women and six children had been deserted by their husbands. He made a note for mention at the next board meeting. He would have to bring it to the guardians' notice in order to have the husbands prosecuted for leaving their wives a burden on the rates.

Next item – application for a clothing grant for the O'Connor family to emigrate. He checked the details – a mother, father, two children. 'One pound five shillings – that'll have to do them as the county can afford no more. At least they have their fare to America paid for by a relative – there's many that haven't.'

Demands on the workhouse had been heavy in the past month. Employment in the town was bad. Some people blamed it on the new railway. Goods were now going directly from Waterford to Rosslare and on to England. Still the winter months were always bad on the quay. Only one vessel had discharged during the week, for example – not enough work for anyone.

His thoughts were interrupted by the arrival of the porter.

'Post, sir. From the local government board by the looks of it,' said the older man, eyeing the envelope in his hand.

'Thank you, Martin, I don't need your help in ascertaining who the post is from.'

'No, sir,' said the porter, touching his forehead as he retreated.

The master opened the large envelope that bore the county-board seal with a sigh. What was wrong now? He was pleased to see that a large bundle of forms was enclosed. He read the accompanying letter: 'Returns are needed for persons in the under-mentioned categories … name and description of each person of unsound mind, number of persons not of unsound mind but who are afflicted with epilepsy …'

So, the clearout was starting. The guardians would be pleased with him. He'd gotten rid of three already and another few were earmarked. Sister Ignatius had given him the list – now where had he put it? He found it safely tucked into the minute book.

'A. Duggan, M. Doyle, R. Murphy …'

R Murphy – he was sure she was the one from Clongeen who threw a fit having refused to live with her husband.

'Didn't hold out much hope for her anyway. Melancholic – plain as day even then.'

*

Rose woke to feel her bed rags being pulled off.

'Up, Murphy, and put these clothes on you – move! Your days of moaning here are over.'

The two attendants grabbed her. Rose's mind felt foggy.

'Shurrup with all that noise,' said someone in a bed nearby.

'Come on, we haven't all day,' said one of the attendants.

Rose tried to concentrate. Were those her own clothes that she saw on the bed? It was her skirt, her petticoat – she had made it herself. She grabbed the clothes, holding them close to her face to see if they smelled of Rosegarland and fresh air.

'Give us them here and get them on you – now!'

Her heart lurched. Was she getting out of here? Why else would they be giving her her clothes?

'Hurry up! Matron's waiting for you.'

Rose tried to concentrate as her skirt was pulled up and the buttons of her jacket closed. Praise God. They must have signed her out. With a few weeks' rest at home and good feeding she would soon be ready to work again. *Glory be to the Father and to the Son and to the Holy Ghost …*

Rose felt herself being half pushed, half carried to the admissions building. Snow was lying on the pathway to it.

'Bloody weather!' said one of the attendants, watching her step. 'It's no sort of a day for going anywhere!'

They were inside the admissions building now; then she was being walked through and out into the cold again. Who would be there to collect her? Bridget? Jack? Patrick even? There was a two-horse carriage outside the door. Was it Leighs'? Had they sent a carriage for her?

She tried to concentrate, her mind battling against her as she looked for familiar shapes and colours. Other men had come out the door behind them.

'Stand up, you bollocks!' Two attendants were supporting a man between them. Was he drunk, drugged, ill? Why was somebody else coming with her in the carriage? Leighs wouldn't like it, them putting anyone else in with her. Then she saw the uniforms. Two policemen got out of the carriage.

'They shouldn't give you any trouble,' the porter said to the two men who stood ready by the carriage door.

'What is happening? Where are you taking me? Am I going home?' Rose said, panic rising in her chest.

The attendants, the porter and the policeman laughed.

'Aye, we're taking you home all right – to a lovely place,' said one as Rose and the male inmate were lifted into the carriage.

Hands tied – what was going on?

The porter slammed the door and the policemen locked each one from the inside. Rose felt suddenly dizzy, everything blurring again.

'Best not to take any chances with their sort.'

'What are you doing?' Rose said, her attempts to catch the door handle abruptly stopped by the policeman on her right-hand side.

The porter tapped the roof with his stick to tell the driver to move on. 'Asylum. Fast as you can.'

Rose felt the blood leave her head and she passed out.

*

The master of the workhouse looked out the window of his front office as the two-horse car clattered down the cobbled street. 'Better update the journal. If I don't do it now I'll forget about it. Now, let me see, what happened this week?

He dipped his pen in the inkwell and started to write in his steady hand:

February 16th 1907
1) Pat F. and Rose Murphy were sent to asylum
2) I sold 8 fat pigs on 11th for 35.16.0 and bought 8 store pigs on 12th for 18.10.0.

19

Coming home

I t was August 2000 and Patricia was pleased. Jack Quinn's headstone in the new cemetery at Clongeen looked very well. Rose's name had been added to that of her brother, with kind permission from Jack's own family. Rose was back home in the Quinn plot – at least in name.

The headstone now read: 'In loving memory of John Quinn, Rosegarland, who died on the 23rd January 1952 and his sister, Rose Quinn, who died the 4th of May 1907, aged 36. Interred in Enniscorthy.'

Patricia felt Rose would now rest easier because she was recognised by family – even if that recognition had happened two generations down. 'If she had lived out her days properly I would have known her,' she thought to herself. 'At least when I was a child, like other friends knew their grand-aunts.'

Closing the gate of the graveyard, Patricia looked over toward the Quinn plot once again. 'Soon the memorial will go up in St Senan's. Then she'll rest even easier,' she thought as she headed for the car.

20

ASYLUM

The journey to the asylum took several hours. The carriage rattled over the rough roads between New Ross and Enniscorthy, the horses finding it difficult to gain speed as snow began to fall and the sharp east wind whipped round them.

'Not a day for a journey like this,' said one of the RIC men as he tightened his uniform under his chin. Only for this he would be back in the barracks in Wellingtonbridge, his behind firmly planted in front of the fire and dare anyone shift him.

The sound of the voice startled Rose. Her head felt heavy and she could remember little of the journey up to now. Where were they? Where were they going? She stirred, trying to look out the window nearest her.

'We're near Boro Hill, missus – we're making good time in spite of the weather.'

The words sounded foreign, the voice distant from her, mixed up with the sound of horses' hooves and the clatter of iron wheels on the roadway.

The other man from the workhouse appeared to be sleeping, sitting opposite.

Rose felt dizzy as the coughing began again. She struggled to search for a rag in her pocket but couldn't – her hands were tied. Panic washed over her, worsening the cough.

The policeman opposite rummaged hurriedly for a rag from the pile under the seat and threw it in her lap at the same time as he and his colleague covered their noses and mouths with their hands.

'This job doesn't pay well enough for what we have to put up with,' thought the second policeman. 'You could catch anything on this job.'

At least the man had been sedated before he left the workhouse so he was giving no trouble. The woman was quiet too but you never could tell. You never knew the minute her kind would lunge at you like a mad cat, eyes spitting fire and nails ready to make red tunnels in your face. It had happened before.

'Doesn't look very robust, though,' he thought. 'The master of the workhouse might have been better leaving her where she was – what are they going to be able to do for her in the asylum in her state?'

The woman hadn't spoken on the journey. Once she'd come to having fainted as they left the workhouse, she sat in the carriage, her shoulders hunched, her eyes closed or looking vacantly into the distance.

The first policeman was glad of the silence when the coughing bout finished. He wondered what the woman had done to be committed. 'Loose with her favours, maybe – she wouldn't be the first, or the last, who got locked up for that.'

She must have been a fine-looking woman in her day, though, he decided, his eyes darting from her head to her toes. Even leaving the workhouse, she stood her full height, some semblance of dignity in the way she carried her body. Her eyes were dull now, though, and sunken in her head.

Melancholia – how many had he seen with that? He shrugged; wishing asylum deliveries weren't part of his work.

*

'Kilcarberry Mills coming into view – we're nearly there, thanks be to God.'

210

The male patient moved in his sleep, turning towards his minder as the carriage rounded a bend into the town of Enniscorthy. The policeman shifted position, wary of the man waking, but settled when his breathing fell into evenness once again.

The second policeman was now looking out the window. 'The Slaney – no swans under the bridge today,' he said to his colleague. 'Must have had a bit of sense and gone somewhere warmer for the winter.'

'Aye.'

The carriage made its way across the bridge, slowing to let other traffic pass, then swung right for the Wexford Road.

'Another few minutes. A hot cup of tea'd go down well now.'

'Aye.'

Rose opened her eyes, panic rising in her chest, their movement unsettling her. The madhouse … The policemen were sitting up and straightening their uniforms now, looking out the window.

The horses' hooves covered another quarter mile of ground.

'At bloody last – the red brick!'

'Lord preserve us from madhouses,' said the other, blessing himself.

'Fine building, though, whoever designed it. Best site in the town too for making an impression.'

'For putting the fear of God into people, you mean.'

Madhouse. Red brick … Rose began to whimper like a child as the horses started the steep climb up to the entrance. She was outside her body again. 'Hail Mary, full of grace, pray for us sinners now and at the hour of our death …'

The policemen said nothing, disturbed by her muttering.

'Whoa!' The drivers reined the horses to a halt, froth at the corners of the animals' mouths now and sweat visible on their coats after the long journey.

The RIC men unlocked a door each and blew on their fingers as they stepped out onto the snow-covered ground, their warm breath visible in the cold air.

'Out!' The first policeman shook the man in the carriage and pulled him outside. The man staggered, then stood, supported by the policeman.

'Where am I?'

'Come on!' The second spoke more gently to Rose, persuading her to step down.

'Hold onto her, for God's sake,' said the first policeman, going ahead with his charge, who occasionally had to be righted from a stagger. 'I'm not running after anyone on a day like this.'

'Hmph! She won't run far – she's not fit to.'

Rose felt herself being half lifted, half pushed along. The wind caught her breath as she walked the ground, making her gasp, then cough.

The policeman let her go until the coughing ceased, turning his head away from her.

'I'll go ahead with this one. He's dead weight with the doping,' called the second policeman.

'Right.'

Eventually the coughing stopped and Rose opened her eyes to look at her surroundings. She felt like a speck beside the huge red-brick building. 'Lord help me!' she said, feeling weak.

'You'll be all right. Come on!' said the policeman, anxious to get her off his hands. 'At least you'll get three meals a day here – more than you got in that other place ...'

*

The clerk's nib scratched as it made the entry in the admissions register. Rose Murphy. From New Ross Union.

Rose stared at the light that seemed to hang from a string in the ceiling.

'It's electricity,' said the older of the two female attendants who held her by the arms. 'We're very modern here in the asylum, isn't that right, Mag?' She laughed.

The younger woman nodded as the clerk smiled and continued to write. The policemen had left the room now having handed over the committal documents.

Rose was still staring blankly at the bulb. Mag Doyle held the new inmate's arm tighter. If the clerk thought she wasn't doing a good job he'd report her to the RMS – that's what Kit, the older woman, said so she'd better do her work properly.

Someone was always watching you and reporting back, she said. She'd have to show willing – she didn't want to make any mistakes, not on her first day. The asylum was a big employer. She was lucky to get a job here – thirteen shillings a year and live-in.

'The electricity comes from the mill across the river,' the older woman, Kit, went on, giving the new inmate a shake. 'It turns into light as it floats across but then you wouldn't understand anything complicated like that, would you? Not when you're a raving lunatic!'

Rose flinched, struggling to remember words once mouthed in Clongeen. 'O God, our refuge and our strength, look down in mercy upon Thy people who cry to Thee …'

'We've a holy one on our hands!'

'Silence!' said the clerk.

Rose struggled to remember more but no other words would come. Contrition – she must be contrite then all this would end. She would wake up and she would be in Rosegarland going about her work like she used to. 'Our Father, who art in heaven …'

Would He listen to her? Was He punishing her for what she had done? Had the devil driven her to go against the will of her family? What had she done? She tried to remember. Had God visited this madness upon her or had she slept in the shadow of the full moon too many times? Luna, lunatic, didn't the word come from the full moon?

The clerk made the entry. More details would be entered once the RMS, Dr Drapes, had seen her. 'The boss is not going to be too happy about being called out on a Saturday,' he thought, checking the date. 'Or about the workhouse trying to unload more rubbish on us.' He glanced at Rose who was coughing again. Chest ailment – he didn't have to be a doctor to know that.

'Get her washed then bring her to the examination room.'

His nose twitched. Was the foul smell coming from her or the attendants? He wondered if the woman had been washed before leaving the workhouse. Usually they didn't bother there, leaving it to the asylum staff when the transferees arrived.

'As if we don't have enough disease and dirt to deal with,' he thought, closing the book and watching the attendants bustle the new inmate out.

*

'Strip or we'll do it for you!'

The washroom was freezing, moisture frozen on the high ceiling and the unplastered walls.

The younger attendant was putting hot water from a boiler in the corner of the room into an enamel basin, the second taking carbolic soap from a shelf beside the washstand.

'It'll be a quick dip for her. I'm not staying in this icebox long.'

Rose's teeth chattered as she tried to undress herself, her fingers fumbling with the fastenings on her skirt. If she blanked her mind would it make it all go away ... The rosary, say it over and over and over ...

'Hail Mary, full of grace ...' Her purple lips started to move again.

'Shut up your mumbling and get on with it!' The older woman left what she was doing to pull at Rose, removing her petticoats, her boots, her torn stockings, Rose's body paralysed with fright. 'We haven't got all day to wait for the likes of you.'

Eventually Rose stood there naked, shame and the cold making her wrap her arms around herself.

The younger attendant looked at Rose, then at her co-worker. 'She's not well. Maybe ... we should cover her up a bit?'

'Listen, you,' said the older woman, grabbing the younger attendant by the collar of her uniform. 'Start feeling sorry for anyone in this place and you'll end up as bad as them, you hear? They're not human beings: they're lunatics. You remember that if you want to survive in this place.'

'Sorry,' said Mag, terrified as the other woman let her go.

'When I started I was like you but I soon got over it. You get them or they'll get you – and never turn your back on them, you hear?'

'Yes.'

Kit shouted at Rose, who stood there naked and shivering. 'The privy is over there if you need it, madwoman – follow your nose and you'll find it!'

Rose walked slowly to the far corner of the room, grabbing the wall as she walked for fear of slipping. Were those purple feet hers?

Mag Doyle dropped the carbolic soap that Kit had left down into the water. 'Use plenty of it – that's what the clerk said.'

The pungent smell of the soap invaded Mag's nostrils, making her stand back momentarily. It had been a long morning. She felt tired already and she wouldn't be finished work until 10 p.m.

Getting the inmates dressed had been a nightmare. She had to search through the stinking pile of clothes that had been taken off them the night before in the dayroom and try to find items that fit each one. 'They should be a standard size,' she thought. 'That'd make this job easier.' That way there would be no searching for the right sizes. Maybe they'd all look a bit better then too.

She'd never forget the sight of the thirty in Number Two ward that she'd dressed – all in brown, rough, misshapen tweed, like thirty scarecrows; the only difference between them was their expressions.

'Get over here!' Kit, the older attendant, shouted, grabbing Rose by the wrist after she had gone to the toilet.

'No point in trying to cover yourself,' she said as Rose tried to hide herself with her hands. 'You'll be stripping off with everyone else here once a week without fail.'

Rose felt herself being shoved forward, her thighs hitting against the table underneath the basin. She felt weak and the coughing started again. The younger attendant handed her a washrag to put to her mouth.

'Goddamn diseased!' said the older woman.

Goose pimples shook on the flesh that stretched over Rose's bones. She started to cough again, her body heaving with the effort. She put the washrag to her mouth to catch the phlegm.

'That's right, keep your filthy germs to yourself,' said Mag, trying to copy her co-worker.

'Now you're getting the idea!' said Kit.

At least this one has manners, Mag thought. She wondered where she had come from, what she had worked at. What age was she? Thirty? Forty? It was hard to tell she was so malnourished. Probably worked in some big house where the staff had to have manners. Not like some of them here who'd shit in their beds and sleep in it. She'd seen that already.

Rose leaned against the table for support, the dry cough coming to an end for now. She took the rag away from her mouth. It was red. Rose's body shook at the sight of it.

'Bloody consumptive!'

Consumptive – phthisis! Her head felt light again as the realisation set in. She grabbed the handles of the basin to support herself. What was the point of anything any more? She was going to die anyway.

'Hurry up, bitch. There'll be hell to pay if the RMS is kept waiting.' Six months maximum she'd give this one.

*

Rose found it difficult to concentrate on the doctor's questions. Dr who? Curtains? Drapes – that was it. The man in black sat across from her in a room off the admissions ward.

She shivered constantly under the blanket that covered the nightshirt she had been put in.

The man kept asking the same question over and over. 'Why have you been sent here, Mrs Murphy?'

She looked around the room to see if anyone else was there. There was no one, bar the charge nurse standing behind her.

'Why have you been sent here, Mrs Murphy?'

'Quinn.'

The doctor made another note in his casebook. 'Why have you been sent here?'

Rose tried to think. She saw faces – Patrick's, his ...

'We are here to help you, Mrs Murphy. To do that you must talk to us. Can you remember why you have been sent here?'

Rose tried to concentrate. 'They put me here,' she said eventually.

'Who are "they"?'

Rose stared at her lap – the dirty grey of the nightshirt scrunched up in her pale palms.

She jumped suddenly, hearing a scream from someone in the ward next door, then noise and clatter and upheaval.

The doctor's voice was still calm, paying the next-door noise little attention. 'Who are "they"?'

'Them. Him.'

'Please explain who you mean. Who is he?'

Rose looked at the ceiling. 'The man,' she said eventually.

'Do you mean your husband?'

Rose nodded, pulling at the sleeve of her nightshirt.

Dr Drapes scribbled some notes. 'You said "they" – do you mean someone else in your family?' He had to strain to hear the quiet 'yes'.

'Why did they commit you?'

The doctor's voice seemed far away.

Commit …

'Answer me, please, Mrs Murphy. I am here to help you.' Dr Drapes made another note. 'You did not want to marry this man?'

Rose was silent.

The doctor scribbled again. Affairs of the heart – how many times had he seen them cause insanity? 'And was there another man that you did have feelings for?'

Rose said nothing again. The doctor's voice seemed to drift.

'And how do you feel toward your family now?'

Rose sat very still, the fingers of both hands clenched, her lip trembling. She looked into the distance. 'Am I insane?'

Ignoring her question, the doctor scribbled again. 'Your family – do you harbour resentment toward your family?'

Rose didn't answer. There was mud on the doctor's boots – it had caked halfway up the toe.

Dr Drapes scribbled again. *Full of ill feeling – does not accept her illness.* 'What day is it today?'

Rose tried to think – day, week, she couldn't tell. The days had run into one another again. What month was it? January? February? How could she tell them apart with no calendar and nothing to live for?

He tested her chest and looked grave afterwards. 'She is to be in observation for two days,' he said, scribbling another note. 'Give her hot baths also to lift her out of her melancholia. Is she eating?'

'Shows little interest, sir,' said the charge nurse.

'Encourage her with some warm bread and milk then. Mind I said encourage. I don't want any accidents.'

'Yes, doctor.'

Dr Drapes left the room. The new inmate had answered very few of his questions. He would repeat the same set of questions the next time he saw her. Asking her why she was confined would be the best strategy for uncovering the continuing presence of accusations against people in the outside world.

*

'Wine?' Dr Thomas Drapes enquired of his guest, Dr Cullen.

'Thank you, yes.'

Dr Cullen, who came to the asylum three times a week to check the physical health of the inmates and also to check on those currently being restrained, was about to have dinner with Resident Medical Superintendent Dr Thomas Drapes.

As usual, he asked for an update on admissions since he had last been in attendance, although if he were being honest Dr Cullen would rather have spoken of other, more light-hearted subjects on such social occasions. His employer might not take it well if he did not inquire, however, and could reproach him for lack of interest in his work.

'Any new arrivals?' he asked.

'Two yesterday,' said the RMS. 'One male, one female. I will be handing the woman over to your care, John. Phthisis, I'm afraid.'

'Ah.'

'She is extremely malnourished and already infected,' Dr Drapes said, filling a glass. 'Not much I can do for her, I'm afraid.'

'Age?'

Dr Drapes handed the glass to Dr Cullen. 'Her record says thirty-two though she looks older. Not that you can trust information given on documentation – some of these clerks are barely literate.'

'Prognosis?'

'A few months possibly. She is melancholic. Not eating either, despite encouragement.'

Dr Drapes looked out the front window of his house, which was situated close to the asylum, and sighed. 'What am I supposed to do, John, when the workhouse just send me their ill and unwanted? They knew she could not live long and that curing her insanity would be irrelevant given her illness.'

'You have told them of the overcrowding here?'

'Yes, but my words have fallen on deaf ears. The reply from the guardians stated that they were overcrowded also.'

'It is difficult to achieve cures in such circumstances ...' said Dr Cullen.

Dr Drapes sighed again, closing the curtains now against the evening chill. 'The best we can achieve is containment. Cure is impossible.'

'It's not like you to be pessimistic, Thomas.'

'No but just occasionally the burden of work weighs heavily on me.'

'That is understandable.'

The RMS seated himself again in the armchair by the fire. 'I was so ambitious thirty years ago,' he said.

'We were all ambitious once …'

'I was going to change the world – cure the mentally deranged. The human mind is a fascinating organ, I thought. Treat these poor souls well, feed them, clothe them, ignore their delusions and concentrate on proper behaviour and they would be cured.'

'It is an admirable goal to aim for.'

'Moral treatment like Pinel and Tuke taught – that was my goal. Now I wonder. Asylums have turned into mere institutions of custodial care.'

Dr Cullen took another sip of his wine. 'The cure rate – what is it?'

Dr Drapes smiled then looked serious again. 'Very low. You think you have achieved something then within months that person is readmitted. And more and more keep coming. Insanity is rife in this country.'

'I have often wondered why that is. Is it the poverty, the diet, God's will? It is hard to fathom it.'

'It is probably none of those things, my good man,' said Dr Drapes.

'Oh?'

'It is the preponderance of bad blood over good.'

'You mean the common people are proliferating too quickly?'

'Correct!'

Dr Cullen smiled. 'Perhaps you should issue instruction to the gentry and the middle classes to reproduce with greater haste.'

'It might solve part of the problem but not all of it.' Dr Drapes looked at the logs crackling in the fire. 'There are those, you know, who think that the only cure is to sterilise the insane.'

Dr Cullen cleared his throat before speaking. 'A little extreme, don't you think?'

'Perhaps. It is not a theory to which the public sentiment has yet been educated, at least.'

'I cannot see that happening.'

'Perhaps not. There is another solution, of course ...'

'Oh?'

'We could redress the situation by discouraging degenerate people of bad blood from marrying. What would be thought, after all, of a cattle breeder who would select a cow who had indications of tubercular disease or a hereditary tendency to lameness? Yet in the case of man marriages are recklessly contracted between individuals who are known to be liable to consumption and insanity.'

'Exactly.'

There was a knock on the door and the maid entered. 'Dinner is ready, sir.'

'Thank you, Nora,' said Dr Drapes, standing up and inviting his colleague to take a seat at the table.

'Thank you,' said Dr Cullen as the maid pulled out a chair for him.

'Still, we must not let all this make us dispirited,' said Dr Drapes as the maid left the room. 'We must struggle on.'

Dr Drapes enjoyed these regular conversations with the local doctor. They kept his mind sharp, reminded him what it was like to converse with the sane. Now he placed his wineglass on the snow-white tablecloth. 'You know sometimes, John, I worry about becoming institutionalised myself,' he said.

'Surely not?'

The RMS sighed. 'It is a concern of every RMS in this country, my good man. It is very easy to be dragged down by the bleakness of the work. That is why we must struggle to maintain detachment of mind, John, the dry light of the intellect,' he said.

'Apt phrase,' said Dr Cullen.

Silence fell as the maid arrived with the soup tureen and placed it on the sideboard, then ladled soup into two bowls and served the men.

'Surely matters are improving for you now that you have attendants sitting the medico-psychological certificate?' said Dr Cullen.

'Would that there were more. Only two have sat the exam so far. The others don't think it worth the trouble for the extra two pounds a year I can pay them but, yes, it is a start, and we now have one charge nurse from Portrane.'

'Yes, of course, that's progress.'

Staffing the asylum had always been a problem – Dr Cullen knew that. Sometimes he despaired of the quality of the attendants. They were employed more for their brawn than their brains, often with serious consequences for the inmates. He decided not to mention the rumour about an inmate being badly hurt last week. No witnesses could be found but who, he wondered, was going to take the word of an insane witness anyway?

'Do you know what one of my counterparts in the Richmond asylum is suggesting?' asked Dr Drapes.

'What?'

'Family care for lunatics.'

'Family care, not custodial?'

'Yes. My esteemed counterpart in Dublin, Connolly Norman, is suggesting that families within the community should be paid to look after the less-disturbed, the imbeciles, the idiots.'

Dr Cullen finished his soup. 'I can't see that working. The Irish like their fools and mad locked up.'

'My feelings precisely. I can't see it happening for a very long time. Take the case of the woman I spoke to you about earlier, for instance.'

'Yes?'

Dr Drapes rang the bell for the second course to be served. 'From Clongeen. Melancholic. She recently married but became agitated when required to live with her new husband.'

'Yes?'

'She was admitted as a dangerous lunatic on a magistrate's warrant, the most extreme way anyone can be committed.' Dr Drapes dabbed at the corners of his mouth with his linen serviette. 'The magistrate's warrant is being used too easily in this country, I believe. It is too convenient for families to get rid of people. I have been writing in the *Journal of Mental Science* on this matter, actually. Lunacy committals are serious matters given the stigma which attaches to admission to the asylum.'

'Yes, of course.'

'I always think the same procedure that applies under the Poor Law in Britain should apply here. Inmates should have to be recertified each year. At least that way they have some chance of getting out.'

'It would seem a fairer way.'

'Families would then be expected to take responsibility for

relatives again, not leave them here to be forgotten about, a burden on the country. Even the ordinary channels of committal are abused. As soon as the harvest starts I find families signing out the relatives they claim were insane, because they need them to work, then the minute the harvest ends they recommit them, swearing they are insane again, or they cite a violent incident and have them committed as a dangerous lunatic if we refuse. It is most infuriating.'

'Indeed,' said Dr Cullen as the maid arrived with the joint of beef ready for Dr Drapes to carve.

*

Mary Quinn knew her husband was in bad form the moment he came home to Rochestown and slammed the half door so hard it shook.

'Your supper is ready,' she said, stopping her eldest son from taking another potato set aside for his father.

There was fresh buttermilk and salted bacon. She would have to make it last as long as possible and what would come after it she didn't know.

'Whisht!' Patrick shouted as the older children started to argue.

'Out and get some sticks for the fire,' Mary said to them, grabbing their coats and ushering them out the door.

'Ah, Ma ...'

'A few minutes – that's all it'll take you. John, you get ready for bed,' she said to her youngest child. 'You'll need a good rest to be ready for school tomorrow.'

When the room was finally quiet she sat down at the table herself. 'You got work today?'

'One of the ploughmen was sick.'

'Oh.'

She didn't wish anyone ill but she was glad her husband was

getting work. At least the spring was coming and they would have money every week – potato sowing, tilling, there would be many jobs on the estate.

'You're very quiet.'

Her husband took another drink of buttermilk, wiping his mouth with the back of his hand.

Eventually he spoke. 'I saw Murphy today.'

'Aye? And what did he have to say for himself?'

Pat Quinn kept his eyes on his tin plate. 'She's been sent to the asylum.'

'Rose?'

The name sounded strange now in the quiet room.

Patrick placed a letter on the table, the envelope crumpled from being in his pocket. Mary opened it and looked at it but couldn't read it. 'What does it say?'

'He got the priest to read it to him. It's from the workhouse. Saying she was transferred.'

'When?'

'Two weeks ago.'

Mary's hand shook as she refolded the piece of paper. 'They must have had their reasons.'

'She was melancholic, it says. She wouldn't raise her head to talk to anyone by the time she went.'

'How do you know all this?'

'He told me.'

The wood crackled loudly on the open fire.

'He's been to see her.'

Mary Quinn sat down in shock. 'To the asylum?'

'Yesterday.'

'I thought he wanted nothing more to do with her.'

'She's been dwelling on his mind, he says. He couldn't rest easy until he saw her.'

'Oh! And … and how was she?'

Patrick Quinn stared at a knot in the table's wood. 'He barely recognised her,' he said quietly.

Mary Quinn's hands crumpled her apron. 'Merciful God!'

'The Rowe one was right about the coughing – she's sorely ill.'

'We must remember her in our prayers,' Mary said, her face now devoid of colour as the words came tumbling out. 'We did what we could for her, didn't we? She threw our help in our faces, didn't she? We were only trying to help, God knows, finding a match for her. Anyone else'd have been grateful for all we done. Her child dying affected her mind – that's what it is. Are we to blame for that?'

Patrick Quinn was silent.

Haven't we burdens enough trying to rear a family, thought Mary? They were the ones who would have to live with the shame of a relative being in the asylum. How would they be able to hold their heads up in the parish again when this got out?

People were still avoiding them after Bridget Rowe's stories about how Rose was coughing in the workhouse. How dare she imply that anyone in their family was consumptive? If Rose was she had picked it up in there.

Mary ladled more buttermilk out of the bucket for her husband, hardly aware of what she was doing. Her hand shook as she placed the mug on the table. 'What else did Murphy say?'

'Nothing. He wasn't inclined to talk.'

'Has he been asked to pay anything?'

'No.'

Mary sat down suddenly, rigid with fright as a new worry struck her. 'The paper – do you think they'll publish her name in the workhouse report?'

Mary could now see the whites of her husband's eyes. Both of them thought of the time when a neighbour had been sent from the workhouse to the asylum. Word had got out from the forge after a neighbour, Tom Byrne, read the paper for all to hear.

'It'll be her married name they'll use, though, won't it, even if they do?' said Mary, feeling relieved. 'That's what she went in under, wasn't it?'

'Aye,' Patrick said, pushing the plate away.

*

Rose screamed as her body was held down in the hot bath.

'It's too hot for her – you know it is,' said Mag Doyle, the new attendant, as she let Rose's arm go.

'Keep her in it!' said the older attendant, Kit Prendergast. 'Hot baths she's to have and hot baths she'll get.'

'Not that hot!'

Rose continued to scream, the shock of the scalding water making her shake.

Mag Doyle grabbed a bucket of cold water and threw it into the bath. Rose closed her eyes, the cold water giving some relief to her stinging skin.

'I'm scalding no one,' Mag said, almost in tears.

'You questioning what I'm doing?' said Kit Prendergast, grabbing her co-worker by the hair.

'No-o-o,' said Mag, screeching with the pain and trying to release Kit's hold.

'Good, else you and me are going to be enemies and being an enemy of mine is not a good idea. You can finish the rest yourself and if someone strangles you when you're bathing them don't shout for me.'

Mag helped the shaking Rose out of the bath. The noise outside the door of the women queuing up to be washed got worse.

'Shut up, youse mad bitches!' roared Kit as she left.

Panic rose in Mag's chest as she got the new inmate out of the bath. The woman was shaking, her skin red now. How would Mag manage them all? Giving the woman the rag to dry herself with, she shouted at the women outside. Frighten them – keep them afraid of you – that's what you have to do.

The woman wasn't drying herself. She was standing there as if she didn't know where she was, whimpering. Mag tried to dry her, making the woman whimper as she touched her hot skin. She dabbed instead. The woman would be all right. Mag could not worry about her. She must not. She had much to do.

Four days working in this place – it seemed like an eternity.

*

The women had been troublesome this morning when they unlocked the doors – fighting, screeching. It's always worse when there's a full moon, that's what the other staff said. Get them dressed; let them out to get their breakfast. She had to stop several of them stealing other inmates' bread, some of them grabbing the huge unbuttered chunks of it. Hunger made them snap and grab.

'Still, it's more than they'd get if they weren't here,' she said to herself.

Supervising the inmates making the tea had been difficult. She had to stir the mixture of tea, milk and sugar in the big boiler with the aid of a sprong fork. The smell of it had made her feel ill. Around the edges she could see the remains of yesterday's porridge. There were also signs of meat scum from the previous day's soup. What inmate was in charge of washing this? She would have to make sure a better job was done today.

It was ten o'clock now and she and Kit Prendergast and another female attendant were rounding up the inmates who couldn't work. Those that were able to work had been sent to the laundry, to the garden and the sewing room. Those who weren't fit or showed no inclination to work had to be taken for a two-mile walk around the boundary of the asylum.

'Lots of exercise – that keeps them tired. Less troublesome that way,' she'd been told.

'Count them out and make sure you do it properly. If you lose one there'll be hell to pay,' Kit shouted at her.

Mag stood at the entrance of the airing yard where they had come from the wards. Fifty-one, fifty-two … sixty. Had she missed one? She hoped not. It was difficult when some of them rushed out together.

'Bring her with you,' Mag shouted at one of the inmates, pointing to Rose. 'Hold onto her.'

The old inmate looked confused at first, then took hold of Rose's arm. 'Come on.'

Rose started to cough, the other inmate rushing her to join the crowd. The raw wind hit her as they left the shelter of the building. She was glad to leave the building behind – its corridors white-washed up as far as the inmates were able, its big, cold rooms, the turf-fires never heating the rooms enough, the smell of the privies. Fresh air …

'Up the hill and turn right along the headland.'

The walk would take them around the perimeter walls. Rose didn't know whether she would be able for it yet she longed to breathe fresh air. The sight of the fields reminded her of Rosegarland. She could see men working in some of them now, ploughing, picking stones. Her breathing became more laboured as the climb began. 'God in Heaven, help me…'

'You go ahead and stop the gaps and be quick about it,' Kit

Prendergast shouted to Mag Doyle. 'We'll stay in the middle and behind.'

Mag cursed to herself. She was being given the hardest job. She'd been told what it was like, trying to stop the gaps like you were stopping cattle from getting away, standing arms out, ready to tackle any inmate who would fight you to abscond. With the asylum farm this size there were always gaps. Walking the path twice a day, most of the inmates knew the weak points better than she did.

'Go on there,' she shouted at the line of women as she reached the first gap into an adjoining field. As soon as the sixty had passed, Mag left the gap and ran ahead of the line; Kit Prendergast, who was bringing up the rear, laughing at her stress and her hurry.

'Move!' The older attendant said as she shoved Rose onwards.

Rose coughed, and faltered again. Several pairs of eyes looked back at her, expressionless.

'Hurry up, there!'

Rose was pulled to her feet. She felt weak, dizzy again.

'Shit!' Mag Doyle panicked as an inmate took advantage of her at the next gap. The red-haired woman was running down the big field towards the road.

'Get her!' shouted Kit and the other attendant.

'Stay here! Move, one of youse, and I'll break your necks!'

Mag was running down the field after the inmate who had absconded. The woman had a few yards' head start on her. Mag ran faster. The inmate ahead of her stumbled. She fell. Mag grabbed her. The inmate started to screech.

'Get back up here!'

The woman tried to hit her but Mag overpowered her, knocking her to the ground.

All the other women were watching, Kit now standing, hands on hips, at the gap.

'You, my lady, are in serious trouble!' Kit said as they reached her, hitting the woman across the face. The runaway whimpered, exhausted now and terrified.

Rose, who stood behind the group of frightened women, started to cough again and collapsed on the ground.

'Turn around, the lot of you! Get up you, you bitch,' Kit said, grabbing Rose's arm. 'If you can't keep up you can stay locked up. Hold onto that other one. It'll be isolation for her. Wait till the RMS hears about this.'

'Don't tell him, please,' said Mag, red faced and agitated. 'I got her back, didn't I? I'm bringing back the same number I counted out, amn't I?'

Kit laughed. 'I told you I don't make a good enemy,' she said, rushing the coughing inmate again. 'Now get this lot back. Coughing their guts up – Jesus!'

'She's ill …'

'Dying if you ask me. It'll be the dayroom and a box for her in the future.'

Mag was trying to hold onto her escapee who was now quiet again, arms tied behind her back with rope that Kit had carried with her. What would Dr Drapes say about her nearly letting someone escape? Would her pay be docked? She dreaded the thought of that – she was getting little enough as it was.

'It's easy for him to criticise,' she said to herself as the group gathered speed going down the hill to the main building. 'Walking the corridors as if he was God Almighty on earth, expecting us to salute him. He doesn't have to get bitten and kicked …'

Rose, at the end of the line, coughed again, feeling the liquid in her mouth now. It was the same taste as when she sucked her finger when it was bleeding, only now there was more of it. Sweat had soaked her clothes by the time she was finally pushed into a chair in the dayroom.

'Get in there and sit down, you useless bitch. Put that other one in the lock up. The rest of you – out to the airing yard.'

Rose fell into the chair. Everything seemed blurred and her chest heaved with each breath.

Lord, let me die ...

*

It was St Patrick's Day in Rosegarland. Bridget Rowe was crying into the sink where she was preparing vegetables for the Leighs' dinner.

Cook stopped what she was doing, seeing the younger woman's tears. 'There's enough water on them carrots without you adding more to them. Come here and tell me what's the matter.'

Bridget blew her nose in the handkerchief Cook handed her. 'Rose has gone to the asylum.'

'Rose? Rose Quinn?'

Bridget nodded.

'The poor lass. How do you know?'

Bridget blew her nose. 'My mother heard it from Father Lyng's housekeeper. The husband came to the priest's house for him to read the letter he got from the workhouse.'

'You'd think it was bad enough her being in there without them packing her off to the other place. When did she go?'

'A month ago. I can't bear to think of her being there. How could this happen?'

Cook stroked Bridget's hair. 'There's no point in fretting over this. Some things we don't understand and we'd do better not understanding.'

'But she's not mad. She worked here for years. You know

what she was like. It was only because she couldn't bear what was happening that she got so wild.'

Cook turned Bridget's face to look at her, stern now. 'Listen to me, girl, you have to stop this going on about Rose. Her family won't thank you for it and the master and the mistress won't thank you for it either. Who are we to know what's right and what's wrong? That doctor said she was mad and we have to abide by that.'

'He was getting paid to say it – he didn't even see her.'

'Hush, I'm telling you. Going on like this will do you no good. If you keep snivelling and sighing and not concentrating on your work you'll have no job. Didn't I cover up for you yesterday when the mistress found a black bit in her potatoes? You should have been concentrating on what you were doing. Rose Quinn is gone – do you hear? There's nothing we can do about it bar remembering her in our prayers. You have to look after yourself. Do you want to get into such a state that you'll be put in the madhouse yourself?'

Cook could see the fear in Bridget's eyes.

'Good. Now get on with your work and don't let me hear any more. What's done is done. It's in the hands of the Almighty now.'

*

'Can I comb your hair, Rose? I likes doing your hair.'

Rose opened her eyes to see Molly, the childish one, looking at her. Rose was in a chair, assisted in walking to it by two other inmates. Now the March sunshine struggled in through the tiny panes of the high windows but she was scarcely aware of it.

Cordoned off in the corner of the room, the attendant was resting, glad she was in a quiet ward. They'd had their ration of tobacco, it being St Patrick's Day. Today would be quiet.

Molly was already twirling Rose's hair, pretending her fingers were a comb. 'We'll get meat today, them says, 'cos of what day it is. You'll have to eat some, Rose. You're too bony.'

The girl's voice came from a distance. Rose felt nauseated. The turf fire at one end of the dayroom was smoking again.

Molly's fingers got caught in tangles and Rose jerked her head but said nothing. Molly was bringing her hair in a clump at the back now, then twisting it into a figure of eight.

'Now you's lovely, Rose.'

Rita, another inmate who had suddenly gone to the window, shouted at Molly to be quiet. Molly left what she was doing to copy Rita who was standing still, listening.

'Music – can ye hear it?'

Molly stayed very quiet.

'It's a band,' says Rita. 'With big drums.'

'Drums, Rose!' said Molly, awkwardly dragging Rose and her chair closer to the window.

'Bagpipes – it must be a band in the town,' said Rita. 'For the parade.'

Rose struggled to open her eyes, the sound reaching her ears now. Piping! Suddenly she was back in Rosegarland, the Leighs' piper waking them all up playing the reveille and sending poultry in the yards and horses in adjoining fields into a sudden scatter.

She stirred in the chair. She could see the piper piping the beef into the dining-room ahead of the butler. What dinner was that? Who was coming for dinner? She struggled to remember. Eventually she saw uniforms. Soldiers, but who were they?

She looked at her hands expecting to see a tiny set of bagpipes in them. Where were they? Who had stolen them? She let out a scream. 'Ted!'

'Shush, for feck's sake!' shouted Kit, the attendant, disturbed from her rest. 'You'll unsettle the lot of them on me. There's no Ted wants anything to do with the likes of you now. Shut up and go back to sleep.'

Suddenly there was a clatter as a nearby chair was knocked over. Two inmates had started to fight over who would stand closest to the window. Screams, snarls and screeches were now sliced by the sound of a whistle blown by the attendant to summon help.

Molly clung to Rose in the chair by the window, hiding her head in Rose's chest until the fuss died down.

Rose felt outside herself again.

'The child,' Rose said, lifting her arms around the girl, tears rolling down her cheeks. 'Child,' she said over and over again as she kissed Molly's head.

21

THE WAY IT WORKS – CATHERINE

The way it works is I see an image like a still photograph and I say, 'This is what I see,' or 'Do you know what I'm picturing now?' and if it's going to flow it flows from that one image.

I say it to someone and they say, 'Oh, right', and then the picture starts to move.

I remember from the asylum image of Rose, I was looking at her from behind and her hair was down and very straggly and then it's as if the image swung round on a camera shot, like it panned out wide, and if somebody said then, 'What are the windows like?' I could turn and see them.

If someone says, 'Is there a fire?' I can actually move around at will in the image and if there is something that they want me to see I will be pulled to that ...

So many people have said to me, 'How do you know it's not the devil that's telling you all this stuff?' My answer is that it's a feeling of love that comes through and I don't think that would happen with something bad. And to be honest, in my teens I had a bad experience so I know the difference.

Looking back on when I was a child I realise now that I always felt different but I didn't know that everyone else didn't feel like I did.

I was constantly afraid of being on my own – in the dark or in daylight – it didn't matter where I was. Even if you left me in the garden I was terrified. I just felt like I was being watched or that there was something there – that was constant.

I don't remember talking about the fear thing at all because I felt that I shouldn't be scared. I just thought people would think I was either stupid or mad. I still feel that sometimes.

Obviously Mum and Dad were aware of my fears because I used to wake up with night terrors all the time. When they'd ask what I was dreaming about, what I was frightened of, I'd say, 'Nothing'. I couldn't remember.

I used to wake up, and still do sometimes, from a dream where nothing is happening but I feel this presence coming in.

I was always drawn to psychic stuff. I'd read books on the subject and I'd read Stephen King. I had a friend who was a goth too – that's where my mind was at the time. As a teenager you hear about things like ouija boards. I was curious about how they worked and having had a fight one day with someone I knew I decided to see what would happen if I set one up.

That evening I took out the Scrabble letters and laid them out like a ouija board and then I got an egg cup. I remember very vividly because I was on my own and I can't blame anyone else for what happened. I stayed at it for about half an hour and I stopped with fright because of what was coming through. I was terrified, freezing cold and shaking.

I felt for about two years after that that I had opened a door and I couldn't close it. That was scary. I had panic attacks after that. I'd be sitting watching TV at night and suddenly I'd think there was something in the corner of the room.

My bedroom was a bad place until my mum had it blessed unbeknownst to me and from then on it became a refuge. I knew that if I could just get to my room and shut the door, whatever it was would stop. It was only years afterwards that I knew she'd had the room blessed.

The panic attacks went on for my two Leaving Cert years. I wouldn't say the fear thing dominated all of my life because I was with my boyfriend, now my husband, at the time. He really carried me through more than anyone else.

I suppose I did become depressed after the bad experience. I was also anorexic at the time so it made that a bit worse. I was lying about my weight all the time and I wasn't eating at all. I was down to picking at food and pushing it round the plate and maybe eating a couple of grapes or an apple a day.

I remember looking at myself in the mirror only once at that time and being happy with what I saw because instead of my tummy going out it went in. I think it had to do with control, not with weight at all.

My mum took me to a psychologist the summer I did my exams. She had watched me one day walking out the door wearing my white shirt and black skirt as I went to work and it hit her how thin I really was and that if she didn't do something I could possibly die. I talked to the psychologist about the food thing, not the fear thing, although I did discuss being apprehensive about going to college and life ahead.

Then I went to college and I met someone there who was anorexic. From seeing that person, I think I realised that this was not the way to go.

In college I got involved in life and living and pretty much put the anorexia behind me. That year the dreams faded away quite a bit too. I still had this thing where if I was on my own, you know, wuh! I was frightened. It wasn't ruling my life, though. I had got over the really bad patch. I had come out of it because I had support from so many people.

The Rose thing was pivotal because I stopped being scared. I never did the medium thing before Rose. Obviously I used to pick up on things, be aware of presences, like a ghost in a house, for instance, but I didn't realise I could pick up messages until Rose.

When I was first aware of Rose it was of someone incredibly sad and incredibly frustrated. She was standing in the graveyard with clenched fists – that was the frustration coming through. She had been trying to get through to my mother for years but hadn't been able; then she found she could do it through me.

Since then I have always felt that Rose is my security guard.

After Rose came along what I used to do when something frightened me was say, 'Rose, just step in for a minute please', and she would push whatever it was away by coming in and having this loving feeling. My mum describes it as white light.

I deliberately did that for a long time because she was such a strong, good presence – a protective force. I remember saying to my mum that Rose has cured me from being scared and I know now that she has.

Going to the graveyard that first time is still vivid in my mind. I drove up in the car with Mum and my aunt Maura. We were chatting away and I was in good form; then I walked in through the gate and it was as if I had hit a wall of emotion. It just came over me, a feeling of incredible sadness, and there was nothing I could do but cry.

Usually when you think you are going to cry you feel it coming on but it hit me like a wall the minute I walked in.

Then I just started to walk and I didn't go near the cross – I just kept going down the path. It was like someone was tugging me towards a particular spot.

I remember standing on the path and looking a little distance up the slope of ground and walking up and just stopping there. I went down on my knees because the weight of sadness was so overwhelming.

Something similar happened to me since on a holiday in Malaysia. My husband and I were visiting one of the tourist traps, a temple full of huge Buddha figures. We took off our shoes and walked round it and as we walked round towards the back of the temple I walked into what I'd only describe as this wall of static electricity.

Obviously it's spiritual energy or whatever. It literally makes my head spin when it's very strong and you get this overwhelming emotion as well – it's like walking into a wall of emotion.

This was so strong that I said to my husband, 'Did you feel that?'

He said 'What? What are you talking about?'

It was that strong.

The temple held the ashes of hundreds of people. They were in urns from the floor up to the huge high ceiling but I only knew that after the experience. I said, 'Oh my God!' I wasn't scared. It was fascinating it was so strong. My head didn't come back right again until I was out in the fresh air for several minutes.

Rose has been very much part of my life since that night in 1999. The day I got married in 2002 I even went to her grave. I had asked the florist to leave one rose in my bouquet loose.

We had a laugh when we went there, though. It was the funniest thing ever. We pulled up at the gate in a silver Mercedes. My father and my brother stayed in the car while myself and Mum got out and walked into the graveyard in all our finery – me in my wedding dress, hair up, make-up, the lot, and Mum in her long, flowing outfit and her big hat.

We went to place the flower on Rose's grave when a noise further over in the graveyard made us look up. A drunk had been asleep on a slab of stone in one corner of the graveyard and the expression on his face on seeing us was priceless. I can ll see him. He must have wondered what the hell was going on.

I don't know if he decided to give up the drink that very minute but I wouldn't be surprised if he did!

22

FINAL JOURNEY

D r Drapes prepared his notes for the board of governors' meeting later that day. He wondered how many would turn up for the April meeting. It was three instead of forty last time – not a figure that suggested support and encouragement from the landed gentry.

He rechecked the admission figures – up again on last month. The governors would not be happy, especially as the number of those released was low again. What was he supposed to do? Some inmates didn't want to leave the asylum even when he said they should.

Where could they go, they asked, if they couldn't find work and families wouldn't or couldn't support them? Back to the workhouse? The asylum was a familiar environment with routine sustenance and employment on the farm or in the gardens or in one of the many workshops.

Dr Drapes rubbed his forehead.

Numbers dead this month? He wrote down the figure three – only one taken home for burial. He would have to discuss the burial plot at the back of the asylum with the governors – how many more would it take? With increased numbers and a bad winter there had been more call on it than before.

It wasn't his fault that it wasn't consecrated ground. Several patients had expressed concern about being buried there and it not being consecrated but what could he do? The chaplain said it was impossible given that paupers of several denominations were buried there.

Dr Drapes wished the governors who had been appointed by the lord lieutenant would take more interest in the asylum and in the work he was doing. Sometimes he wondered if they were watching for signs of madness in himself.

Some of them, he knew, thought he had too much to say for himself. The publicity about the patient who had died after he injected him with hyoscine hadn't reflected well on him either but he'd like to see them try to deal with what he had to deal with on a daily basis.

How was he supposed to keep control of intractable patients, especially now that restrictions had been placed on the use of the plunge bath and the duration and temperature of cold showers?

'Relics of a barbarous age,' one of the inspectors had said in his report.

Dr Drapes wasn't at all sure that he agreed. Punitive measures were justifiable under certain circumstances – he had even written an article about it. He doubted if any of the governors had read it, however, even though he had furnished them with copies.

It was difficult to get the staff to lead patients into a healthier groove of action, to repress morbid acts or habits. 'With such overcrowding and understaffing how am I going to make inmates less destructive, less unclean, less slovenly, more orderly in eating and devoid of bad sexual habits?'

A knock on the door interrupted his thoughts.

'Enter.'

It was his clerk. 'The apothecary has been, sir. Wants you to check the delivery of drugs, sir.'

'I'll be there presently.'

'Thank you, sir,' said the clerk, retreating.

Dr Drapes completed his notes for the meeting then removed his large bunch of keys from a desk drawer and left the room. He checked the contents of the new delivery cupboard, which the apothecary would need for mixing the prescriptions. Good, all he had ordered had arrived.

He felt optimistic when he looked at the cupboard's contents. Some drugs could radically transform a patient's behaviour. 'Moral treatment is not enough,' he said to himself. No amount of board games and dancing and ball playing and work therapy made a difference to the intractable patient. He was coming to rely more and more on these medicines to help him control the inmates.

The clerk read out the list delivered. 'Opium and hyoscyamus to procure composure and sleep, chloral hydrate for restraint and bromides for the epileptics, sir.'

'No sulphonal?'

'No, sir. You cancelled that last time, sir.'

'Yes, of course.'

How could he have forgotten? His colleague in the Richmond asylum in Dublin, Connolly Norman, had written to say that he had changed his mind about the sleeping drug sulphonal. He said he now considered it dangerous – it had poisoned the kidneys after continued administration, resulting in death. Better to forget about that one, then.

Dr Drapes wondered what the future held in terms of drugs. He could only see treatment improving as more were developed.

Would there be more mood-altering drugs that one day would enable lunatics to live in the community? Would the big walls that surrounded asylums ever come down? Would it be like Connolly Norman wanted – people with mental disability living among the general community? He doubted it very much. Not with violence continuing to be such a problem. It was in every asylum – between inmate and inmate, inmate and keeper and sometimes between keeper and keeper, when alcohol was over-indulged in.

'Recruits are of such poor character – that is the problem,' he thought to himself. 'They cannot exercise the required forbearance.' Stopping their pay didn't work either – it just led to insubordination from the rest of the staff.

Sometimes inmates injured one another, too. Only last week he had wanted to prosecute two of them for assault. His pleas had fallen on deaf ears – the lord lieutenant's office telling him that the function of a district asylum was to contain the violence within it.

He picked up his pen to add a note to his next article for the *Journal of Mental Science*.

'Excitement and disorder must be kept in subjection,' he said to himself. 'These are as harmful to the mental invalid as microbes are to a patient with a wound or sore. The asylum must be the context of a readjustment of the patient's mental and social world. This is what will lead him back to good thought and correct action.'

He must ask the governors about investing money in improving the sanitation in the place. There were so many things that needed improvement.

'It is not good for lunatics to see undiversified white walls in corridors and dayrooms,' he wrote. 'Such an air of bleakness and desolation prevails, more calculated to fix than to remove the awful disease under which it labours.'

How could inmates be well with such insufficient heating, with such bad sanitary conditions and such little activity? How could he explain to husbands and wives and family members of inmates why they had died?

Memories of such a conversation with a husband lingered.

Where was he from – the man he had spoken to a few days before? Clonegal? Clongeen? No, it was Carrig-on-Bannow. The wife, an inmate, was from Clongeen – that was it.

The husband had been shocked by her physical illness, by her nearness to death, when he saw her. What could the doctor do but tell him that she had been ill before she was transferred to the asylum. That it was God's will and that he must try to accept it.

*

Rose could hear the shutters close on the dormitory windows. Everything went dark. Several women screamed and shouted, objecting to the enforced darkness on long spring evenings.

Conscious now, Rose prayed for sleep. She had been placed in a bed in a far corner of the ward alongside another woman who did not go to the dayroom any more. The corner for the dying, Rose knew that. The doctor no longer bothered her – the attendants neither. Occasionally the kinder one, Mag, tried to give her 'goody' by spoon but Rose turned her head, making the food dribble down her chin and onto the straw pillow.

'Rose?'

Whose voice was it?

Molly was standing at the foot of the bedstead, eyes wide and hollow.

'Into bed or it'll be the worse for you,' said Kit, the attendant. 'Go near that one and you'll not live long yourself.'

Rose heard Molly cry out as she received a slap across the head and heard her uneven gait slump back to her bedstead.

Rose's body was in a sweat. The fever was present all the time now, her limbs feeling as if their insides had melted, taking away the strength to lift them.

'Hail Mary full of grace, the Lord is with thee. Blessed art thou amongst women and blessed is the fruit of thy womb, Jesus, pray for us sinners now and in the hour of our death ...'

The dreams came often now, mixing up the faces in her head. Was it in such a dream that she had seen the man she married standing across from her, sad-eyed and staring, as he twisted his cap round and round in his hands?

The coughing started again, Rose almost choking as it continued and her emaciated body shaking for many minutes after it stopped. How long had she been here – two months? Three months? She did not know. The pain in her chest was heavy, her breathing difficult. She felt too weak to move now.

'Dear sweet Jesus, take me ...' she said, her voice lost in the noise of the high room with the thirty beds.

*

Ted Jameson scrunched up the letter his employer had received from the asylum. The date stamp said 1 May. He had appealed to Mr Leigh for information. As a governor of the asylum, surely he could find out about Rose's state of health.

'Not looking good, old chap,' said his boss. 'Seems she picked up phthisis in the workhouse. Not long for this world, I'm afraid.'

Ted felt ill. 'How long?'

'Weeks, days maybe, according to the RMS. Decent sort of chap, Drapes – went to the trouble of finding out for me.'

When the master had left him Ted headed for the stables. He found Jack Quinn in the second stable. 'She is going to die in that place, do you hear?'

Jack Quinn stood there, ashen-faced and speechless.

The stable door hit the wall as Ted slammed it shut. Ted tried to calm himself. What would he do? What could he do? He couldn't just let her die in Enniscorthy without her knowing that someone cared for her.

Jesus!

He wished he could take her back to Rosegarland and let her die in peace. Perhaps he could get a message to her at least – something to let her know she wasn't forgotten.

He made the decision. On his next day off he would borrow a horse and go to the asylum.

*

Rose lay on the iron bed, her breathing laboured and erratic. Her face was grey and small, her lips colourless and ringed with dried spittle that cracked if she tried to speak.

Although it was daylight outside, the room off the dormitory for the dying was in semi-darkness. A single bulb hung from the ceiling over her iron bed, making it easier for the attendant to see her.

'The child ...'

Mag Doyle stood at the end of the bed. Don't get too close – that's what she'd been told. Still, how could she see any human being like that? She went to the basin of water in the corner and dipped a mug in it. Going back to the bed, she lifted the dying inmate's head with her left hand, holding the cup to her lips with the other.

Rose moved her lips, sucking at the water. Some of the water ran down onto her chest.

Mag laid her head down on the pillow.

Rose's lips moved again. 'The child ...'

Mag tried to think of the woman's name. Rose, that was it. 'What child, Rose?'

Had Rose had a child out of marriage? That would explain her ending up in this place. Any woman who even thought of lifting her skirts for a man could end up here, never to be seen again.

Rose's hands tightened momentarily on the threadbare

blanket, her knuckles protruding from the white skin.

'She's not at peace. How the hell could she be, dying in a place like this?' Mag thought, frightened now by Rose's sunken eyes and protruding cheekbones. Her breathing was becoming more laboured. 'It won't be long now,' Mag thought, wishing there was someone with her.

The death rattle rose in Rose's throat as the angelus bell rang.

Mag stood there for a moment looking at the strange, still eyes. The room was silent, all the other inmates locked out for the day.

She walked over and brought her left hand down over Rose's eyes to close them.

'Another one for the pauper plot,' said Kit Prendergast, seeing what was happening as she came in, keys clattering. 'And one less for us to look after.'

'Rest in peace, Rose,' said Mag to herself before running out the door.

*

At first they wouldn't tell him where the graveyard was.

'There has to be one. Where else is she buried if she wasn't brought home? She must be here. Show me where the graveyard is or I'll get my employer, who's a governor of this place, to get you sacked.'

The porter didn't like this fellow. Who did he think he was coming in here demanding to see the pauper plot? Too uppity for his own good. What would he want to be going to the plot for, anyway? Fat lot of good it would do him.

'I'll send an inmate with you to show you where it is.' The porter stopped to grin. 'Don't worry – I'll send one of the quiet ones.'

*

The elderly man with the childish face waited eagerly for instructions.

'You're to show him the plot, do you hear? The last grave dug there.'

'Yessir.'

Ted Jameson walked up the steep laneway from the asylum behind the man with the trousers that were too short for him, exposing his ankles. They turned right to walk down the headland of the field under the farmyard, the high boundary wall of the asylum on their left. Men picking stones in the field below them stopped to watch them as they made their way through the entrance to the plot.

'A bit of a field – that's all it is,' Ted said to himself as he entered by the lower gate. He wondered how many people had been buried in the plot. The place was built in 1868 – thirty-nine years earlier. Was it dozens? Hundreds? More?

The older man pointed at the freshly dug ground visible on the left-hand side. 'Them's the graves,' the man said, smiling. 'Them's the graves!'

Ted Jameson knelt on the damp clay, his body heaving as he said a prayer for Rose Quinn. 'Our Father, who art in heaven …'

Then he placed a bunch of bluebells at the head of the grave. 'May you be remembered some day, Rose. May you not rest until you are.'

23

BIG DAY

It was October 2000 and a crowd was gathering now for the special ceremony. Patricia was delighted to see so many people arrive. Relatives, friends, neighbours, staff and patients from the hospital – they had all come to attend the unveiling of the memorial.

The graveyard behind St Senan's hospital looked so much better now. The new gate didn't creak. The few small iron crosses that Catherine had seen the night she connected with Rose had been freshly painted and were standing now, sentry like, against the back wall.

The ditch on the lower side was trimmed and the ivy cut back from the two high stone walls, where the glass embedded on top now glinted in the autumn sunshine.

The weather was exceptional for 20 October.

'God is smiling on us,' someone said.

'Rose is smiling on us,' Patricia said.

The sound of bagpipes broke the Friday afternoon stillness. It was Jim Gordon, the piper from New Ross Pipe Band who she had asked to play, tuning up in the field below. At the end of the service he would play 'The Battle is O'er'.

'Because the battle is over,' she thought.

The granite headstone stood ready to be unveiled but the covering didn't have to be removed for Patricia to know what it said: 'Sacred to the memory of all those people buried in this graveyard many years ago.'

'It's about time they were mourned properly,' she thought. 'If I've done nothing else in my life I'll have done this.'

She glanced at the white cross where the framed poem she'd written for Rose hung. She remembered the blue flowers that had appeared beneath it on the day of the pattern. They shouldn't really have surprised her. They were simply another detail that had been proven correct – another remarkable connection. There had been so many between Rose and herself that she felt inextricably linked to her. She thanked God for Catherine, the 'key'.

The bishop of Ferns, Brendan Comiskey, was coming in through the gate, ready to perform the blessing. The priests and the members of the hospital management were lining up for the ceremony to begin. Patricia felt a great calmness descend as silence fell. Rose was at peace now – she was sure of it.

The bishop began to speak: 'In the name of the Father, the Son and the Holy Spirit ... On this beautiful afternoon we have been called here to this serene place to honour and to pray for everyone, to pray for all alive and for all those who minister to the less well off.

'I often think there are no such things as coincidences. There are only God-incidences.

'We ask now for your prayers for those people buried here – they surely are with God if anyone is. I also encourage people in hospital to remember when the Lord said a cup of cold water given in His name would not go unrewarded. How much more is the love and care and attention I see when I visit St Senan's hospital.

'Now we ask God's blessing on all here and on God's holy ground. Lord, look kindly on these graves. We ask your angels to guard them.'

As the last notes of 'The Battle is O'er' fell on the Enniscorthy air Patricia felt that Rose was at peace. Almost every Quinn relative was here today. Rose already had one of the things she had asked for through Catherine – recognition by family.

In the days to come she would have the other – her story told. The letter in the newspaper had already made her story known and there would be more to come.

The world would know that a woman named Rose Quinn existed.

24

MORE COINCIDENCE

The programme *Forgotten People* was broadcast two days after the memorial was unveiled.

Audience reaction suggested that Rose's story had struck a chord. What, I wondered, would people who'd listened say if they knew the full story? Would I ever be able to tell it?

One of the people who contacted me afterwards was a woman named Mary Farndon. She was a native of Enniscorthy, formerly Mary Whelan, and her grandfather, Patrick Whelan, a shoemaker, had died in Enniscorthy asylum in 1926, at the age of fifty-seven. Meeting Mary was to bring another startling connection to the story.

Her grandfather had been committed as a drunk, suffering from 'the shakes', she said. Mary, a retired nursing sister who spent most of her working life in Birmingham, England, believes it was not alcohol abuse that led to his family committing him but Parkinson's disease.

'No one, not even the doctors, would have understood the condition at the time. The family, in fact everyone, would have feared anyone who appeared different to the rest,' says Mary.

She had an elderly neighbour's anecdotal evidence of visiting the asylum as a child with her grandmother. 'She remembers his hands were shaking all the time,' said Mary. 'He couldn't hold a cup. Even if he had been committed as a drunk, he wouldn't have been drunk for seven years.' His death certificate stated the cause of death as 'spastic paraplegia'.

Although she had never known him, Mary spent years trying to find out where he was buried. She wasn't able to. Her grandfather had not been spoken of within the family – quite remarkable given that her father, also Patrick, worked as a cobbler in St Senan's hospital for thirty-three years. Many other family members also worked there in one capacity or another over the decades.

Although she had never met him, even at the age of seventy she was eager for information about him. Her search for him had been confused by the fact that the hospital maintained he had been discharged. 'That meant he could have been buried anywhere. I searched church records all over town,' she said, 'but nothing came of it. Even on historical-society outings, if we were visiting a place near an old cemetery, I'd be climbing over walls to see if I could find his name on a headstone but we never had any luck. He was originally from the Tombrack area of Ferns. I checked records there too but there were none.'

Could we meet up? Yes, she would love to meet Patricia. She was delighted to hear that someone had been able to get information from the hospital. It gave her hope that now she could do the same.

A few days later we sat in Mary's sitting-room talking. The character similarities between Patricia and Mary were quite striking. Both were concerned about the injustice done to their relatives.

'I always thought it was dreadful that we couldn't find his grave and that he was forgotten about like that,' Mary said. 'It must have been so painful for him and people like him to be put in and left there. So often people were admitted for reasons they wouldn't be admitted for today.'

On Mary's kitchen window-sill, as on Patricia's, there lay a pile of small stones, souvenirs of places she'd visited. 'I always bring back stones I like the feel of or the look of – better than souvenirs you'd buy,' said Mary, pouring tea.

Mary's father had been actively involved in the Troubles, on the side of De Valera, just as Patricia's had.

The real revelation was still to come, however.

As we sat there in the sitting-room with Mary and her husband, Peter, we looked through the extensive family-tree research that he had done. Peter is English and had traced his roots back to 1200. The bound book on our knees was substantial evidence of his endeavours.

Patricia looked at the entry relating to Peter marrying Mary. Peter Farndon marries Mary Teresa Whelan. Year of birth – 1929. Day of birth – 11 July.

A tingle ran down our spines again.

'The eleventh of July – it's the same as mine and Rose's,' Patricia said.

'There's a coincidence,' said Mary.

'Fascinating,' said Peter.

The coincidence was remarkable, another one in a long line. What did this mean?

At that very moment I believed there could be a huge number of former inmates of St Senan's who had scores to settle with the world, doing it through members of their family two generations down.

'Perhaps your grandfather has been a restless spirit, too,' I said.

'Perhaps,' said Mary. 'Even though I never knew him there's always been something driving me to find out more about him. I get emotional thinking of him locked up there, forgotten about. The fact that he wasn't talked about within the family was hurtful too.'

Mary remembered poetry written by her father when he

was in Kilkenny jail. 'My father wrote poetry about a lot of things when he was there and one lovely one to his mother but his father was never mentioned. He was conspicuous by his absence.'

Having spoken to Patricia, Mary immediately contacted the hospital. Was there information about her grandfather?

Within days, the senior nurse in charge of the research, Hugo Kelly, had come up with the information that, yes, Mary's grandfather had died in the asylum in 1926. He had been buried in St Mary's, the graveyard in Enniscorthy town. This was probably because his family had been able to contribute to the cost of his burial. He had been buried, however, in an unmarked grave. The details were in the St Mary's cemetery records, the plot recorded only by numbers on a map.

Within weeks, Mary and members of her family, in particular her cousins Kathleen Murphy and Breda Sheils, who likewise wanted to find the grave of their grandfather, had had a headstone erected on the spot in his memory.

Records also came to light of a grand-uncle and two grand-aunts who died at a young age, unknown to the family before, who had been buried in the same grave.

In 2003 Mary also received a document showing that her grandfather had been signed out of the asylum on 21 September 1906 by her grandmother. Her knowledge up to that suggested that he was committed in 1919. Perhaps this had led to the hospital originally saying that he had been discharged.

As yet, she does not know if he had been there before and why or if he had been committed again between 1906 and 1919.

Whatever the situation, he was almost a contemporary of Rose's.

25

LOOSE ENDS

The interest in Rose's story did not come to an end with the broadcast of the documentary.

Many people I spoke to had stories of neighbours being put in the asylum or the 'mental' for what we would now term incorrect or inappropriate reasons. They never left. Women who'd had children, brothers who'd fought over land, people who were 'a bit simple' simply being carted off in the night. Were the walls of St Senan's screaming with the stories of powerless people?

As far as the spiritual or psychic connection element of the story went, though, would I ever be able to tell it?

Having done so much research into the asylum era too, my instinct was to try to reconstruct Rose's life. Could I do it based on all the psychic and factual information I had?

Given that what had happened to Rose could have happened to thousands of people in Ireland was it not a story that should be told?

There would be things I couldn't say, though – I knew that; things I would have to hide unless Patricia's daughter, Catherine, agreed that I tell the real story. It wouldn't be an easy disclosure for her – such gifts weren't always spoken openly about. Family and friends didn't know as yet – how long would it be before she felt able or confident enough to admit what she could do?

*

One of the stone walls that we had come up against while researching information about Rose was finding a record of her admission to the workhouse in November 1906.

Frustratingly Wexford library had no minute books for New Ross workhouse for that winter. That still remains the case, the records having been lost somewhere along the line of almost a century.

A few months later, though, Jarlath Glynn of the library staff unearthed the minute book from New Ross workhouse for February 1907 – the month we knew for definite Rose had been transferred to Enniscorthy asylum. Would Rose's name be mentioned there?

It was. The master of the workhouse, David Meany, had entered details of her transfer to the asylum. She, along with another man, Pat F., had been transported to the asylum by horse and closed carriage on the sixteenth.

The entry for the week also recorded that eight fat pigs had been sold for thirty-five pounds sixteen shillings and three store pigs bought for eighteen pounds ten.

There was something shocking in the matter-of-factness of the entry. Sitting there that day I couldn't help but be disturbed by it. People, pigs – with the amount of detail for the latter, the pigs seemed to take precedence.

Maddeningly, there were no details of why Rose was transferred and no mention of when she had been admitted.

Again the lack of information was frustrating but at least we had another piece of solid knowledge.

*

Patricia's obsession with bagpipe music had always suggested that there was a connection with Rose, especially after the airport incident. Patricia's interest in this kind of music is all embracing. She travels all over the country to hear piping bands play, knows the name of every band, can tell you what level they play at. Such is her love of piping she even sponsors a trophy each year now in memory of her father, John.

Was there any kind of piping connection with Rose? The possibility is there. Research into the history of the Rosegarland estate threw up the fact that the Leigh family had a charter for a piper since the 1600s.

That meant it was more than likely that someone who worked on the estate in Rose's time was also a piper. He would have played on important occasions and when the family were entertaining guests. The supposition made sense – Patricia's interest was profound: there had to be a connection.

Further research also showed that F. R. Leigh of Rosegarland – Rose's boss – was also on the board of governors of Enniscorthy asylum, as many of the landed gentry were, although attendances by gentry were not always high.

F. R. Leigh was also a local magistrate, again as many landed gentry would have been at that time. Was he the magistrate who had signed Rose's committal form? This has yet to be verified.

*

A copy of Rose's doctor's case-notes was also received by Patricia from the hospital under the Freedom of Information Act in 2004.

The records show that she didn't sleep very well, was moody but clean of habit and language. In general appearance she was 'palid and of phthisical aspect' when she was admitted.

She had not attempted suicide, the admission records state, menses had been absent for four months and her lung respiration was harsh.

She was tube-fed once with milk and egg on 18 February, as she did not eat all day.

She was never in the habit of taking drink, the notes said, and had never been in an asylum before.

One entry stated that the doctor read her a letter from her sister. Rose cried but would not send any message home.

Her temperature went up each evening and she regularly refused to be examined.

When her husband came to see her on 9 March she would not speak to him. He told the nurses that he was 'taken in when he married her as he did not know that she was insane but he now hears that she had not been well in mind for some time'.

On 22 March she was brought down from ward number five because 'she was getting up and going to the windows'.

By 5 April she was taking little food and refusing to let doctors even take her pulse, stating that they were trying to poison her.

She was last examined by Dr Drapes on 27 April. No entry was made regarding her condition in the final week of her life.

The entry on 4 May 1907 states that she died at twelve noon of pulmonary phthisis.

*

Confirmation of the date of the eviction came in 2005 via a Leigh family connection. Patricia had just known that it was in the 1880s. A newspaper cutting from 26 November 1881 bore testimony to that difficult day for Rose and her whole family, stating that the eviction of Patrick Quinn was a particularly hard case. He owed over £20 in rent as he tried to feed a family of ten on poor, marshy land in the townland of Newcastle.

*

We had also learned that it was unlikely that Rose had a priest at her burial, especially in a paupers' graveyard. Somehow, however, we had visions of her at least having a coffin.

Information that later came our way suggested that the bodies were brought from the hospital to the graveyard in a 'trapdoor wagon' – coffin-less. The wagon was parked over the already-dug grave, a fastener underneath the cart pulled back and the bottom of the cart – two hinged sections – opened to let the body fall directly into the grave.

26

RESEARCH AT ST SENAN'S

I t all started with Rose. Prior to Patricia Quinn's enquiries
about her great-aunt at the former Enniscorthy asylum, it
had not been deemed necessary to assign staff and space to
the preservation of patient records from the asylum era.

Following a written question being tabled in the dáil to
Minister for Health Micheál Martin in February 2000, however, hospital management decided to assign a senior staff nurse
with an interest in history the task of finding Rose Quinn.

It was an opportunity clinical nurse manager Hugo Kelly
welcomed. For thirty of his forty years nursing at the hospital
he had been putting records and artefacts from former times
away in safe places whenever he came across them – in the
basement, for instance, and in any available storeroom he
knew of.

'I was a bit of a magpie,' he says. 'I knew the records would
be important some day as this hospital, like all other former
asylums, is part of our social history.'

Along with the right to trawl the records for Rose Quinn
or Rose Murphy (her married name), hospital manager Jeanne
Hendrick also granted Hugo's wish that he be allowed to log all
available records at the hospital. Thanks to this permission patients, or inmates as they were then known, can now be traced
from 1868 up to the 1950s. Two rooms on the top floor have
been assigned as museum space.

It is a remarkable collection. On bookshelves near one door

stand the ancient minute books of the board of governors of the asylum, all filed chronologically and dating from 1868, when the asylum first opened.

Beside this bookcase hangs a typed agenda for the board meetings. 'The local landlords were on the board until after 1898,' says Hugo. 'The local councillors took over after that. They met every month and made all the decisions related to buying supplies and paying bills and recorded how many were admitted and discharged during that time. A house inspection by the governors was also part of the monthly meeting and the minutes were published in the local paper.'

In the early days, he says, commodities such as milk, bread, butter and vegetables were bought in but later the asylum's own bakehouse and farm supplied such foods. Inmates worked on the farm, with work considered part of the cure.

The first person to be admitted to the asylum was a labourer from Courtown. He arrived at Enniscorthy asylum along with seventy-five other Wexford natives who had been inmates of the Carlow asylum, now St Dympna's hospital.

'There was big pressure to open an asylum in Wexford,' Hugo says. 'Kilkenny, Waterford and Carlow asylums all had Wexford people in them, the workhouses and the jails too. There were a lot of people classified as insane in jails at that time.'

The faded but still legible ink of the admissions book records the names of sailors and shoemakers, of farmers and fishermen admitted to the asylum.

'Mental illness, or insanity as it was called then, knows no barriers,' Hugo says. 'We're all human, regardless of what profession in life we take up. The reasons given for the insanity in the admission records often includes loss of a loved one or loss of money. Drink too was often a supposed cause.'

After extensive study of the Enniscorthy records Hugo believes that very few people were admitted to the asylum without reason. 'I only came across five or six people – two of them clergymen – who had "insanity questionable" written on their records. My experience is that the committal rules were very stringent and that no one would be sent in here on the whim of anyone else. The insanity was mostly divided into two categories – mania and melancholia. Rose Murphy was classified as suffering from chronic melancholia and phthisis when she came here.'

Tranquillisers and antidepressants developed in the 1950s were what made the huge difference to patients' quality of life, he believes. 'Male nurses had started being trained in the 1930s too so there were more nurses with qualifications coming in all the time. The days of keepers and attendants were over.'

On one wall of the third-floor museum hangs a certificate of competence given to one Lizzie Doyle in 1905 from the association of medico-psychological science. This certificate, given to Hugo by a descendant of Lizzie's for preservation in the museum, testifies to Lizzie having 'attained efficiency in nursing and attending upon insane persons'.

One of the signatories is Resident Medical Superintendent Dr Thomas J. Drapes, who came to Enniscorthy in the 1870s as assistant RMS. By the time Rose was admitted Dr Drapes had been in Enniscorthy for twenty-three years.

Hugo wishes that Dr Drapes' handwriting had been more legible, however. 'If it had been my task would have been a lot easier,' he says, pointing out some of the very difficult-to-read words.

One display item is a handwritten letter dating from 1900 from Inspector of Lunatics S. P. O'Farrell. There is no record of what triggered this correspondence. The letter reads: 'I feel

I cannot too strongly urge on the committee the importance of employing as attendants persons of intelligence and good character.

'The attendants are the very backbone of the asylum and on their character and conduct may depend the happiness and good treatment of the patients.

'Looking to the, in many respects, highly skilled nature of their duties which they have to perform, it is evident that well-educated persons should be selected for the positions, that systematic efforts should be made to train them in the method of performing their duties and finally when they are trained it is sound economy to endeavour by good treatment and liberal wages to retain them in the institution instead of allowing them to seek better employment in similar institutions elsewhere.'

Apart from letters, documents and rulebooks, Hugo has also put on display many artefacts from the hospital, dating from the opening of the asylum to more modern times – the male and female wing keys, for example, made by the firm of Gibbons & Co. of Wolverhampton, take pride of place. Serious regulations, of course, surrounded these keys. If a male attendant or nurse was found in the female wing he was immediately sacked.

Items on display also include tools used for post-mortems, calibrated medicine bottles, syringes, anatomy diagrams, a map of the hospital's drainage system and an earthenware 'Dr Nelson's improved inhaler'. This resembles an old whiskey jar but still smells of the asthma medication it once contained.

Forceps for delivering babies also occupy a space on a table, proving that births took place in the asylum.

Various types of mouth 'gags' are there also – items used for opening the mouths of reluctant eaters.

On another table sits a set of shoemaker's lasts – one for men's shoes, one for women's. 'They were Patrick Whelan's, who worked here as a cobbler for a lot of his life.'

The walls also bear witness to the lives of many staff at the hospital – people remembered by a valued collection of memory cards and union cards from later years. One undated photograph rescued from the last RMS's office shows a group of female staff resplendent in white starched aprons and highly shined shoes.

Hugo Kelly, a native of Enniscorthy, joined the staff at St Senan's in 1960, coming in to train as a psychiatric nurse immediately after finishing school. He has recently retired after forty-four years' service. 'There were 550 beds here when I came, though the place was originally built for 350. The figure now stands at about 150. A lot of people are treated in their own homes now.'

One remarkable part of the research for Hugo involved his discovery that his great-grandmother, Brigid Kelly, had been an inmate of the asylum. 'I didn't know anything about her being here. My grandparents, like most older people at the time, didn't talk about the past so finding a Brigid Kelly with an address I knew was a surprise. It struck a chord with me that she had walked the corridors of this place just like I had and yet I never knew she'd been in here. I keep her grave tidy now in St Mary's cemetery.'

Hugo is glad that there is now more openness about psychiatric illness. 'It's great to see family members coming and going, supporting people through their illness. It often wasn't that way. Often patients weren't visited at all but it's better now. A lot of the stigma is gone. Years ago there was a lot of secrecy. I don't think it was secrecy for secrecy's sake.

'It was about protecting the person who was in the hospital.

Nothing was said about them being there so that they wouldn't suffer the comments of neighbours when they came out. It was usually more about what the neighbours would say than the family themselves being ashamed of the illness.'

Since the records were opened for details of Rose Quinn a few people have contacted the hospital for information about relatives who were there. 'The number hasn't been big but at least now all the records are in order if they are ever needed,' says Hugo, closing the door on his work. Work that records a past gone but, thankfully, not forgotten.

Appendix 1

OTHER ASYLUMS

The practice of burying patients abandoned by their families to asylums in unmarked graves in dedicated plots on asylum property was widespread.

In the south-east, for instance, a graveyard was attached to St Dympna's psychiatric hospital in Carlow. Records for people buried there cannot be located, according to a hospital source in 2000. There are no individual headstones for the deceased. The graveyard ceased to be used around the mid 1940s.

In County Tipperary, St Luke's psychiatric hospital in Clonmel also had a paupers' plot.

In counties Kilkenny and Waterford, St Canice's psychiatric hospital and St Otteran's psychiatric hospital did not have burial grounds attached. Burials took place in nearby graveyards.

Some psychiatric hospitals hold annual commemorative services and have erected memorials to the dead but, in many cases, the names of the dead are unknown.

Further afield in the west of Ireland a spokesperson for the Western Health Board said it would be possible, by examining the records, to say how many patients have been buried but 'it would prove impossible to identify each and every person interred'.

A North Eastern Health Board spokesperson said there was a private cemetery at St Davnet's hospital in Monaghan, used from the 1920s to 1972. It was well maintained and there was a plaque commemorating the dead. Graves were unmarked, however, and, from an initial search, there did not appear to be a burial record.

St Brigid's psychiatric hospital in Ardee also had a private cemetery with a single headstone erected in it. It was in use from 1933 until 1985.

St Ita's in Portrane, County Dublin, has a cemetery dating back to 1896. It was closed in the 1980s. Graves were not individually marked and a map indicating the locations where individuals were buried was destroyed in a fire. However the hospital had records of the names of those buried there. These are used whenever relatives of these people seek information. There is a central crucifix in the cemetery, recording the fact that former patients were buried there, and an annual blessing ceremony is held.

A Southern Health Board spokeperson said the former psychiatric hospital, St Raphael's, in Youghal was the only one in the region to have had a private cemetery. Records had been kept since 1966 and, while graves were unmarked, the names and locations of those buried there from that time were known.

St Loman's in Mullingar also has a plot on former asylum grounds. Small crosses bear numbers to represent those who died. A plaque was erected by hospital management in February 2005 in memory of those buried there.

Appendix 2

MENTAL HEALTH LEGISLATION – A LONG ROAD

1800

Responsibility for lunatics was vested in the lord lieutenant's department. The Dublin House of Industry was the main centre.

1816

Robert Peel, chief secretary for Ireland, initiated an enquiry into the provision for lunatics and idiots throughout Ireland.

1817

The lord lieutenant in Ireland was instructed to establish district asylums throughout the country. Each area was to finance its own asylum. Ten were initially built. Twelve more were built between 1852 and 1869. Ireland was the first country in the western world to have a system of public asylums.

1838

The Irish Poor Law Act 1838 was introduced 'for the effectual relief of the destitute poor in Ireland':

>> workhouses were opened in each poor law union
>> a dispensary service was started
>> infirmaries in workhouses meant the beginnings of a national state-run hospital system
>> workhouse affairs were controlled by a board of guardians. This consisted of elected local representatives and *ex-officio* members
>> property owners in each area had to pay a 'poor law rate' to meet the cost of the workhouses

1838

The Dangerous Lunatics Act was introduced. This meant that two justices of the peace could commit a person – the second usually signed automatically.

1846–7

The Great Famine ravaged Ireland.

1851

The Irish Dispensary Service was established. The country was divided into dispensary districts, each with a salaried medical officer whose first priority was to treat the poor. This doctor was responsible to the board of guardians of the poor law union.

1862

Children from workhouses were now 'boarded out'.

The authority of the RMS (Resident Medical Superintendent) was established conclusively: laymen, known as 'moral governors', no longer ran the asylums.

1863

Registration of births, marriages and deaths was initiated to establish accurate statistics in the fight against disease.

1867

The Dangerous Lunatics Act (Amendment) was passed. A medical examination was now required. Evidence provided by the person seeking committal had to be given on oath ('an information' had to be sworn). Admissions continued to rise after this date, however, due to the high fees paid to doctors for the committal of dangerous lunatics and because families saw the asylums as a means of ridding themselves of 'troublesome' or ill relatives.

1868

Enniscorthy district asylum was opened. It was built to house 300.

1878

The Public Health Act was introduced. Authorities were given the power to destroy unsound food, supervise slaughterhouses and isolate persons suffering from certain notifiable diseases. The death rate from the principal epidemic diseases – smallpox, typhus fever, typhoid, measles, diphtheria, whooping cough, scarlet fever and diarrhoea – declined from 2.8 to 1.5 per thousand between 1882 and 1906.

1890

The Mitchell Committee Report highlighted the judicial committal, considering it an order of indefinite detention. No mandatory review of the condition and status of a person detained under the Dangerous Lunatics Act took place.

1896

The first purpose-built hospital for those with TB opened at Newcastle, County Wicklow.

1898

The Local Government Ireland Act meant that infirmaries came under the control of the newly created county councils. 'Now that the Irish were in charge of the care of their own insane they were no more generous than the ascendancy governors who had for so long based their parsimonious management of the asylums on the just rights of property and on the belief that institutions for pauper patients should reflect the grimness and discomforts of poverty'.

1901

Over three per cent of females died within one month of admission to asylums and almost another three per cent within three months. Twenty-five per cent of all deaths in asylums were attributed to phthisis or TB of the lungs. The average age of death was thirty-nine.

1904

TB accounted for almost sixteen per cent of all deaths in Ireland.

1908

The Royal Commission on the Care and Control of the Feeble-minded recommended that all insane persons be transferred from workhouses to asylums.

1912

Peamount hospital opened in July.

1925

Statutory sanction was given to the change of name from lunatic asylum to mental hospital.

The commission recommended the repeal of all lunacy laws and simpler procedures for admission, including voluntary admission, which would safeguard the rights of the patients.

1930s

Analeptic drugs were used to induce convulsions in schizophrenic patients.

1940s

Psychotherapy was developed as a method of understanding and correcting the distorted communicating process of the psychotic patient. Electro-convulsive therapy (ECT) was also introduced

1945

Under the Mental Treatment Act:

» patients were no longer committed on the order of two peace commissioners (previously justices of the peace)

» medical certification was needed

» patients could be admitted either as a voluntary or as a detained patient

» detained patients fell into two categories – temporary patients (those who required up to six months of treatment but were considered unsuitable to be voluntary patients) and 'persons of unsound mind'

» persons of unsound mind could be detained indefinitely

» a legal obligation was imposed on the hospital authorities to discharge a recovered patient

» visiting committees were appointed to hospitals

» relatives or friends were given the right to appeal to the minister for the discharge of the patient

» the right of any person to apply to the minister to have

the patient examined by independent medical practitioners was established

» the Inspector of Mental Hospitals was given special powers and duties to ensure that there was no abuse of the detention arrangements

» treatment, under this act, could also be given without consent

Under the Public Health Act TB and VD were not classified. New measures were introduced to prevent the spread of infection. Children who were ill had to be kept away from public places. Infected people could be arrested for not taking precautions against spreading the infection to others. Allowances were paid to people undergoing treatment. Mothers were educated.

1950s

Drug treatment became available and the chlorpromazine group of drugs was introduced. This had a major impact on the treatment of schizophrenia and other serious psychotic conditions, reducing the intensity of disturbed behaviour (see Robbins).

1960s

Antidepressant drugs such as imipramine and amitriptyline proved effective, as did Tofranil and Tryptizol (see McDermott). Carbritol and paraldehyde were also used as sedatives. Largactil was used later. Phenobarbitone was used for the treatment of epilepsy.

1961

More patients were being treated at outpatient clinics than within hospitals.

1962

By the end of 1962 almost 60 per cent of the in-patient admissions were on a voluntary basis. However in 1961 the Irish provision of 7.3 psychiatric beds per 1,000 population appeared to be the highest in the world.

1965 and 1966

Government commissions of inquiry proposed the inclusion of short-term psychiatric units in general hospitals.

The terms 'idiot' and 'imbecile' disappeared from use. 'Mentally handicapped' was used instead.

The Mental Health Association – a voluntary body to represent the interests of people with mental illness – was set up.

1970

The health boards were established. A network of services for the mentally ill was created outside the mental hospital. A community psychiatric-nursing service was established.

1981

New mental health legislation was introduced but not implemented.

1984

The landmark 'Planning for the Future' report recommended:
  » a further extension of community based services
  » the development of the long-term goal of treating all admissions in the psychiatric units of general hospitals
  » that old institutional mental hospitals were unsuitable for the delivery of a modern mental health service
  » that the concept of a comprehensive community-orientated psychiatric service be developed

1986

Health Minister Barry Desmond announced plans to close Carlow and Castlerea mental hospitals.

1992

A green paper on mental health was introduced.

1999

The Mental Health Bill was published in November 1999.

Inspector of Mental Hospitals Report by Dr Dermot Walsh stated that 'drug prescribing in some locations is often arbitrary and made without regard to appropriate clinical diagnosis. The number of patients, particularly long-stay patients, who are on numerous drugs simultaneously, often at high dosages, was striking. In some instances, prescriptions had not been reviewed for some considerable time.'

2000

In this year it emerged that more than seventy people had been held against their will for more than thirty years. Two had been detained for more than sixty years (source: Labour Party).

2001

The Irish Mental Health Act brought Irish legislation in relation to the detention of mentally disordered patients into conformity with the European Convention on the Protection of Human Rights and Fundamental Freedoms. The Mental Health Commission, established in 2002, will be the main vehicle for the implementation of the provisions of the Mental Health Act. The commission has indicated that one of its priorities will be to put in place the structures required for the operation of the mental health tribunals.

2004

Mental Health Association members held a meeting with the minister of state at the Department of Health to highlight concerns of the groups to develop strategies for investment and reform in mental health services. The minister was urged to ensure that proceeds of lands attached to mental health services are reinvested in the health services.

The budget for 2004 included no additional investment in mental health services with the exception of one million euro allocated to the central mental hospital. The mental health budget in 2004 represented just 6.8 per cent of the total non-capital health budget.

The minister subsequently announced that he had asked health boards to carry out audits of all their property holdings so that unused land could be identified.

A new inspector of mental health services, Dr Teresa Carey, was appointed by the Mental Health Commission in January 2004.

2005

The statutory body established under the 2001 Mental Health Act, the Mental Health Commission produced a landmark discussion paper entitled 'A Vision for a Recovery model in Irish Mental Health Services'.

If this becomes policy it will herald a radical change in the way mental health services are delivered in this country.

The recovery model emphasises the importance of mobilising the person's own resources as part of treatment.

Partnership and equality are emphasised in service provider/user relationships. Psychiatrists and mental health professionals would adopt a coach or personal trainer role rather than an authoritative one.

The Mental Health Commission is committed to issuing a policy document in the near future.

2006

'A Vision For Change', the Report of the Expert Group on Mental Health policy was launched by Minister for State Tim O'Malley.

One of the key recommendations is the closure of all remaining mental hospitals and the reinvestment of the funding generated from this into mental health services.

It also recommends non-capital investment of 21.6 million euro every year for the next seven years.

Mental Health Ireland (formerly the Mental Health Association of Ireland) has asked that 'Vision for Change' become 'not just another report' as this would be 'a tragedy for services users and for the country'.

Appendix 3

IN ROSE'S TIME

1870

» Under Gladstone's Irish Land Act the government is to lend two-thirds of the purchase price to any tenant who wished to buy his farm, repayable over thirty-five years. At this time a hundred thousand Irish farmers have less than fifteen acres.

» Water closets come into wide use.

1871

» Bismarck becomes chancellor after German unification.

» Composers Gilbert and Sullivan begin their twenty-year collaboration.

1872

» The Ballot Act introduces the secret ballot in British elections – tenant farmers no longer have to vote for the candidate their landlord favours.

» The pennyfarthing bicycle is in general use.

» Stanley finds Livingstone: *Dr Livingstone, I presume?*

1873

» German troops withdraw from France after France makes its final war indemnity payment.

» World depression begins as wheat prices fall.

» The Irish Home Rule League is formed.

1874

» The first Remington typewriter is sold.

» The first Impressionist exhibition is held in Paris.

1875

» Charles Stuart Parnell is elected MP for Meath.

» Britain, France and Germany embark on rearmament programmes.

1876

» The Battle of Little Big Horn – Custer's Last Stand – is the last major North American Indian victory.
» Alexander Graham Bell invents the telephone.
» Mark Twain's *Tom Sawyer* is published.
» A survey of Irish land is carried out – almost all the land belonged to 10,000 individuals.

1877

» Irish nationalist MPs begin a policy of obstruction in the House of Commons.
» Parnell is elected president of the Home Rule Confederation.
» Anna Sewell's *Black Beauty* is published.
» Tchaikovsky's *Swan Lake* is first performed.

1878

» Under the Red Flag Act mechanical road vehicles are limited to a speed of 4 m.p.h.

1879

» The Land League is founded in Ireland by Michael Davitt. Parnell is invited to be leader.
» Austria and Germany enter into the Dual Alliance.
» Edison produces incandescent electric light.
» The first steam tanker for transporting oil operates on the Caspian Sea.
» Winter in Ireland is the wettest and coldest of the nineteenth century.

1880

» There are 10,000 Irish evictions; the term 'boycotting' comes into use. Land League meetings are attended by thousands.
» Parnell is elected leader of the Home Rule party.
» Pasteur develops preventative immunisation for anthrax.

» Tenant farmers took over the boards of guardians of the asylums.

1881

» The second Irish Land Act is passed. Parnell advises tenant farmers not to pay rent until their cases are heard by the land tribunals set up by the act. Land tribunals were to be set up to fix judicial rents that would remain unchanged for fifteen years. Parnell is arrested for his criticism of the act.

» Flogging in the army and royal navy is abolished.

1882

» The Phoenix Park murders in Dublin spark another Anglo-Irish crisis. The IRB is discredited and the Home Rule party now becomes the dominant force in Irish politics.

» The Irish National League is set up.

» Italy joins Germany and Austria to form the Triple Alliance.

» Mount Krakatoa, the volcanic island near Java, erupts.

» Robert Koch, the German bacteriologist, discovers TB bacillus.

» Sherlock Holmes appears for the first time in Conan Doyle's *A Study in Scarlet*.

» R. L. Stevenson's *Treasure Island* is published.

1883

» The Statue of Liberty is presented to the USA by France.

1884

» The Gaelic Athletic Association is founded.

» The Scramble for Africa begins after Europeans meet at the Berlin Conference to lay down rules for Africa's colonisation.

» The Reform Act in Britain gives the vote to all male householders who owned or rented a single room.

1885

» The Ashbourne (Land) Act lends five million pounds to

Irish tenants to buy their farms, repayable over forty-nine years.

» Marx's *Das Kapital*, volume two, is published.

» Russian goldsmith Fabergé produces the first of his jewelled Easter eggs for the tsar of Russia.

1886

» Gladstone introduces his first Irish Home Rule Bill – it is rejected and government falls.

» Daimler produces a four-wheeled motorcar.

» Thomas Hardy's *The Mayor of Casterbridge* is published.

1887

» Freud uses hypnotic suggestion.

» Gold is discovered in South Africa.

» The Balfour Act reduces Irish land rents.

1888

» The Suez Canal opens to ships of all nations after the Convention of Constantinople.

» The Eiffel Tower is completed for the Paris Exhibition.

» Van Gogh's *Sunflowers* is painted.

1889

» Jerome K. Jerome's *Three Men in a Boat* is published.

1890

» Kitty O'Shea's divorce case damages Parnell's standing.

1891

» Parnell dies.

1892

» W. B. Yeats and John O'Leary found the National Literary Society to promote Irish literature, folklore and legends.

1893

» The Gaelic League is founded to stop the decline of the Irish language.

» The second Irish Home Rule Bill is passed.

1896

» Irish women win the right to be elected to boards of guardians.

1898

» The Abbey Theatre is founded.

» Under the Local Government Act grand juries are to be replaced by county and district councils. Few landlords win seats. Women get the right to vote for local councils and to sit on district councils, though not on county councils.

1899

» An *Claidheamh Soluis* is published by the Gaelic League and edited by Patrick Pearse, 1903–1909.

1900

» The Home Rule party is reunited under John Redmond.

» A more extreme nationalism emerges, linked to cultural revival.

» Queen Victoria visits Ireland.

1901

» The first Picasso exhibition is held in Paris.

» Roosevelt becomes US president.

» The first safety-razor blades are launched by Gillette.

» Marconi sends his first transatlantic radio transmission.

1902

» Women's foot binding is abolished in China.

» Irish MPs are involved in violent scenes in the House of Commons.

1903

» The Wyndham Land Act sets a hundred million pounds aside for land purchase, with landlords to get eighteen to twenty-seven times their annual rent and tenants to get sixty-eight years to pay off their loan.

» Scott of the Antarctic reaches the furthest point south.

» Pope Pius X is crowned before a crowd of seventy thousand in Rome.

» The Wright brothers make the first heavier-than-air flight.

1904

» The Irish nationalist leader John Redmond calls for Home Rule.

» The UK and France sign the Entente Cordiale.

» Charles Rolls and Henry Royce agree to make cars.

» The Trans-Siberian Railway is completed.

» Puccini's *Madame Butterfly* is performed.

» Trinity College Dublin admits women to its degree courses.

1905

» Seventy-five thousand Russian workers strike – Tsar Nicholas promises reforms.

» French writer Jules Verne dies.

» Anti-semitic riots break out in Warsaw.

» Einstein propounds his Theory of Relativity.

» The Wright brothers make a record flight of thirty-eight minutes.

1906

» There is a Liberal landslide in the British general election. The Irish rejoice at first, hoping for Home Rule, but as the Liberals have a huge majority they are in no hurry to introduce it.

» Mount Vesuvius, Italy, erupts, killing hundreds.

» The *Lusitania*, the world's biggest liner, is launched in Glasgow.

» Eleven suffragettes are jailed for demonstrations in London.

1907

» Home Rule for Ireland is on the British Liberal government's agenda – and criticised in Dublin and London.

» Robert Baden-Powell launches the Boy Scout movement.

» J. M. Synge's *The Playboy of the Western World* is staged.

Bibliography

Barrington, Ruth, *Health, Medicine and Politics in Ireland 1900–1970* (Institute of Public Administration, Dublin, 1987).

Clancy, Prof. Luke, *Life Events and TB* (interview 2004).

Finnane, Mark, *Insanity and the Insane in Post-Famine Ireland* (Croom Helm, London, 1981).

Jones, Greta, 'The Campaign against Tuberculosis in Ireland 1899–1914' in Malcolm, Elizabeth and Jones, Greta (editors), *Medicine, Disease and the State in Ireland 1650–1940* (Cork University Press, Cork, 2000).

Kearnon, Kenneth and O'Farrell, Fergus (editors), *Medical Ethics: The Future of Healthcare in Modern Ireland* (Columba Press, Dublin 2000).

Lonergan, Eamonn, *St Joseph's Hospital, Clonmel: An Historical and Social Portrait* (Eamonn Lonergan, Clonmel, 2000).

Malcolm, Elizabeth, *Swift's Hospital: A History of St Patrick's Hospital 1746–1989* (Gill and Macmillan, Dublin, 1989).

Malcolm, Elizabeth and Jones, Greta (editors), *Medicine, Disease and the State in Ireland 1650–1940* (Cork University Press, Cork, 2000).

McDermott, Joe, *St Mary's Hospital, Castlebar: Serving Mayo Mental Health from 1866* (Western Health Board, Mayo, 1999).

Murphy, Imelda (editor), *Clongeen through the Ages* (Clongeen Historical Group, Wexford, No date given).

Reuber, Markus, 'Moral Management and the "Unseen Eye": Public Lunatic Asylums in Ireland 1800–1945' in Malcolm, Elizabeth and Jones, Greta (editors), *Medicine, Disease and the State in Ireland 1650–1940* (Cork University Press, Cork, 2000).

Reynolds, Joseph, *Grangegorman: Psychiatric Care in Dublin since 1815* (Institute of Public Administration, Dublin, 1992).

Robins, Joseph, *Fools and Mad: A History of the Insane in Ireland* (Institute of Public Administration, Dublin, 1986).

Ryan, Annie, *Walls of Silence* (Red Lion Press, Kilkenny, 1999).

Tumbling Walls: The Evolution of a Community Institution over 150 Years (Midland Health Board, Portlaoise, 1983).

Walsh, Oonagh, '"A Lightness of Mind": Gender and Insanity in Nineteenth Century Ireland' in Kelleher, Margaret and Murphy, James H. (editors), *Gender Perspectives in Nineteenth Century Ireland* (Irish Academic Press, Dublin, 1997).

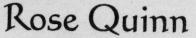

Rose Quinn

11/7/1870 - 04/5/1907

Discarded, Disowned
A Desolate Feeling
Suffering
Untold
But a special person

A person with dignity
A person with feelings
Dealt with a cruel hand
But loved

Loved and cherished by Someone Greater
Taken from the suffering to love and peace

And now
Years later
Found
Your story unfolding

A special person in my family
My purpose
To say
You were special
You were loved

Your life was of value
An expression of sorrow
For treatment by family
And thanksgiving to the Greater Power
For your life
For a special Rose